City of God in Several Voices:
Brazilian Social Cinema as Action

Edited with an Introduction by
Else R P Vieira

Critical, Cultural and
Communications Press

CCCP
Nottingham
2005

City of God *in Several Voices: Brazilian Social Cinema as Action*
Edited by Else R P Vieira

The right of Else R P Vieira to be identified as editor of this work has been asserted by her in accordance with the Copyrights, Designs and Patents Act, 1988.

First published in Great Britain by Critical, Cultural and Communications Press, 2005.

ISBN 1 905510 00 4

Cover photograph by César Charlone.

First edition

Printed by Antony Rowe Ltd., Eastbourne, England.

Table of Contents

To Breno
Above all, I trust you

Acknowledgements

My respect is due to the children of Cidade de Deus, who grow up, if at all, believing that the hissing bullets of the narco-traffic are natural, and to their helpless parents, trapped in the *favela* by poverty, for the dignity with which they accept the drama of their personal lives being laid bare to the world. A very special word of affection goes to them on this last day of 2004, in the hope that this book might somehow contribute to brighter prospects forming on their life's horizon.

I warmly thank Fernando Meirelles, the world-renowned director of *City of God*, for constant availability, generous support and remarkable cordiality amidst his less than human life rhythms.

My particular thanks go to M V Bill, foremost hip-hop activist in Brazil and community leader of Cidade de Deus, for taking his time to write his contribution over the holiday, and to CUFA (*Central Única das Favelas – The Favelas' Central Union*), for opening my eyes to their sensibilities and aspirations.

Luis Nascimento and Renato de Souza, actors from *City of God* and key players from the *Nós do Cinema* [*We in Cinema*] Project, and Ana Cristina Cunha, its public relations representative, have been an endless source of help; the open smile with which they welcomed the 'London Professor' to their project was captivating.

The tracing of sources in Brazil has been greatly facilitated by Professor Bernardo Mançano Fernandes, President of the Brazilian Association of Geographers. My gratitude is also due to Professor Harold A. Veeser for his timely and ever cordial orchestration of logistical support from the United States.

My thanks are also due to Edson M. Lopes and Thomas Laborie Burns, former colleagues in Brazil, and Juliet Line and Maurice Blackford, for their Herculean translation task; to Heather Herrera and Rob Colson for crucial editing assistance; Marco A. Durães and Joe Elwood for indefatigable graphic assistance.

Siobhan McGuirk, Project Research Assistant, has enlivened this and other joint ventures with invaluable support, unflagging commitment and professionalism. I thank her warmly.

Credits are due to *The Guardian* of December 19th 2002 for first publication of Walter Salles's contribution, originally entitled 'On a wing and a prayer', reprinted here with the author's permission; *The New Left Review* for first publication in English of Roberto Schwarz's originally entitled 'City of God', reprinted here with the author's permission; *The American Cinematographer* for permission to reprint Jean Oppenheimer's contribution, originally entitled 'Boys from Brazil'; *Third Text*, vol. 18, issue 3, 2004, 239-250, for first publication in English of Lúcia Nagib's 'Talking Bullets: The Language of Violence in *City of God*', reprinted here with the author's permission; *Revista Sinopse* (published by CINUSP – Cinema da Universidade de São Paulo), for permission to translate and to publish Leandro Rocha Saraiva's 'Cidade de Deus: maestria e contradições'; the daily *Jornal do Brasil* for permission to translate and to publish Ely Azeredo's 'O olhar de "Cidade de Deus"'; *Revista Sinopse* (published by CINUSP – Cinema da Universidade de São Paulo), for permission to translate and to publish Ismail Xavier's 'Humanisadores do inevitável', here enlarged; the daily *A Tarde*, of Salvador, Brazil, for permission to translate President Lula's text, originally entitled *Cidade de Deus*; the newspaper *Nomínimo.com*, which first published Luiz Eduardo Soares's text 'Cidade de Deus e do Diabo', also available on his personal website (http:luizeduadosoares.com.br), here reprinted in English translation with the author's permission; *Viva Favela* (www. vivafavela.com.br) for permission to translate and publish M V Bill's 'A bomba vai explodir' and 'É possível construir uma nova mentalidade'; the daily *O Estado*, in which Maria do Rosário Caetano's report 'The young authors of *Cidade dos Homens* publish a book with script notations for cinema and TV' was first published, reprinted here in English translation with the author's permission; *Cadernos de Antropologia e da Imagem*, in which an earlier version of Márcia Pereira Leite's 'The *favelas* of Rio de Janeiro in Brazilian film (1950 to 2000)' was first published and whose updated version in English translation is reprinted here with the author's permission.

Preface
Arnaldo Jabor

City of God is not simply a film. It is an important fact, a crucial event, a borehole in the conscience of the country. We do not screen this film, it looks at us. Like an epic of the war of the wretched who were given life in and from Paulo Lins's book. Our life as spectators, with clothes, food, a girlfriend at our side, and then a pizza, has become ridiculous. The film is a blow to our sense of normality. It shatters our point of view. We Brazilians have become a nation of the guilty, our faces looming behind those children with automatic weapons killing one another.

While misery was sweet, no one worried about it. It was as though the poor had no inner life. We could romanticise them, laugh at them, patronise them, everything. But television, which democratises consumption, brought to light this miserable yet desiring mass. A brutal string of expression pulsates in the funk dance-halls – violence as hunger and language. The cultural industry has taught these poor its language and they have learned to desire it. Cocaine and arms traffic fuelled its fulfillment.

City of God is not a lachrymose picture of the *favelas*; it does not bear a single trace of sentimentalism. The film does not show what happened, it shows what is happening now, relentlessly, while we screen it and read between its lines. These are clear signs of our own chaos. They point directly to the sordidness of our dominant class, and to what are but tales told by politicians of kindness and nationalistic ideals, full of sound, signifying nothing. The film bears witness to the fact that we are unprepared to solve social tragedies, even if the political will were there.

After cocaine dumped millions of dollars onto the world of misery, the lethargic acceptance of exclusion has become hunger for consumerism; the acceptance of slavery disguised as a 'job' has become the invasion of the 'white' country. It is no longer inferiority, it is difference. Now it is blow for blow. We exist, they exist. It is the upsurge of another world, not as decadence or threat, but as a sinister culture, with awful values, all under the sombre cloak of death. We now look death in the eye. The tragedy of the Brazilian periphery was an ignored earthquake, to which no one sent rescue squads.

Our awareness of the problems of crime has always been skin-deep. And we could only say 'the horror!' But this film steeps us deep into the blood of those slaughtered, it plunges us into everything that we have always detested seeing. As I revisit my meditations on the film when I first saw it, I remember vividly that, when I left the cinema, I felt like shouting all over the streets: 'And then? Will not anyone do anything? Thousands of children are killing one another. And shall we go on talking about criminality as a matter for the police?' Those armed children are above good and evil. Yes, indeed they are.

The film is the revelation of a social, ethical and physical mutation. We need new concepts to understand this problem which is the State's as well as society's. Forty years ago maybe there was a hygienic, assistance-based solution. But today, the rhetoric of class struggle, awareness-building and citizenship has been rendered ineffectual. Too late. They have already 'developed their awareness' on their own, and in another direction. Who is going to solve the problem? And on which budget, with what right, with what powers? And who can ever say that they still want us to 'save' them? And then I wonder, 'what to do?'

Fernando Meirelles, with the collaboration of Kátia Lund, has created a masterpiece – extraordinarily well-produced, well-directed and well-shot. But, at stake, as we leave the theatre-house, it is not a matter of saying, 'I liked or I disliked it'. One does not qualify the discovery of a disease. *City of God* breaks with the laws of the normal spectacle; it betrays the cultural industry and throws into our faces not a message but a sentence. We are doomed to live with this tragedy, it will grow on like a tumor which we are not prepared to cure, because we are a part of it.

More than three million Brazilians all over the country saw this film in mesmerised terror. It has already prompted changes in political conduct, because it set off a crucial process of awareness – within and beyond the misery belt – that no one can stop now. *City of God* shows that there is a hell here, beyond Rio's Ipanema or somewhere behind São Paulo's Gardens. This film has forever unmasked us.

City of God premièred in Brazil in 2002, during the presidential campaigns. It demanded an immediate political response. Film critics, of all generations, reviewed it and commented on *City of God* as a film that has broken with all the patterns of Brazilian cinema. It also caused heated polemics disseminated by the country's media. Spokesmen and major activists from the *favelas* took the floor and voiced their views and sentiments regarding the film. The director has been in constant demand, in Brazil and elsewhere, to say more about what went on behind the scenes. It has become an integral part of academic curricula and University debates both nationally and internationally. A little over two years after its launch, it has generated books, theses and various academic papers. It is this panorama of studies and responses to the film, predominantly those from Brazil – voices ranging from the *favelas* to Brazil's President – that this book, the first one in English on *City of God*, makes available to readers the world over.

From São Paulo, on January 27th, 2005

Translation by Else R P Vieira

Introduction:
Is the Camera Mightier than the Word?
Else R P Vieira

In January 2003, when *City of God*, directed by Fernando Meirelles and co-directed by Katia Lund, premièred in London, the BBC honoured me with an invitation to join him in a debate on the film. One week earlier, the launch of my own work – a virtual museum of the artefacts of the culture of landlessness in Brazil across various media (Vieira 2003) – had taken place in the House of Commons. Although we were pursuing different trajectories, our work converged in the sights and sounds of the dispossessed and socially excluded in Brazil. The interviewer's questions featured the film's great success and the heated political issues it raised on its release in Brazil the previous year; the possible connections between this and the landmark victory of President Luiz Inácio Lula da Silva at the ballot box; the image of Brazil it portrayed; and what solution could be envisaged for the problem of marginalisation in Brazil. Part II of this book is in many ways an elaborated reply to these questions. Lula's own response to the film is the first of a series of statements on its social, political and aesthetic impact. This first President from the Workers' Party in Brazil's history watched *City of God* during his campaign; he expressed his view on the government's lost social role and insisted the then President screen the film. The anthropologist, political scientist and former National Secretary of Public Security Luiz Eduardo Soares elaborates on the tripod of neglect by the authorities, police brutality and the tyranny of the drug dealers who have settled in the *favelas* (slums, shantytowns) and have been attracting young children into the trade.

Cutting across hierarchies, social divides, and discursive frontiers, the book includes the views expressed by many diverse voices. The spokesman for the *favela* Cidade de Deus [City of God] discusses in three texts the view that the undeniable political benefits that the community derived from the film need to be weighed against the stigma created for those unrelated to the drug trade. Paulo Lins, who also grew up in Cidade de Deus and wrote the bestseller of the same name *City of God* (1997) that inspired the film, in turn spawned by an anthropological research project on criminality, offers a disclaimer to the view of this stigma, redirecting the polemics towards social mobilisation and the need for the creators of such social chaos to be ashamed, not the *favela*. Part II also features a survey of the publications that *City of God* has generated (Chapter 19). The impact of the film on television language, themes and patterns of beauty is the thrust of Leandro Rocha Saraiva's contribution, which further highlights the social fabric of the *favela* in the film's continuation in the television series *City of Men*, an off-shoot from the film, one episode of which was directed by Meirelles and Lund (Chapter 17). The original cast's contribution to this manuscript highlights their post-*City of God* engagement with film production as social and political action through the project *We in Cinema*, derived from their training as actors, to offer disadvantaged communities the empowering experience of film. It also projects the internationalisation of their platform through the *Get Together* project and its international experience, *Get Together England* (Chapter 17). The first film they produced, during Lula's campaign, is eloquent. It reflects commotion in the country at the prospect of change but also the specific one of the *favela* responding to the experience of film. The original cast of *City of God* wanted to produce their own film but did not have any money. The very poor Rocinha *favelados* gathered whatever they could and backed the production. The film's three characters embody three political evils in their view indecision, authoritarianism and disguised authoritarianism while, through the themes of misery and social conflict, they enter into a dialogue with the now deceased exponent and main expositor of the political 1960s *Cinema Novo* [New Cinema], Glauber Rocha.

This book does not seek coherence where there can be no coherence. It does not seek a unifying discourse in its orchestration of Brazilian voices and reverberations in other countries. The dissenting voices were all invited to speak and I respect those who did not respond to the invitation. No attempt was made to incorporate only consensual voices. In fact, one of its objectives is to explore the polemics surrounding the film in Brazil and elaborate Lins's view that its social action is derived from the intense debates it generated on poverty, racism and violence.

The various processes involved in the making of the film are analysed in Part I. Co-producer Walter Salles[1] highlights the leading visual metaphor of *City of God*, whereby a most obscure character, a chicken, is singled out to represent a community or so many communities of people trapped in an unjust country (Chapter 1). A long statement by the director Meirelles covers the pre-production stage of *City of God*, including the writing of the script of a two-hour film out of the 700 pages of a panoramic novel with over 200 characters; it also explains in detail the very careful process of conveying realism through the cast, which eventually led to the search for and training of a number of amateur actors from the *favela*. But these *favela* actors were also expected to supplement what was in the script with their voices through the technique of improvisation, to the same extent that the professional actors were expected to 'de-interpret' their performance (Chapter 3). To this major issue of voice I will return while also advancing the view of the film as a palimpsest in which important traces of its teamwork production are inscribed.

Brazilian film is increasingly seen as the creator of conditions for the silent actors in society to articulate their own voice and for the 'filmless ones' to produce their own image. *Domésticas* [*Maids*] (2001) can be seen as Meirelles's first experimentation along these lines. His specific use of the technique of improvisation in *City of God*, in my view, could well be related to what Carlos Alberto Mattos, in another context, has referred to as the increasing demand that, in the last decade, Brazil has placed on its audio-visual production in terms of the authenticity of

---

[1] Walter Salles's career as a director features the award-winning *Central Station* (1998), *Behind the Sun* (2002) and *Motorcycle Diaries* (2004). In Britain his films have won a BAFTA Award for best film not in the English language.

the voice and of the image, to which its strong documentary tradition has responded with radical experimentations (2003). Those familiar with *Central Station* (Walter Salles, 1998) will remember the mass of illiterates who cannot benefit from the reach and power of writing, but whose voice and plight reverberate the world over as they dictate letters through the audio-visual medium. Fernando Meirelles follows the demand for authenticity in terms of actors, but, again in my view, asserts the film's social action also through the negotiation of the power of the voice.

City of God is a film also constituted by several discourses. In fact, it could be described as a mosaic of images or a palimpsest of voices adding new layers of meaning without erasing the previous ones. The book by Lins casts in fictional language the interviews he carried out in the *favela* as part of his anthropological research on criminality in Cidade de Deus under the directorship of Alba Zaluar. The analysis by Roberto Schwarz, a major literary critic who also advised Lins on editing matters, stresses its artistry in expressing an anthropological study on criminality, the demise of a major social type, the *malandro* (a Brazilian trickster) and the emergence of armed drug dealers. The evolution of the drug trade in Rio de Janeiro is taken up in Part III by a sociological study ranging from the equally folkloric numbers racketeers through to the invasion of the *favelas* by the armed gangs and, more recently still, by narco-guerrillas dispersed from Colombia and elsewhere (Chapter 21). But, returning to the book, Lins himself refers to the artistic and fictional voices which added rhythm, plot and suspense to the vast research he carried out not only in the *favela* but also in prisons, several newspapers and archives (Chapter 16). Lúcia Nagib, in her intersemiotic analysis (Chapter 5), reveals how the marked poetic language of the novel was masterfully transposed to the visual language of the film. Conversely, Leandro R. Saraiva's first contribution to this book advances the view that the demands of the film script entailed a loss of the anthropological substance and a shrinking of the immense social fabric of Lins's book.

City of God, according to Meirelles, was self-financed and conceived for a national audience. But, because of its later distribution by Miramax, it was eventually cast in the international circuit. Its avatars in fact epitomise the challenges increasingly faced by Brazilian cinema today: complying with the social pressures within and with the expectations of the market without. It also entailed a different apprehension of it; critics throughout the world have in fact identified a wide range of Latin American and international voices in the film. *City of God* in fact speaks many and at the same time no idioms. Orphanhood is the metaphor suggested by the critic Ruy Gardnier to express its affiliation to many traditions and at the same time to no one specific tradition. Such a syncretic dimension of its film language is enhanced as it draws upon a constellation of internationally recognisable film images. Juliet Line explores the sophisticated interweaving of Christian symbolism and Hollywood's dramatic techniques that, in her view, embellish the film, at the same time undermining its social critique; she also foregrounds the internationalisation of the *malandro* (Chapter 9). Following a reverse trajectory, Miranda Shaw interrogates the Anglo-Saxon critics' facile and exclusive framing of *City of God* within the gangster genre and how this may have channelled a non-recognition of the important social and political tradition of Brazilian cinema embedded in it (Chapter 8). Jean Oppenheimer's very detailed study stresses how the camerawork achieves realistic effects, conveys a sense of change across the decades and constructs a visual poetics (Chapter 4). In her specific analysis of César Charlone's cinematography, she picks out, for example, the gas lorry hold-up, which evokes the gunmen of Westerns on horseback running alongside a stagecoach. Yet I would rely on Homi Bhabha to argue that there is a certain blurring of the western image when these 1960s boys rob the gas containers and the money to provide for the poor population. A social message is added to the western, deriving from the Brazilian tradition of 'honourable bandits' represented by the *cangaço*. This, in my view, is an example of what Bhabha calls mimicry (1994: 86) which permits identification of the image but disturbs, locates a crack that discloses what I would describe as the intentional ambivalence of *City of God* persistently breaking the audience's expectations. To this strange familiarity I will return.

City of God's production of social knowledge and its poetics of exhibiting violence in the *favela* are interrogated by the Brazilian critic Ivana Bentes who implies that it could have remained closer to the aesthetics advanced by the exponent of the 1960s *Cinema Novo,* Glauber Rocha (Chapter 10). Márcia Leite, in turn, presents an analysis of the films on the *favela,* ranging from major ones in *Cinema Novo* to others from the 1990s; her contention is that representations of the *favela* in Brazilian film tend very much to reflect the ideology of whoever is behind the camera (Chapter 20). Still contextualising the film within Brazilian cinema, Ismail Xavier focuses on productions from 2000 onwards and explores, through Buscapé, the thematic connection between *City of God* and other films in their endeavour to offer roads to humanising the country or to present images as alternatives to violence.

In 'Seen *God*' (below), I shall present an overall picture of the repercussions of the film, which does not pretend to be exhaustive but which highlights the multiple readings and framings it received beyond Brazil. It is hoped that the reader, by entering this polyphony, will also engage in the debate and assess the achievements of *City of God*. To what extent has it pushed the frontiers of the world's and of Brazilian film-making? By so doing, how successful has it been in advancing the social agenda of poverty, exclusion, violence, and racism? How successful has it been in partially using a universally recognisable film language to take a national reality across frontiers? What have been the consequences of its remarkable national mobilisation and international success for Cidade de Deus and other *favelas* in Brazil? What cinematic and social knowledge has it produced? Does the use of some of the conventions of an international film language clash with the demands on the audio-visual within Brazil?

I espouse Ismail Xavier's perception that *City of God* is another film in the commercial circuit that looks at life in extreme conditions and tries to show a road to liberation, while 'reflecting its own image of cinema as a means of salvation in the face of a social order of inequality, concentration of power and violence' (Chapter 12). Meirelles, in my view, moves the social agenda forward with a different concept of the aesthetic, a different level of engagement, and a different view as to how to change history, but with a conviction shared wih most Brazilians of the need to change. His starting point is not the revolutionary political platform as was the case with those in *Cinema Novo*. Yet he dedicated years of his life to the *City of God* project and put into it whatever money he had made in his previous career as a commercial director and his remarkable talent to draw attention to an object. Meirelles is an intuitive man of action. So the question to be addressed concerns not what his political views are but how the film conveys a message, how it mobilises and what it achieves. Ultimately, the question to be addressed concerns the achievement of the commercial film in advancing a social cause.

Throughout this introduction, I have been highlighting examples of the familiar rendered strange. I would like to suggest now, for future elaboration, that rather than shocking, he resorts to various forms of defamiliarisation [*ostranemie*], related to the perception of a work of art, as described by Šhklovskij, as a typical device to render the familiar unfamiliar, thereby triggering non-automatic perceptions.[2] For Šhklovskij, when we lose our sensation of the world, only new forms of art can change the mode of perception, for example, by displacing an object from its customary context. A pervasive pattern of recognition, non-recognition and mis-recognition in *City of God* impedes the automatic, uncritical view of a situation that now demands heightened perceptions. Three main producers of the effect of defamiliarisation, to which I later return, are in fact presented right at the beginning of the film: a floating voice unattached to a body on an imageless black screen; the narrator Buscapé shooting the audience; and the chicken whose human attributes are reminiscent of fables. These three plunge us into the world of the *favela*. Special effects of sight further expose this social wound in the body of Brazilian history, a wound which took on unimaginable proportions when ruthless armed drug dealers settled in the *favelas*. What the distant Brazilian ear cannot or does not want to hear is rendered eloquent by this remarkable technical production that stings the social conscience.

After 'Seen *God*', drawing upon the shuttle effect of my double residence in Brazil and Britain, I invite the non-Brazilian reader to share with me a passage into Rio, starting with my own awareness of a changed configuration in the city. Prompted by sounds or by images both seen and unseen in *City of God*, I shall point out possible entrées to the film in terms of its strategy of inviting the audience in but breaking its expectations. On this journey I shall highlight a crisis of authority and a shifting power system through the metaphor of a Christ-less Rio and through the politics of the (im)proper name; such an instability seems to signal a society undergoing profound changes. The floating voice in search of a body will address the need for a revision of the social actors in the Brazilian imaginary (in the Lacanian sense) and cultural theories. The imploring eyes of a chicken will be used to advance the view that the film frequently resorts to devices of defamiliarisation to break automatism in

---

[2] For a discussion of *ostranemie* and other concepts related to Šhklovskij, see Steiner (1984: 44-67).

the perception of a reality that is now different. Other devices of defamiliarisation will be also pointed out as I suggest that the film may have been disturbing to many Brazilians as its powerful sounds and images strike a hard initial blow at two pillars of Brazil's imaginary and self-identity: that of a predominantly pacific country whose relations are based on cordiality; and that of flexibility in situations of conflict, of which the *malandro* [trickster] is so emblematic. It also interrogates Brazilian racial democracy (a third pillar of the country's imaginary). Resonant of Ionesco, my title, 'A Director in Search of One Hundred Black Actors', highlights the imbalance of a country that has an approximately 50 percent black population, which is reputed to have the second largest black population in the world, second only to Nigeria, yet suffers a drought of black actors. The workshops for the training of the actors will be analysed as the site for the creation of areas of permeability across the polarised class system of Brazil and for the negotiation of the power of the voice. A camera shooting the audience will focus on the politicisation of the look of the 'filmless' ones demanding 'to-be-looked-at-ness' and, by extension, 'to-be-listened-to-ness'. For this purpose, I here mobilise the politicised elaboration of the concept of the gaze by Laura Mulvey, but move it away from its psychoanalytic bias in terms of gender. It is like the Althusserian voice that hails the other who, by turning around, acknowledges the call (1971a: 163). The concept is here invested with a social reading and with the agency (not victimisation) of the one being looked at. It further suggests the removal of the walls, be they between image and audience, or the *favela* and the city. Finally, 'The Power and Pains of Visibility' addresses the political gains of the film vis-à-vis the sense of uncomfortable exposure.

This trajectory is in many ways a return to my earlier work on Carolina de Jesus (Vieira 1995), a poor, half-literate woman in the *favelas* of São Paulo who lived off paper collected from litter bins and who, in the late fifties, wrote herself into power – her diary, which was eventually published with the mediation of a reporter. Gayatri Spivak's challenge in 'Can the Subaltern Speak?' was at the time and remains particularly illuminating for my purposes. When this national celebrity became an international one, St. Clair, her translator into English, for sure echoing the revolutionary ethos triggered by the Cuban Revolution, struck a prophetic note in his preface, 'If there should appear a Brazilian Fidel Castro, and if he should give these hungry illiterates guns...' (quoted in Vieira, 1995: 115). 'Not guns, not the immateriality of words the subaltern speaks' (Vieira, 1995: 115) is a self-quotation that reflects my contention that the pen is mightier than the s/word. Today the power of writing must contend with the power of high technology and the image. In this light, this introduction will be, in many ways, a rewording of the challenge *City of God* today poses to the audience – is the camera mightier than the word? Or the overpowering guns?

'Seen *God*': National and International Readings and Repercussions

This is the title of a preview of *City of God* which quotes part of the film's title and also hails it as Number 1 Absolute for the Toronto Festival (2002). This was found, at the time, amidst Kevin Smith's writings, sent to Bráulio Mantovani and later to me. The Canadian critic Jeffrey Wells's punning with the religious dimension of the film's title is taken further as he suggests that it is a divine study of a self-enclosed criminal society and its sympathetically drawn characters. This 'descendant of the Warner Bros gangster films of the 1930s', 'with shootings a plenty', nonetheless surprises with a 'sad, sickening, emotionally crushing' ending, after 'a total turn on from start to finish'. Like Rio's Christ, the expected but unseen is the pattern that *City of God* establishes in the various film languages it speaks. Its ingenuity and artistry are as unequivocal as the certainty that it will be framed anew and will break with the audience's expectations in different countries.

The film's international success comes as no surprise to those already familiar with its calibre that garnered it the Cinema Brazil Grand Prize for best cinematography, director, editing, picture, screenplay, sound, and actor. It also received glowing praise in Cannes. If the film's success in the Anglophone world, where it was nominated for four Academy Awards, and won several other prestigious accolades,[3] comes as no surprise, its categorisation does. When it was first launched in London, *The Guardian*'s influential *Guide* listed it as the number one pick of the week – an astounding distinction considering the second and third films on the list: Scorsese's *Gangs of New York* and the second instalment of *The Lord of the Rings* (*The Two Towers*). It described it as an 'outstanding Brazilian thriller that brings a freshness and energy to what's essentially a familiar story in an unfamiliar location'. This box-office success that outperformed *Goodfellas,* the film to which it is frequently compared, had other details added to its description in the *Guide*, such as 'exhilarating Brazilian thriller zipping through 20 years of youthful gang rivalry in Rio's poorest neighbourhood... the result is a blend of *Goodfellas*, Tarantino and *Amores Perros*'. The 'outlaw' point of view did not seem to be disconcerting to the British; for them, *City of God* was perhaps one more star in the constellation of films dealing with violence, but one that added a touch of originality to a well-worn theme. It was the familiar rendered strange.

The citation of one of the awards received in Cuba sets it squarely within the tradition of socially committed films: 'for approaching the explosive theme of social exclusion, using an ambitious, complex and involving style of narration, without moralising or condoning violence.'[4] In the Havana Festival, the film also won the Glauber Rocha Award, a prize that aligns Fernando Meirelles's achievement with that of the most celebrated filmmaker of *Cinema Novo* (or perhaps of Brazilian Cinema),

---

[3] In the United States: for best foreign language film from the New York Film Critics Circle and from the Las Vegas Film Critics Society; for best sound editing in a foreign feature from the Motion Picture Sound Editors; amongst others. In Britain: the British Independent Film Award for best foreign film. In Canada: the Toronto Film Critics Association Award and the Vancouver Film Critics Circle award for best foreign film. Data obtained from *The Internet Movie Database* (http://www.imdb.com).
[4] In France a similar reading can be found, in what is considered an epic with Naturalistic parallels in Zola. See *Télerama* no. 2774, March 12th 2003, 38-9.

who was the theorist of the revolutionary *An Esthetic of Hunger*,[5] which articulated the Brazilian departure from the glamorous Hollywood films of the 1960s towards a gritty social and political orientation.[6] *Cinema Novo* is the movement in Brazilian Cinema with which Fernando Meirelles's *City of God* is most often compared.

Readings of the film by over three million Brazilians who saw it in the month following its première in August 2002 variously stressed criminality, sheer poverty, violence, or, if amalgamated, the explosive, perverse process of drugs and guns empowering a desiring mass of the destitute Brazilians. The eminent critic Ely Azeredo defined it as a 'film of rupture'. It was Azeredo, in 1961, who gave Brazilian filmography the designation *Cinema Novo* in reference to Glauber Rocha's *Barravento* [*The Turning Wind*]. In his contribution to this book, Azeredo points out that *City of God* is a fictional film that radicalises the drug peddler and user's point of view of the early *Cinema Novo* film by Ruy Guerra, *Os Cafajestes* [*The Unscrupulous Ones*]. He notes that, while rendering visible a new aesthetics that moves audio-visual products about the *favelas* away from the sequential narrative, from the documentary tradition, and from the demand to present a comprehensive picture, its outlaw point of view pulls the spectator into a web of interlocking stories and into the labyrinth of a ghetto-like *favela*. 'Mesmerised terror' is how Arnaldo Jabor summarises his response to the film in the preface to this book. Similar ambivalence reverberates in Azeredo's commentary that *City of God* is 'seductive, disconcerting, and sometimes shocking.' Ambivalence, in fact, seems to be the common denominator of Brazilians' responses to the strange familiarity of *City of God*.

The *Favela*: A Presence in a Christ-less Rio

Also in 2003, after a long absence, my eyes re-established contact with Rio, this glittering city in my native Brazil. Something unusual caught my attention – the marked symbolic presence of the *favela*, for decades an urban outsider, on the 'asphalt.' The trope of the asphalt has been given increasing currency as a class marker by those who live in the usually unpaved *favelas* uphill; it distinguishes the *favela* from the affluent urbanised areas benefiting from access to all services. As I stopped at the traditional Sunday handicraft fair in Ipanema – the neighbourhood in Rio celebrated for its upper class beach culture and beauty, epitomised by the tall and tanned 'Girl from Ipanema' – wherever I turned, in every size, style and hue, there were paintings of the *favelas*. Heading towards the beach, the canvases with the *favela* motif were still a most visible presence with the folkloric vendors swarming the city's black and white pavements. Strikingly, on the coastal avenues, very poor children, as quick as a lightning, while the light was red for the drivers,

---

[5] For an understanding of *Cinema Novo* and the related aesthetics of hunger see chapters by Shaw, Bentes and Leite in this book. For the seminal texts on the two topics, which gave currency to the title in English as *An Esthetic of* Hunger, see Johnson, Randal and Stam, Robert (1995).

[6] Glauber Rocha shares the orientation towards the social and the political in Latin America with other cineastes such as Fernando Birri, Fernando Solanas, Octavio Getino, and Julio García Espinosa.

were literally taking up the asphalt and displaying their juggling talents to those inside the cars. Each act was very brief, not much longer than one minute. It was not Carnival, these children were not dressed in costumes, they were not feigning wealth, they were not living the fantasy of seizure of power, and they were not occupying the street as a figurative space. Risking their lives in this radical traffic light performance, maybe they were and still are begging both for alms and recognition.

The cameras in many recent Brazilian films have been sweeping over the *favelas*, catching Brazil's and the world's eyes, making ever more visible the burgeoning of these quintessential sites of exclusion, as if they were self-contained cities within the metropolitan sprawls of São Paulo and Rio. Sophisticated technology brings the real to the life of the screen. Exclusion as a social *locus* is rendered visible in its magnitude *and* diversity even for the eye that does not want to see.

Favela is a word that shares with 'shantytown' or 'slum' the meaning of squalid habitation, or the class reference with shantytown, namely, the depressed area where the very poor live. But this book gives world currency to the word *favela* because it describes more than a geographic place inhabited by poverty; it highlights a number of other dimensions and connotations. It conveys a strong sense of marginalisation and the socio-economic condition of those disenfranchised by modernisation policies. The *favelados* or *favela* inhabitants are individuals 'who reproduce the fundamental inequality of Brazilian society ... and [who are] expressions of a restricted, hierarchised and fragmented citizenship' (Machado da Silva, 2002: 223-24). Vulnerability and extreme discomfort mark out their lives. They are those who have to cope with constant threats because, deprived of a place to live, they occupy space irregularly; they are thus exemplary of the survival strategy of the undesirables. The *favela*, in the eyes of many, is a cancer to be extirpated because it brings down the price of properties in the region. A 'museum of misery' or 'a controversial postcard' are the metaphorical terms Ivana Bentes has introduced for the *favela* as a not yet overcome historical stage of capitalism (Chapter 10). In turn, *neo-favela* entered current Portuguese through Paulo Lins and Roberto Schwarz (see Chapter 2) to denote the *favela* that displays all those features plus the armed drug traffic. 'Cityscapes of exclusion' is the term I have already advanced to account for the sheer size of the bourgeoning *favelas* and the wall, real or symbolic, that separates them from residences in the more affluent parts of the cities.

Earlier representations of the *favela* have been condemned for having romanticised it, thematising the lively music and rhythms it produces; the celebrated film *Black Orpheus* by Camus (1959) is a case in point. It has also been glorified for the football talents it has produced. Many have perceived the *favela* as a Mecca for hedonism, even if this is the short-lived pleasure of Carnival. In fact, shifting representations of the *favela* somehow correspond to its own shifting dynamics and to the ethos surrounding those behind the camera, as Márcia Leite's panoramic analysis reveals (Chapter 20). Meirelles subsumes the two views in *City of God*. Violence is an undeniable presence in the *neo-favela*, but he also brings out its sense of *jouissance*: a place full of colour, ubiquitous music and weekly balls. This representation, he declared to the Argentine newspaper *Clarín*, upset many middle class viewers in Brazil who expect depictions of the *favela* to be sad and poor (2003). This is yet another example of Meirelles's strategy of breaking automatic readings.

City of God is a name that evokes the prominent image of the Christ on a high hill as an icon of the city. But it is the *favela* that has become a major presence in a now Christ-less Rio. Deepening contradictions bedevil the lives of today's *favelados*. While the neo-liberal mode of capitalism has potentialised social exclusion and made economic inequality abysmal in Brazil, television (the sets are increasingly affordable or accessible) has democratised the appeal of consumption. Television seduces this 'miserable yet desiring mass', in the words of Arnaldo Jabor. Desire meets the power of arms and drugs, increasingly forced upon the small ones by the interests of the dealers. The tripod interest-power-desire is perversely closed. To name is to make exist, yet the figure of Christ does not make an appearance. City of God, the name of this *favela* on the western fringes of the city, was improperly called from the beginning a 'housing project'; it is in fact a very simple and very poor housing area constructed by Governor Carlos Lacerda between 1962 and 1965, and where Paulo Lins and his family were re-housed after the floods of 1966. Roberto Schwarz points out that it was the result of bungled planning by this reactionary Governor (Chapter 2). As Lins spins the social memory of City of God, he makes those deprived of the recognition warranted by a legalised residence symbolically exist as residents of the city. A common popular saying is that God is Brazilian. But the reality rendered visible and audible by the film deconstructs Brazilian popular memory. It will be recalled that, with great fervour, children in City of God hold hands and pray to the Lord before beginning a slaughter. The celebrated yet invisible image of the Christ might be witnessing, from the distant heights, a new generation of violence and drug traffic being born. But the blessed figure remains unseen in and from City of God.

City of God and the Politics of (Im)Proper Names

A profound irony inhabits the title of the book, which later becomes the title of the film, *City of God*. The *favela*, increasingly pushed into the state of a ghetto, continues to efface the 'proper' promised in the name of the 'housing project'.

The year 2003 is also a reference for Ruy Castro's book *Rio de Janeiro* (2003, English translation 2004). His playful survey of the history of Rio brings to light what I would refer to as the politics of misnaming Rio. He recounts how in the summer of 1502 the Portuguese fleet commanded by Gonçalo Coelho sailed into the Guanabara Bay for the first time; the Florentine chief pilot, Amerigo Vespucci, confused the bay with a river mouth and named it Rio de Janeiro, shortly after shortened to Rio. This same Vespucci saw in Rio a paradise-like masterpiece of nature.[7]

---

[7] Here is Castro's account: 'a riotous display of hills and mountain-ranges, beaches, inlets, islands, dunes, sandbanks, mangrove swamps, lagoons and forests, all this under an endless blue sky [...] inhabited by happy, sunburnt and

Foreign eyes have in fact, for centuries, according to Castro, constructed an imaginary of the Marvellous City, ranging from an Eden to a kind of sexual Mecca. Yet, the subtitle *Carnival under Fire* and the prologue to his book bring out the real, striking the keynote that alterations in the panorama of the city no longer arise from foreigners' projections, but from a new presence, the projectiles of drug gangsters. As already prefigured by the title of the book, parallel to the festivity that epitomises pleasure and fantasy, the gangsters have unleashed a wave of violence in the city's outskirts, setting fire to buses staging shoot-outs with the police in the *favelas* and setting off cinema-like car chases (p. 1).

Not 'fantasy', but 'cavalry' is the word chosen by Soares to describe the tyrannical imposition of allegiance by the drug and arms dealers settled in the *favela,* drawing young addicts into the trade; a shift from 'blessings' to 'malediction', emblematic of the corrosion of values and of the inversion of the system of power in a community previously ruled by other forms of authority, finds a correlative in the now ironical undertone of its name (Chapter 14). 'The City of God and of the Devil', the title of his contribution, names a malevolent presence as a sharer in the power system of the city.

The tag to the name of the *favela* (the Devil) also carries a major echo for the Brazilian ear, that of Glauber Rocha's 1964 *Deus e o Diabo na Terra do Sol* [*Black God White Devil*]. It is sufficient for our purposes here to refer to its two alternative manifestations of power emerging in lieu of the ineffectual established ones: *cangaço* (social banditism), a marginal form of protection developed in the poorest areas of Brazil's Northeast, and Messianism, the social movement based on the conviction that a divine entity will be sent to spread justice and peace amongst men.

To the renegotiation of power, this time in the actors' workshop, we will return.

A Floating Voice in Search of a (Theoretical) Body

> '"Dadinho" o caralho, meu nome agora é Zé Pequeno, porra!'
> '"Li'l Dice", my ass, my name now is Li'l Zé. Fuck it!'

The DVD version of *City of God* released in Brazil opens with the threatening sounds of a disembodied masculine voice over a black screen. The voice, attached to no particular bearer invades our reality; as Slavoj Žižek would have it, it 'flows freely in space, towards some addressee, function[ing] as a stain or blemish, interfere[ing] like a foreign body' (1999: 15). This initially meaningless presence without a body – a floating signifier, as it were – is later attached to that of the ruthless drug dealer Zé Pequeno [Li'l Zé], a tyrant, previously named Dadinho, who as a child had already 'killed his thirst to kill'. At 18 he is re-baptised in a *Quimbanda* rite of passage, a type of black magic that legitimises his

---

amoral people [...] who spent all their time singing and dancing in the sun [...] sleeping in hammocks by moonlight or in romantic straw huts' (pp. 9-12).

route to evil.[8] He emerges from the ritual as Zé Pequeno, a change in name that unleashes all evil, imaginable and otherwise. His previous name, Dadinho, insinuates a certain playfulness in his taking chances with life. The christening, as it were, of Zé Pequeno is like an imprecation, which, through irony, foretells the magnitude of crimes to come. Besides trivialising death, Zé Pequeno introduces a menacing and profound change into the natural hierarchies and values of the *favela*. The small children's perception of the gangsters as idols is suggested in the film by the positioning of the camera, always shooting them from low angles (see Chapter 4). A perverse hierarchy in the drug business, built upon the exploitation of small children, begins with pre-adolescent delivery boys who are later promoted to lookouts, then to soldiers, and finally to managers, the boss's right hand.

Lúcia Nagib correlates (nick)naming and authoritarianism within the *favela* itself (Chapter 5). For her, those nicknames sum up the characters' lives and immobilise them within poverty's hierarchy while reflecting the prejudices of life described in ready-made phrases. I would like to supplement her point by drawing attention to one other detail, that of the mismatched names that also populate *City of God*. The Trio Ternura [Tenderness Trio], made up of the three bandits Cabeleira [Shaggy], Alicate [Clipper] and Marreco [Goose] achieve notoriety from a hold-up in a motel. Upon Zé Pequeno's death, he is soon replaced by Giant, a small child, whose mismatched name points to premature criminality, inasmuch as it foreshadows a long trajectory of marginality. The otherwise crude protocol of naming in the *favela* through a physical attribute – of which Cabeção [Melonhead] is but one example – can also be seen as a sign of the negation of individuality and social visibility outside the *favela*, which only exists in the press for the wrong reasons. Newsworthiness, albeit for the wrong reasons, renders those individuals notorious or, as Schwarz elaborates in Chapter 2 with reference to Lins's book, a perverse mechanism against social exclusion is set in motion when, through the media, inhuman acts take on positive value.

Renaming is also emblematic of a change in social ethos. At stake is a sense of transformation not only of Zé Pequeno's identity, but of the Brazilian social actors, more specifically that of the folkloric *malandro* (to whom we return). It also brings out shifting religious values, from the pervasive *Umbanda* (that restores the balance of energies) to the more surreptitious *Quimbanda* – that uses the same deities, but with opposite purposes – to promote the benefit of the individual through the destruction of the others. Film language has rendered palpable this anomalous floating voice of transformation. Yet this singularity deals a blow to the Brazilian ethos of cordiality and flexibility. Both the changing ethos and the new social actor demand that the country revisit some of the pillars of its national identity and broaden its epistemologies of the social.

Schwarz, who has contributed important scholarship on Brazilian

---

[8] The more popular ritual of *Umbanda* or *Candomblé* in Afro-Brazilian culture, meant to restore to balance energies in disarray, would have been more natural and traditional in Brazil.

culture and its forms within the framework of the peripheral development of capitalism, has taken the lead and underlined the transformations of the older slum-world order under the pressure of the narco-traffic wars, and the parallel developments in police violence and corruption. Relying on Antonio Candido's 'Dialética da malandragem' ['Dialectic of Trickery'], Schwarz shows the early *malandro* to-and-fro between order and disorder; in a crescendo, the gangster emerges on the scene of the *neo-favela* (Chapter 2). Line picks up the thread and sees the early *malandros* in *City of God*, the Trio Ternura [Tenderness Trio], as initially sharing some of the features of the honourable bandits of the Northeast, the *cangaceiros* (Chapter 9). Soares, it will be recalled, stresses the new type of evil arising from the later combination of drugs and arms and the tyranny of the drug dealers (Chapter 14).

'Who is going to solve the problem?' and 'And on which budget', are questions taken up by Arnaldo Jabor as he revisits, in the preface to this book, his meditations on the film after first watching it. 'What theoretical framing?' is my own epistemological echo. Schwarz bridges power and class structures in his materialist analysis of the book that gave rise to the film (Chapter 2). The drug dealers exercise control over the *favela* but the opulence that the trade generates is not there; class exploitation is further implicit in his naming of other absences: 'the higher spheres of drug- and arms-trafficking and the military and political corruption that protect them' as well as 'the real-estate speculators and public administrators that ensure the *favela*'s segregation from the rest of the city'. His description of the lifeless Little Joe (equivalent to Li'l Zé in the film), the once powerful gang leader in the *favela*, further suggest the potential of a class-race intersection:

> Dead on the ground, the cunning, violent lord of life and death is a gap-toothed youngster, under-nourished and illiterate, often barefoot and in shorts, invariably dark-skinned in colour: the point on which all injustices of Brazilian society converge (Chapter 3).

The class-race intersection also punctuates Ismail Xavier's analysis of the film in 'Angels with dirty faces':

> The film reveals the role played by the fabric of emotions spun from intense, frustrated desire bringing to the fore the resentment that lies beneath such shocking forms of aggression. It gives powerful expression to the feelings of class and racial disenfranchisement that create a subject under siege in a society swamped by images of glamour and sex appeal and a rhetoric of advertisements intent on the exploitation of mimetic desire, a rhetoric that gives elegant new forms to old associations of aggressive virility, the accumulation of goods and power (2003:30)

In his contribution to this volume Xavier highlights the intimidating drug dealer as a social symptom and '*as a sign of the victory of the market over the State reduced to impotence'* (his emphasis). This second analysis of *City of God*, however, pursues a different trajectory. Casting the film within a constellation of other Brazilian productions of the last years, he focuses on characters who, like Buscapé, manage to bypass the shortcut of drug-dealing as a way out of poverty.

The voice that anticipates the images of *City of God* lays bare not a wound but multiple wounds in the body of Brazilian history and cultural theory. Other voices will variously respond to the wound and to the wounded. But the first response does not come from a voice. It comes from a camera in the *favela*.

A Camera Shoots the Audience: Demanding Visibility and Technological Inclusion

As part of the new aesthetics ushered in by *City of God*, a camera, when the film starts, is aimed at the audience – shooting the viewers straight in the eye. Via the camera, the eyes of the audience return the look and a negotiation is set in motion. Looking at the audience through the viewer is the narrator Buscapé [Rocket], a Cidade de Deus boy. Through him, the audience is looked at and is unavoidably implicated in the images of the perverse encounter of dire poverty, drugs and arms; the audience becomes complicit with what is documented and presented. The camera becomes a weapon against the violence of non-recognition or mis-recognition. It is a demand for social visibility in the structure of the film. From then on, Buscapé is also the one who guides the spectator through the *favela* (see Meirelles, Chapter 3), delineating a path through its meaning and its characters, and at the same time constructing the symbolic power of the film and of the image, a point to which we return.

The camera is additionally a technological metaphor representing alternatives in life beyond dire poverty or drugs. Thinking of other protagonists in the film, mention is made of Bené [Benny], the 'good' bandit, the one who bears traces of humanity; hence his decision to abandon his life of drugs. Yet, at his farewell party he is shot dead, thus reiterating the recurring situation whereby there is little escape from evil and anonymity – even if your name invites you to do so. The good, the bad and the photographer (not the ugly...) is my own rendering of a society structured around excluding binaries, but which allows for a third that is empowered by technology to break the confines of class and race. For the *We in Cinema* project, film and technology are weapons against exclusion from job opportunities and to break down barriers between social classes. Technology becomes social intervention.

Technology is a point at which Fernando Meirelles departs radically from Glauber Rocha's hard-hitting films intended to 'break the paradise of inertia of the public', and shock them into awareness through the use of rudimentary equipment and techniques (Rocha, in Johnson and Stam, 1995: 179). Meirelles signals a new conception of representation, which is the use of sophisticated technologies to render visible and realistic the more intangible aspects of culture. Sound in Meirelles's film is also seductive. The samba tunes of this scene also grip the audience, making it feel a part of the action, until the initial scene strikes a note of disaster and the audience retreats, only to slip back in when a change in scene recovers its grip. The overall thrust of Ivana Bentes' contention is that the film's aesthetics neutralises the shock. What I would like to suggest is that, even though the comparison between *City of God* and *Cinema Novo* yields interesting results, there is a sense in which Meirelles's production 40 years later can be seen within its own rules of representation and as a different way of approaching the social problems of Brazil.

A Feathered Protagonist: Defamiliarising Perception

In the initial scenes, the audience's look is also met with the imploring eyes of a chicken – her legs tied, her fate sealed as suggested by the sound of a knife being sharpened. This visual intrusion serves as yet another chronicle of a death foretold. That is, until something unexpected occurs. She breaks free of the strings round her legs and dashes off, believing that she is fleeing her fate – only to face the frantic chase of the armed gang under the command of Zé Pequeno. Walter Salles has described our feathered protagonist as a traumatised chicken in a crossfire. And he goes on to ascribe a symbolic meaning to the chicken: she stands for so many Brazilians trapped in an unjust country. With her eyes turned towards the audience, the chicken fixes the spectators in a plea to be looked at and looked after. The history of this trauma is thus never only the *favela*'s; it shows that we are implicated in one another's trauma.

But there is another dimension to the chicken that brings us back to the strange familiarity that punctuates the film. This scene is, up to a point, a common one in Brazil, the preparation of the Sunday dish *frango ao molho pardo*, like *frango à cabidela* in Portugal, that is, chicken cooked in a sauce thickened with its own blood, which requires it to be slaughtered at the time of cooking. But this familiar scene is rendered unfamiliar as her fate is not the pan, but the crossfire of dealers or the police. It will be recalled that the British audience had its perception sharpened by the familiar story rendered strange by a change in setting; for the Brazilians the familiar setting was rendered unfamiliar by a change in film language. Katia Lund hints at this possibility when, in an interview with Vicente Lou in London, she states that film also provides the spectators with other ways of perceiving something or someone they have always looked at but not seen (2004: 21). The point of view of the chicken is a reminder of the effects achieved by fables through the use of animals endowed with human qualities to enable a distancing reflection on everyday life. These three not only invite the audience in – they plunge the Brazilian audience into the world of the *favela* at the same creating a distancing effect – they invite one to recognise and also to mis-recognise. In this way, the audience is invited to look at the *favela* with fresh eyes and to develop a critical stance on the situation.

A Director in Search of One Hundred Black Actors

Upon entering the *favela* Cidade de Deus, on the western fringes of Rio, one notices that its population is 95 percent black. This point is confirmed by *favela* spokesman, M V Bill, the founder in Cidade de Deus of the political party PPPomar which stands for *Partido Popular Poder para a Maioria* [Popular Party Power to the Majority], the first political party for blacks in Brazil and increasingly one of the most important militant black groups in the country. It is also called *Partido Negro* [*Black Party*], and confronts racism as the basis for the marked social inequalities in the country. This eminently respected member of the *favela* community does not accept the label of artist, because he has not lost his sense of his social place, for which in fact he has been awarded prizes by UNESCO and also Rio's and Barcelona's Citizen of the Year. His objective is not to gain the world's recognition, but to struggle against the violence of the non-recognition of his community. As such, he has denounced the racism of, for example, television programmes that have only white actors. The exclusive membership of blacks in the PPPomar party is explained as the wish not to continue to have the rights of blacks defended by whites. *Trafficking Information*, his first CD, conveys the reality of his community from the point of view of the unhappiness of those who have no connection with the drug traffic, but who sleep on the floor at night for fear of stray bullets.

A different trajectory led Fernando Meirelles to a similar realisation of the under-representation of blacks in the Brazilian media. His policy differs from M V Bill's assertion of race and the exclusive membership of non-whites. Rather, Meirelles projects a class-race intersection. As he explains in Chapter 3, he wanted the spectator to have a direct relationship with the characters. And he wanted actors who would know how to interpret the characters, which presented a problem. Brazil, with its abundance of white, middle-class actors, has a dearth of young black and/or mulatto actors. As a result, Meirelles looked for talent in the *favela* communities of Rio, having short-listed 200 out of 1000 interviewed.

The review of *City of God* in *Black Filmmaker* (02/03) does not fulfil the promise of addressing the issue of race announced by the journal's name. Violence is the theme that it privileges. An earlier example of unfulfilled promises is Camus's *Black Orpheus*, a world-renowned film about Rio's *favelas*. The legend of Orpheus transposed to the *favelas* conveys music as a cultural force in a world full of passion; solidarity seems to fill the vacuum of racial politics. However, the film exoticises the black population by casting them as the exception, when, in fact, blacks account for about half of the country's population. Others have denounced Brazilian television for framing the blacks within sports or dance or in subaltern roles (maids, drivers, and so on). Brazilian film, in turn, tends to present caricatures or stereotypes of blacks.

Race in Brazil has historically intersected with class and determined the standard of living and all that socio-economic status entails: access to housing, education, health care, consumption. It has also produced certain stereotypes of criminality, licentiousness, *etcetera*. In fact, the racialisation of good and evil that has accompanied Brazilian history and to which the film draws attention seems to have passed unobserved by many. Such racial framing has been epitomised by the equation 'preto de alma branca' [black with a white soul]. *City of God* draws attention to the ideology of whitening as a road to virtue through the 'good bandit'. Bené is a 'whitened black' whose decision to leave the life of drugs and arms is signalled by his dyed blonde hair. White 'outside' and wearing a fashionable shirt, he constructs the image of whiteness and glamour prioritised by society. Ironically (or deterministically?) he is shot dead before fulfilling his aspirations.

The review in *Film Comment* by Alcino Leite Neto has, in turn, stressed that the film's impact derives mostly from the performances in a film that features one of the largest black casts ever seen in a Brazilian film (2002: 11).

The *favelas* have been burgeoning with historically and successively marginalised people, the blacks being a case in point. But it is film as a reconstructive project that I shall be looking at with reference to the workshop.

The Actors' Workshop: Negotiating the Power of the Voice

The blacks are the most affected by the logic of capitalism's unequal and contradictory development which has hit Brazil hard and has accentuated the differentiation between those who have access to the modes of production and can contract wage labour and those (a large part of the country) who are impoverished. Capital does not recreate with the same intensity that it excludes.[9] The actors' workshops in many ways straddle the asphalt-*favela* binary, creating a link between the entrepreneurial class, fully integrated into the capitalist system, and those who have been excluded by capital. Casting off the persona of the commercial director, Meirelles dived headlong into the daily training of actors in workshops in the *favelas* for months. There the country's social extremes – perhaps the country's most successful commercial director and those trapped by abject poverty – find a meeting point in performance art. He describes this process at length in Chapter 3.

This is perhaps also the place where the strategy of team working becomes visible and the traces of other voices are rendered audible. Katia Lund's knowledge of the codes of the *favela* resonates through the script and the training of the characters. This started in 1996 when Michael Jackson made a video in Rio and she mediated the negotiations with the drug trafficker Marcinho and the Inhabitants' Associations; this experience was the catalyst for her production of the documentary *Notícias de uma Guerra Particular* [*News from a Personal War*]. And then there is Guti Fraga's long-standing work with theatre in the *favelas*. This actor and stage manager was already living in the Vidigal *favela* and recognised that there was so much untapped talent there. Upon his return from New York, where he staged Marília Pera, he was inspired by the way that off-Broadway shows produced non-mainstream work with high artistic merit. He decided to set up an actors' workshop, *Nós do Morro* [*Us from the Hill*], which has now over 300 students. Success is based on the principle of intense training and a mixture of plays about life in the *favela* and the classics.

The pre-production workshops enabled the professionalisation of

---

[9] This aspect of capitalism has been highlighted by Bernardo Mançano with reference to the rural landless workers (in Vieira, forthcoming).

these talented people from the *favela*. Implicit in their activities is the recognition of the source of creativity Brazilians derive from being great improvisers. But for them to find a channel into the world at large they need to go through the discipline of professionalising inborn gifts; 'controlled spontaneity' is the way Cristophe Narbonne describes the effect achieved (2003: 36). Meirelles also mentions their training to remain undisturbed by cameras glued to their faces. Conversely, in a two-way flow, the rigorous world outside learns to appreciate their creativity.

Half the word we say already belongs to someone else. This is the basic principle of dialogism established by Bakhtin which is apposite to describe the process whereby the pre-defined voice of the script opens itself to the voice of the other which empowers itself in the process. From another perspective, a certain resonance of Paulo Freire complements Bakhtin's dialogism with the articulation of the expression of the underprivileged (1998). For this Brazilian pedagogue, to speak the word is to generate words from the universe of the discourse of the oppressed. As the actors-cum-creators speak their words and listen to the words from their same circle of culture, they re-existentialise their world and position it in relation to another world. Crucial for Freire is reading the word to read the world. Improvisation, looked at from this perspective, is empowering; it enables the *favelados* to be co-creators of the script and narrators of their (hi)story.

The workshops established a pattern which, upon completion of the film, enabled the participants to start a film-making project as a reconstructive process: the *Nós do Cinema* [*We in Cinema*], a media-arts non-governmental organisation described in Chapter 18. In an attempt to reweave the fabric of a society that tends to exclude and disqualify the poor, the unequivocal trajectory of the *We in Cinema* project and of its off-shoot, the *Get Together* project, has been the development of integrative strategies and the search for solutions based on recognition and positive representation. The remarkable talent of the group, already evident in *City of God,* has been increasingly recognised in Brazil through the focus of the Project on positive representation. New life paths for many have thus been opened up. Suffice it to mention a few facts relating to those in the original cast and who make up the administrative body of today's *We in Cinema.* Luis Carlos Nascimento, the coordinator, has competed for the prize of distinguished work with technology as a weapon against social exclusion; he also conceived and implemented the project 'Theatre Literature' in schools, which, in addition to putting on performances, distributes books and promotes debates with the playwrights. Recently he directed the award-winning short film *Cidadão Silva* [*Citizen Silva*] (2003). Renato de Souza, the president of *We in Cinema*, is now finalising his internship in editing at Urca Films; he has long contributed to the *Ex-cola* Project aimed at rehabilitating the citizenship of street children, particularly those who sniff glue.[10] He has

---

[10] The pun in the name of the project is untranslatable into English, but an explanation renders explicit the agenda of presenting alternatives to drugs that feeds into this and into the *Nós do Cinema* projects in general: the word for school

also been an actor in feature films, including the award-winning *Quase Dois Irmãos* [*Almost Two Brothers*], and the TV series *Cidade dos Homens* [*City of Men*], recently aired by the BBC. Mention is also made of Leandro Firmino da Hora, Li'l Zé in *City of God*, who is today studying Biology at the Santa Úrsula University. He has worked as interviewer for the documentary on the actors of *City of Men,* among other roles in television, and has directed a polemical short film on medical neglect.

This examination of the outcomes of participation in *City of God* parallels another major debate in Brazil, namely the assignment of quotas for black people to give them greater access to University. Several studies have been conducted that reveal that the professional performance of blacks does not differ from that of whites, the same holding true for their incomes, once they manage to enter the job market. But the marked difference resides in the conditions of access for the blacks (whose race, as has been seen, also tends to be class-marked) to the job market; they lack social competitiveness. That access to the job market cannot be dissociated from mastering technology is the key idea of the *We in Cinema* group.

The widely seen and recognised talent and professionalism of the members of *We in Cinema* has altered racial and physical concepts of beauty and respectability. Thus, not only providing a life path for individuals, it also goes further, providing positive representation and constructive role models for millions. The efforts of the group, nationally and internationally, to promote a space for non-prejudiced engagement with disadvantaged groups, are also remarkable.

Ismail Xavier, in this book, presents the overall pattern into which this initiative fits, namely the politics of NGOs [Non-Governmental Organisations], which provide artistic training as a means of education for citizenship, a process that involves the individual's self-affirmation and the recovery of self-esteem. Further still, as exemplified by such characters as Buscapé or the mythological figure of Orpheus, he points out the important role of Brazilian film today in humanising barbarism.

The Voice from the Wound: The Power and Pain of Visibility

I was very moved when, on the last day of 2004, M V Bill, upon my request, dedicated some of his precious time to revisit his meditations on what he considers to be the major issues interconnecting the population of the *favela* Cidade de Deus and the film *City of God*. The thrust of his argument is that the film made the *favela* into a protagonist in world history, but no dialogue was established with the community beyond the actors. Two years before, at the height of the debate surrounding the film in Brazil, M V Bill had used the website *Viva Favela* and other media to draw attention to these issues. The first time he summoned the *favela* population – the prospective winner of the 'Oscar for violence' – for a collective interview was when the film was nominated for the Academy Award. He thinks that a more aggressive rhetoric was unavoidable in order to make the community move the discussion beyond

---

in Portuguese is *escola,* which is pronounced the same as *ex-cola*, meaning 'formerly glue'.

issues of verisimilitude between the film and the *favela*. Two days later he took the floor again. The more celebratory agenda was then the unprecedented mobilisation of all sectors of society and the number of new partnerships and official commitments in response to the first message.

But what was also wounding, in his view, was the way this reality was told. Visibility was given to the talented young ones in the actors' workshop but, contrary to the expectation of dialogue with the *favela* in general or with its political leadership, there was no sharing of a history of which they were protagonists. If their voice had been heard, in their view, the social focus of the film would have been enhanced; if greater contact had been established, the film would also have given them the chance to change their reality. They had also expected the film to be presented to the *favela* before premièring in the cinemas, but their lives were first exposed to the world, not to themselves.

Cidade de Deus, he stresses, is still waiting for an expression of affection from those involved in the film whose countless achievements include its having triggered changes in the reality it depicted. They do not expect individuals to solve the immensity of their problems, but, in their view, there could have been a gesture of recognition. It is this symbolic debt of the voice that the *favela* claims, a word of affection.

The film *City of God* has been perceived by many as an event that provoked the responses of institutionalized power and this is seen to highlight its role as a social film. But their interrogation of the government's policy is incisive. What Spivak has referred to as strategic essentialism (1984-5) seems to explain what gives force to this political voice from the wound. They refer to the government's granting of resources to 'the men of the asphalt' to narrate the history of a population that is not even granted the bare minimum of dental care. Will their story continue to be narrated by others? Why are the chances not given to them to become narrators themselves? Even if the *favelados* want to tell their own (hi)story, they lack competitiveness and never get the grants, so they will remain those forever narrated by anthropologists and film-makers.

A sorrowful voice of Otherness cries out from the wound, trying to tell the world of a reality or truth that was unavailable, signalling the moral discomfort of those in the *favela* who have no connection with the drug problem. The exposure of violence humiliated the self-esteem of the *favela*. Visibility can be a poison and a remedy. The film, which became an event in Brazil, in turn interacted with the best-selling book by Lins that preceded it, mobilising public authorities and the population. The cure, as in psychoanalytic processes, can only be attained through the disclosure of the object; it could only be obtained by making the wound available (Žižek, 1999: 272).

The Camera or the Word? Overpowering Guns

Carolina Maria de Jesus wrote in her diary:

'They', the unnamed crowd, understand, 'those who live and degrade themselves there in hunger, mud, litter and bed'; 'big-tummied children' and a 'thin dog' understand the misery 'better than us'. 'But they won't say anything. They cry, they scream, they fight, they love, love of all kinds, they swear, they commit suicide, they clench their stomachs, but they don't say anything (quoted in Vieira, 1995: 103).

Unlike the majority of illiterates living in the *favela* in the 1950s, who had their own sign-system but were aphasic towards or, perhaps, in the eyes of, the nation, those from Cidade de Deus and other *favelas* will speak to the nation. M V Bill, in fact, solicits class and racial identification and solidarity for a counter-hegemonic expression of the *favela*. They will also demand to-be-looked-at-ness and to-be-listened-to-ness. They will demand writing. And they will demand technology, the deficit of which has become a means of subalternisation.

Buscapé, through technology, establishes a link with the world outside and the *favela* City of God. He follows the path laid down by his predecessor, Paulo Lins, the writer who gave fictional expression to the social fabric in mutation of City of God, a pattern, in turn, previously established by the empowerment through writing of Carolina Maria de Jesus. In the meantime, the problems of exclusion she depicts have been aggravated. Many many more need to write themselves into being, as Henry Louis Gates Jr. would have it. Rendering the problem and the trauma explicit, as Meirelles has done, can be a step towards a solution. Yet the complexity of the problem demands many more voices and images, many more heads.

'Is the camera mightier than the word and the sword?' is the question that has hovered over our journey. The voices in this book, disparate as they may be, in unison seem to imply the need for the recovery of the social and political ethos. Cidade de Deus, before Paulo Lins's book, was an open letter that no one cared to read. The camera and the sound technology of Meirelles's *City of God* further hit our eyes and ears with the magnitude of the problem of dire poverty encountering drug traffic, in our days unimaginably aggravated as it has fallen into the hands of global narco-guerrillas. The power of Lins´s writing must meet another constellation of accessible instruments of communication and of articulation of power. Many now also face the need to film themselves into being.

The *neo-favela*'s demand for to-be-looked-at-ness implicates the Brazilian audience – but not only them – to position themselves in relation to the global problem of drugs and the historical vicissitudes that transformed the always poor but solidarity-driven, more hedonistic and folkloric *favela* depicted by the films of the 1950s and 1960s into a battleground of narco-traffic or, more recently, narco-guerrilla. But songs and words traffic information too.

Out of solidarity with all in a traumatised *favela* – and against the 'talking bullets' – the chorus of voices in this book speaks *with* them and with Meirelles's camera.

A Postscript: *We in Cinema* as Social Action

This book, conceived to mark the first visit to Britain of the original cast of *City of God*, looks at both *City of God* and the productions of the *We in Cinema* group as part of the tradition of cinema as social action in Brazil. For the visit, *We in Cinema* made a special short film, initially called *People Not in the News,* as part of the agenda in Brazil of providing visibility to those whose identity has been negatively constructed, to those devoid of an image, the 'filmless' ones. Along the way, the focus was redirected and the film is now called *Vida Nova com Favela* [*New Life with Favela*].

The short film, directed by Luis Carlos Nascimento, interpellates the governor of Rio who, in the 1960s, during the dictatorship, created a politics of exclusion and isolation of the *favela*, of which Cidade de Deus is an example. To remove one *favela* is to create another. Such policies, in turn, establish a dialogue with another process of modernisation based on the late 19th century positivist whitening of the black race which, it stands to reason, is a form of denial of race. The film spells out routes for the valorisation of the *favela* production and of racial affirmation. Its characters are a hamburger delivery boy, a Mãe-de-Santo (a figure from *Candomblé*, the Afro-Brazilian religious manifestation) and also the flag-bearer of the Mangueira Samba School. These influential characters have become a reference for the *favela* in that they embody the view that the world is possible. The delivery boy lives in the most violent community, the Complexo do Alemão, where Luis himself was born and grew up. This complex embodies 16 *favelas*, where over a million people live in 200,000 shacks. It displays the lowest level of human development in Rio.

Vida Nova com Favela bears traces of the autobiographical. A major problem that the director has faced in life, and which he shares with others in the *favela,* is that they could have their professional dreams, work hard towards them, but these were *a priori* aborted because their physical type did not conform to the images projected by society.

When asked about the impact of the *City of God* experience, he said that, above all, it made him realise that he could dream. Film enables one to become the protagonist of one's own dreams. One films today that one is, say, a teacher, and then begins to construct one's history from one's own dreams. For those actors, it is in the recovery of the possibility of being through acting that the social action of their cinema mostly resides.

References

Althusser, Louis. 'Ideology and the ideological state apparatuses'. In: *Lenin and Philosophy and Other Essays.* Trans. Ben Brewster. London: New Left Books, 1971.

Bakhtin, M. M. *The Dialogic Imagination.* Ed. M. Holquist. Trans. C. Emerson and M. Holquist. Austin, TX: University of Texas Press, 1981.

'Losing my religion'. *Black Filmmaker.* V. 5, no. 18, Dec-Jan 02/03, 14-

15.

Castro, Ruy. *Rio de Janeiro*: *Carnival under Fire.* Trans. John Gledson. London: Bloomsbury, 2004.

Delorme, Gérard. 'La spontanéité contrôlée de Fernando Meirelles'. Interview with Fernando Meirelles. *Cahier Critique,* no. 313, March 2003, p. 36.

Derrida, Jacques and Bennington, Geoffrey. *Jacques Derrida.* Chicago and London: The University of Chicago Press, 1993.

Fernandes, Bernardo Mançano. 'Occupation as a form of access to the land'. In: Vieira, Else R P (ed). *The MST: Movement of the Rural Landless Workers of Brazil*: *Introductory Essays.* Nottingham: CCC Press (forthcoming).

Freire, Paulo. 'Reading the word and the world'. In: Freire, Ana Maria Araújo and Madedo, Donaldo (eds). *The Paulo Freire Reader.* New York: Continuum, 1998, pp. 163-85.

Gardnier, Ruy. 'Editorial'. *Contracampo.* March 2003.

Gates, Jr., Henry Louis *Figures in Black.* New York: Oxford University Press, 1987.

Johnson, Randal and Stam, Robert. *Brazilian Cinema.* New York: Columbia University Press, 1995.

Leite Neto, Alcino. 'Discovery: Fernando Meirelles'. *Film Comment.* V. 38, no 4, Jul/Aug 2002, 10-11.

Lou, Vicente. 'Interview with Katia Lund'. *Leros.* October 2004, pp. 21, 23.

Machado da Silva, Luiz Antonio. 'A continuidade do "problema favela"'. In: Lúcia Lippi Oliveira (ed.). *Cidade*: *história e desafios.* Rio de Janeiro: Fundação Getúlio Vragas, 2002.

Mattos, Carlos Alberto. 'Em busca da voz legítima'. *Cinemais,* vol 36, October/December 2003, 79-84.

Meirelles, Fernando. *Interview for El Clarín.* In: 'Polémica en el festival: el realizador brasileño contra quienes lo denostan'. *El Clarín.* 9 March 2003.

Mulvey, Laura. 'Visual pleasure and narrative cinema'. In: Mulvey, L. *Visual and Other Pleasures.* London: Macmillan, 1989.

Rocha, Glauber. 'An Esthetic of Hunger'. In: Randal Johnson and Robert Stam (eds). *Brazilian Cinema* (Expanded Edition). Columbia University Press, 1995, pp. 69-71.

Rocha, Glauber. 'The tricontinental filmmaker: that is called dawn'. In: Randal Johnson and Robert Stam (eds). *Brazilian Cinema* (Expanded Edition). Columbia University Press, 1995, pp. 77-80.

Spivak, Gayatri C. 'Can the subaltern speak?' In: Patrick Williams and Laura Chrisman (eds). *Colonial Discourse and Post-Colonial Theory*: *A Reader.* New York, London: 1993, pp. 66-111.

Spivak, Gayatri C. 'Criticism, feminism, and the institution', interview with Elizabeth Gross, *Thesis Eleven* 10/11 (November/March), 1984-5: 175-8.

St. Clair, David. 'Translator's Preface'. In *Child of the Dark*: *The Diary of Carolina Maria de Jesus.* New York: Signet Classic, 1962, pp. 7-15.

Steiner, Peter. *Russian Formalism*: *A Metapoetics.* Ithaca and London: Cornell University Press, 1984.

Télerama no. 2774, March 12th 2003, 38-9.

The Internet Movie Database (http://www.imdb.com)

Vieira, Else R P. 'Can another subaltern speak/ write?' In: Mark Millington and Collin Heywood (eds). *Renaissance and Modern Studies. Special Issue*: *Minorities and Minority Discourse*. Vol. 38, 1995, 96-125.

Xavier, Ismail. *Allegories of Underdevelopment*: *Aesthetics and Politics in Modern Brazilian Cinema*. Minneapolis, London: University of Minnesota Press, 1997.

Xavier, Ismail. 'Brazilian Cinema in the 1990s: The unexpected encounter and the resentful character'. In Nagib, Lúcia (ed.). *The New Brazilian Cinema*. London and New York: I.B. Tauris, 2003, pp. 39-63.

Xavier, Ismail. 'Angels with dirty faces', *Sight and Sound*. January 2003, 28-30.

Žižek, Slavoj. 'The undergrowth of enjoyment: how popular culture can serve as an introduction to Lacan'; 'A hair of the dog that bit you'. In Wright, Elizabeth and Wright, Edmond (eds). *The Žižek Reader.* Oxford: Blackwell, 1999, pp. 11-36, 268-82.

PART I
THE SIGHTS AND SOUNDS IN
F. MEIRELLES'S *CITY OF GOD*

1. A Traumatised Chicken in Crossfire
Walter Salles

The film begins with a chicken who knows too much. We are in City of God, a *favela* (a Rio de Janeiro slum) in the early 1980s. A gang of young drug dealers is preparing the local stew. This chicken knows that she is dead meat and tries desperately to escape. The tragicomic scene that ensues determines the tone of *City of God*, a Brazilian film by Fernando Meirelles, co-directed by Katia Lund. The fleeing animal is chased and fired at by the young hoodlums until fate leads her under the wheels of a police car.

A clash between the young princes of the *favela* and the police is imminent and promises to be bloody. It will, however, be frozen in time, as Meirelles takes us to the 1960s and 1970s in the same locale. Based on a true account by Paulo Lins, a writer born and raised in the place that lends its name to the film, *City of God* does not offer the comforting and touristy image of the Brazilian slums that Marcel Camus's 1959 film *Orfeu Negro* [*Black Orpheus*] sold to the world. This is about a nation within a nation, about the millions of *olvidados* [the forgotten] that are statistically relevant, but scarcely represented on screen.

Rarely has a film created such heated debate in Brazil. The country's current leader, Luiz Inácio da Silva, at the time the socialist presidential candidate, urged the then president, Fernando Henrique Cardoso, to see *City of God* in order to understand the extent of the urban tragedy in Brazil. Cardoso did. Arnaldo Jabor, one of Brazil's most important intellectuals, wrote that 'this is not only a film. It is an important fact, a crucial statement, a borehole in our national conscience'.

After I directed the Oscar-winning *Central Station*, our small production house had the opportunity to help a few films by upcoming Brazilian directors. The decision to be part of *City of God* was defined by the trust we had in Meirelles and his co-director, but also because few films could shed more light on the social apartheid of Brazil.

There are more than 40,000 violent deaths a year in Brazil, more than three times the total number of deaths in Kosovo. Many of these deaths in our urban areas are the result of confrontation between drug gangs, or between dealers and the police. What *City of God* achieves is the possibility to understand how we got to this chaos.

In the 1960s, families of immigrants expelled from their land in the Northeast of the country found an illusory refuge in the slums in Rio de Janeiro. The marginalised youth living on the fringe of society at that time had to bend to strict familial codes and rules. The drug was marijuana, which inspired a contemplative, 'romantic' lifestyle. Gun use at the time was sporadic and the ends justified the means.

In the 1970s and 1980s everything changed. The first large drug dealers appeared and outlaws ceased to lead a nomadic life and settled their businesses in the heart of the *favelas*. These dealers began to control the communities in which they operated and created a parallel system of justice within their borders. Cocaine became the drug of choice and the .38 was traded for the AK47 and other machine guns. The death toll grew dramatically and the dealers became younger and younger. It was hell.

City of God follows several real characters, whose lives started and ended within the *favela*'s perimeter during these three decades. Bené [Benny], the cool marijuana dealer, Zé Pequeno [Li'l Zé], a merciless killer, and Buscapé [Rocket], the innocent eye, Lins's alter ego, a young black kid who manages to break the country's social and race barriers – at a price.

Most of the film's actors are kids from amateur theatre groups in *favelas*, or non-actors found in a year-long casting effort in these communities. The directors rehearsed them for more than six months before the shoot and improvisation was encouraged. Like other directors in Brazil, I am used to working with non-actors, but I still do not know how Meirelles and Lund managed to achieve such a sense of realism.

Do not expect pity or redemption. There are no such things in *City of God*. This is the depiction of a world where people have been forgotten for too long by the Brazilian ruling classes; a world where the state does not provide proper health or education services. In fact, the only items it provides freely are bullets.

Now for the present: a time when the *olvidados* got tired of being forgotten, a time of diffuse, uncontrollable violence. '*City of God* is not only a portrait of our *favelas*, it is also our portrait, at 24 frames a second, our faces blurred with the faces of 10-year-old children holding machine guns. All the manifestations of our chaos become visible. This film will be seen by the whole country in terror, and I believe it will cause transformations in the political arena,' says Jabor.

There were also dissonant voices in Brazil, arguing that the film gives the impression that *favelas* are populated only by drug dealers. They are not. In fact, an immense part of the Brazilian population has been the victim of this present state. This is when we realise that the chicken caught in the crossfire at the beginning of *City of God* is not only a chicken. It is the reflection of so many Brazilians trapped in an unjust country.

2. Paulo Lins's Novel *City of God*
Roberto Schwarz

The 'City of God' – there is no irony in the name – is a slum of some 200,000 inhabitants on the western edge of Rio de Janeiro. It is famous for the unending shoot-outs between drug gangs and police – an uncontrollable, escalating war, emblematic in various ways of wider social developments in Brazil. A few years ago, a remarkable novel depicting the life of the place appeared. Its author, Paulo Lins, was born in 1958 in Estácio, a black district of Rio, close to the docks; after the disastrous floods of 1966 he was rehoused with his family in the City of God. This development scheme – a product of bungled planning by Carlos Lacerda, the notoriously reactionary governor of the time – was still quite new. Lins went to school there, and carried on living in the *favela* while he studied at university. He knew the local gangsters – delinquents he had grown up with – and they came to trust him as someone who could mediate with the community on their behalf.

The most reflective and artistic circles in the *favelas* were alert to the subterranean cultural ferment against the military dictatorship in Brazil. By the seventies, discussions about popular music had become a locus of opposition, a form of political debate. On a much smaller scale, something similar occurred with poetry, where a subculture of casual colloquialism and mimeographed leaflets, passed from hand to hand, operated as an antidote to official censorship and conventional publishing. Some of these circulated in the City of God. In the early eighties the anthropologist Alba Zaluar, arriving to make a field study of the new criminality, provided another opening and source of intellectual energy. Lins became her research assistant responsible for interviews. It was in the course of this investigation that he acquired the formal discipline and range of empirical knowledge that would make his novel a work of quite another cultural order.

Five hundred and fifty pages long, *Cidade de Deus* appeared in 1997. The explosive nature of its themes, the scope and difficulty of its ambition and its unprecedented form of internal narration marked it out immediately as a major event – a work pushing back the frontier of literary possibilities in Brazil. It traces the world of what Lins calls the *neo-favela*, underlining the transformations of the older slum-world under the pressure of the narco-traffic wars, and the parallel developments in police violence and corruption.

Epic of the Street
The teeming, quasi-encyclopaedic scale of the novel's recreations of this process is reminiscent of the great gangster movies; but the story opens, subtly enough, with a scene of popular life. Young Barbantinho is sharing a joint with a friend, and daydreaming of a future as an ultra-fit lifeguard on the beach. Not one of those lazy loafers who let the sea carry people away – he would make sure he took every chance to keep fit, even running back from the beach after work: 'Need to keep at it, feed well, swim as much as possible'. Illicit activities coexist, calmly and

5

guiltlessly, with altruistic impulses, modest ambitions, punctuality and respect; keeping up with the latest health fads while trusting in the protective powers of Yemanjá;[1] emulating the good example of his father and brother – also lifeguards. A degree of hesitation is introduced in the following pages, as this hopeful, conformist outlook is cast in doubt by the poverty and unemployment – and the first corpses, floating down the river. Quite another facet of popular life is about to predominate; but the contrast between the two, potentially surfacing at any moment, has a structural function, as if to suggest a historical perspective.

It is when the gangsters erupt onto the scene with the first armed robbery that the novel picks up the mesmerising rhythm that will drive it to the end. Any serious reading of *Cidade de Deus* depends on raking the measure of this relentless dynamism. The figures in the action-packed foreground are lit up, as in a thriller. Revolvers in hand, the Tenderness Trio – Duck, Nail Clippers and Long Hair – tear across the playground into Loura Square to emerge 'opposite the Penguin Bar where the truck loaded with cylinders of domestic gas is parked'. The driver tries to conceal his takings but they order him – 'the worker' – to the ground then kick him in the face. Does the class description make their violence more reprehensible, or does it collude in jeering at the sucker who had tried to fool them? Impossible to tell. The ambivalence of the vocabulary reflects an instability of viewpoint, embedded in the action – a kind of con-artist's to-and-fro between order and disorder, to adapt, for our times, the terminology of Candido's 'Dialética da malandragem' ['Dialectic of Trickery'].[2] Besides, the robbers themselves now hand out the cylinders of gas to the frightened bystanders, who had been trying to slip away from the scene but who now, instantaneously, carry the whole consignment away.

All is as clear as it is complex. Choreographic exactitude fuses with a blurring of good and evil. Cops and gangsters, exchanging fire, both put 'half a face round the edge of the corner' [*meia cara na quina da esquina*]. The internal rhyme and acute visualisation suggest not only art as a concentration of life, but life as a process inspired by TV series that are watched by criminals and police alike. In the escapes and chases that follow, the *favela* is a series of crumbling walls, backyards and alleyways, where one character, setting off round the block to surprise a second from behind, comes face to face with the third he did not want to meet. The tension and danger, the vivid settings – seemingly made for such encounters – create a certain empathy; but any sense of adventure is

---

[1] Translator's note: Goddess of Yoruba origin.

[2] Translator's note: 'Dialética da malandragem', 1970; see Antonio Candido, *On Literature and Society*. Princeton, 1995, pp. 79-103. Candido's essay is a study of the novel by Manuel Antônio de Almeida, *Memórias de um sargento de milícias* (1854-55), taken as an example of a dialectics between order and disorder profoundly characteristic of Brazilian popular existence. The Princeton editors decline to translate *malandragem* – roughly, 'roguery' – which refers to the specifically Brazilian figure of the *malandro*, a layabout and trickster, living on the edge of legality. He is often portrayed as Zé Pelintra, Joe the Rogue – a black man, whose skin-colour denotes poverty but who wears a natty white suit, two-tone shoes and a slouched hat.

undercut by the sheer brutality of what goes on. In the end, one is left with a kind of stunned comprehension.

Less palpable is a quasi-standardisation of sequences, a sinister monotony in their variation. First come the drugs, or some other diversion. Then the boys set off for a hold-up, maybe with killings; for a rape, or some other sexual revenge to knock out rivals from another gang, or from their own. Going out for a good time – to play football on the beach, or to stir it at some party – always runs into complications and the same brutal outcome: one of the book's most disillusioning themes. Finally, after the violence, escape – on foot, by bus, in a stolen car or taxi, – and then holding up, till the necessary twenty-four hours have passed. Shut up in some room, the *bichos-soltos* [animals on the loose] knock back milk or do some drugs, to chill out and get some sleep.

Dynamics of Escalation

For all the constant repetition, there is a sense of crescendo – although nobody knows where it is leading: and here the novel confronts us with the inescapable nature of our times. The overall rhythm of the book depends not so much on points of inflexion in individual lives – although there is no shortage of these – as on escalations that take on a collective meaning. For example: an attack on a cheap hotel disintegrates into slaughter while, on the same night, a man revenges himself on his mistress, hacking to bits the white baby to which she has just given birth; on another corner, a worker mutilates his rival with a scythe. There is no link between these crimes; but the next day, the City of God emerges from anonymity, hitting the front pages as one of Rio de Janeiro's most violent zones. In their own eyes and those of the city, the gangsters' importance has grown. The hotel attack – which had only degenerated into a bloodbath because the boys were so nervous – becomes a newsworthy event, an elevation of the hoodlums' authority and that of the terror they inspire. A new mechanism of perversely inflating integration has been set in place: the most inhuman acts acquire positive value once they are reported by the media – which, in turn, become a kind of ally in the struggle to break the barriers of social exclusion. '"Gangsters got to be famous to get respect", Long Hair told Little Black.'

Another instance: Little Joe is badly disturbed by his friend's injuries. He strikes out at random, murmurs incomprehensible prayers, wants meat bought for a barbecue, and readies his gang for war with heavy doses of cocaine. Next day, they set out for the kill, eyes bulging and teeth on edge. But their craziness has an unexpected logic: its victims are the owners of corner drug joints – 'smoking-mouth'.[3] Revenge is Little Joe's pretext to move up from robber to local drug boss. Now his concern is to impose order within the terror, so as not to deter customers from outside. Just as, on the night of the hotel attack, their blunders pushed disorganised robbers onto a higher level of integration, so here, a random outburst of personal rage triggers the unification of local power and business. The immense disproportion between immediate cause and

---

[3] Translator's note: *Bocas-de-fumo*: places where marijuana and other drugs are bought and sold.

necessary outcome in the novel is one of those conjunctures in which the inexorable weight of contemporary history makes itself felt.

Such haphazard episodes slowly distil into a periodisation, shared both by the internal order of the fiction and by Brazilian reality: from individual robbery to organised gang, from improvised assaults to regular drug-trafficking, from simple revolvers to specialist weapons (at the height of gang-warfare, Little Joe tries to buy ex-Falklands rifles), from seizing odd chances for the control and management of a territory. In successive waves, the violence grows, the age of the assailants drops. It soon comes to seem logical that seventeen-year-old leaders should dispatch ten or twelve-year-olds – freer from vigilance than the older boys – to shoot down the eighteen-year-old owner of another *boca-de-fumo*. With tears in their eyes, the children accomplish their mission, to earn the status of *sujeito homem* [real men] and the esteem of the rest of the gang.

What are the frontiers of this dynamic? The action takes place within the closed world of City of God, with only a few forays outside – mainly to prisons – following characters' destinies. Events are portrayed on a grand scale but the space in which they unfold is far more limited than the social premises on which they rest. The higher spheres of drug- and arms-trafficking, and the military and political corruptions that protect them do not appear; their local agents, if not gangsters themselves, are scarcely any different. The real-estate speculators and public administration that ensure the *favela*'s segregation from the rest of the city barely figure either, save for odd glimpses – though there are quite enough to suggest that they, too, are all the same.

This limited compass functions as a strength in literary terms, dramatising the blindness and segmentation of the social process. On their own patch – that of the excluded – the gang leaders are powerful figures, men with brains and hard experience who can withstand the highest level of nervous tension. Yet they are still poor devils, dying like flies, far from the opulence that the drug trade generates elsewhere. This dizzying oscillation in our perception of their stature gives literary form to an overall social fracture, reproduced within the criminal world. Dead on the ground, the cunning, violent lord of life and death is a gap-toothed youngster, under-nourished and illiterate, often barefoot and in shorts, invariably dark-skinned in colour: the point on which all injustices of Brazilian society converge. Crime may form a world apart, with a spell that lends itself to aestheticisation; but it does not dwell outside the city that we share. It is this that prevents aesthetic distancing, that forces us to a committed reading – if only out of fear. This is a literary situation with peculiar properties of its own.

Locked into the action, the narrative viewpoint captures its instantaneous options, logic and dead ends. Pressures of danger, of necessity, bear down on the characters with the immediacy of breaking news. The result is a kind of irremediable reality and an absurd, stress-induced form of objectivity that cuts the ground away from any moral judgment. Yet *Cidade de Deus* refuses the exoticism and sadism of commercial gangster fiction. The closure of the horizon here is a calamity, although its implications are left for the reader to assess. It becomes

8

immediately comprehensible, for example, why young children should start out by mugging pregnant women and the elderly. It is perfectly rational to beat up the disabled and steal what they have got. It is quite understandable why prostitutes should pull knives when they cannot find clients; why gangsters live on their nerves; why so-and-so 'has never had sexual relations with a woman of her own free-will'; why the best get-away vehicle after a crime is a bus – 'a black who takes a taxi is either a gangster, or at death's door'. The subject matter could be grist for sensationalism and black humour; it is treated in quite another spirit here.

The tight focus gives no respite from this murderous sequence of events. As maximum tension becomes routine, the trivialisation of death pushes us far beyond any thrill of suspense towards a disabused, all-encompassing standpoint, only one degree removed from mere statistics; a point of view focused rather on the decisive, supra-individual parameters of class. To be intimate with horror, yet still need to be able to see it from a distance – if possible, an enlightened one: this is our situation today.

Scientific Stamp

As in nineteenth-century Naturalism, *Cidade de Deus* owes something of its boldness of range and conception to an association with social enquiry. Under a different historical constellation, the findings of a vast and highly relevant research project, Zaluar's 'Crime and Criminality in Rio de Janeiro', have been fictionalised from the perspective of the objects of study – and (without promoting any political illusions) with a corresponding activation of a different class's point of view. This is in itself a significant move. In addition, the reordering of materials produces a distinctive tone and vigour, powerfully at variance with 'well-wrought prose'. The systematising, pioneering force that lends the book's cartography its specific weight is closely related to its origins both in scientific works, and in a team. On the final page, as in film credits, the author thanks two of his companions for their historical and linguistic research. Artistic energies of this sort have no place in the comfortable conception of creative imagination cultivated by most contemporary writers.

If the methods of interviewer and researcher contribute to the artist's schematisation, they also stamp his material with literary unevennesses which themselves have wider implications. The worker, the con-artist, the hoodlum, the drop-out, the go-between are no longer defined within stable, separate roles. They are elements – some, legacies from the past – of a new structure, still in formation, that is to be investigated and understood. It is within this totality that precise yet mutable new distinctions and relations begin to distil, bestowing on the fictionalisation its fine-textured relevance. The subjective testimony of the field-notes sets up an immediate complexity. There is the boy who would rather listen to gangsters' talk than pray in the Assembly of God with his father; the *bicho-solto* who is so in love with a pretty black girl that he dreams of becoming a manual worker. 'Slaving on a building site – never', says another; then he turns believer and starts work for a big

9

construction company; his faith helps to keep at bay 'his feelings of revolt against the segregation he had to suffer for being black, half-toothless and semi-literate'. The relational world set up by the play of these positions stands at the intersection between the logic of everyday life, imaginative literature, and society's systematic effort to know itself.

Another aspect of this composite art finds form in the intervals between the action, in passages that explore the present or recapitulate the past. Such explanatory gestures owe their origins to the Naturalist narrative but here they take on quite a different register. Unadorned field data, evoking the harsh efficiency of the scientific report, combines with the sensationalist tone of popular press – mined for factual documentations and ideological raw material – and the brutal terminology, at once obtuse and bureaucratic, of the police. This thick mixture, laden with its cargo of degraded and alienated modernity, has played a real part in the universe of its victims. Social policy has long worked on, if not improved, the terrain on which they are abandoned. The playground – the 'Leisure'– the gangsters tear across was undoubtedly the contribution of some town planner. In Lins's work, the overriding gravitational force of the drug trade in the *neo-favela* serves to deflate a whole complex of explanations, once scientific and now *bien-pensant*: the alcoholism of the father, the prostitution of the mother, the disintegration of the family and so forth. In the circumstances, such reasoning takes on an outdated, unreal look, even though soaks and whores are everywhere. A set of naturalist sociological causalities is integrated, as one ideology among others, within a discursive web that has no final word; and that operates, in turn, as an element in a wider mystery, formed by the huge business of crime, with its amorphous boundaries, and by the laws of motion and contemporary society – on whose effective shape such explanations have nothing to report.

Dialectics of Song

The vivid transcription of popular speech – lively and concise, almost to the point of minimalism – offers a contrast to this mortar, up to a point; yet it can also seem, through its very brutality and repetition, its purest and simplest expression. But the most daring stand in the language of the novel is its quite unexpected – perhaps risky – insistence on poetry. The verbal resources of *samba* are combined with a delinquent, Concretist word-play – the book takes its epigraph from Paulo Leminski – opening a seam of popular potentialities.[4] '*Poesia, minha tia*', begins Lins's own eulogy to poetry, with a rough caress – *tia* is aunt, but here, rather: my baby, my old lady, my whore – that defies translation:

> *Poesia, minha tia*, blaze against what they say is – bullet-blast the phonemes of the prose. Speak the word that swells beyond its bounds, that talks, acts, happens; staggers from the shot. From a toothless mouth, a gaping cavity: our alleyway plans, our deadly

---

[4] Translator's note: Paulo Leminski, 1944-1989. Born in the southern state of Paraná, Leminski used the stylistic devices of Concretism to create an irreverent popular poetry.

choices. The sand shifts on the ocean floor. Absence of the sun darkens even the jungle. Iced strawberry-crush melts the hand. The word distils in the mind, takes soul as it's released from lips to ear – but sometimes, sound-magic cannot leap to the mouth. It's swallowed dry, choked in the stomach by black beans and rice, defecated instead of spoken.
Speech fails. Bullet speaks.

The deliberate and insolent importance of the lyrical note in Lins's world, in the face of the crushing weight of misery that conditions it, is a distinctive gesture: a movement of refusal, difficult to imagine in a less heterodox author. It is tempting to wonder about the connection between this improbable lyricism and the strength of mind required to change the class viewpoint of a social enquiry, from scientific object to subject of the action.

'All is true', announced Balzac, at the beginning of a novel full of the wildest flights of imaginations.[5] Lins, too, is concerned not to deny the part of fiction in his work, but to sharpen its powers of prospection and demystification. Faced with the task of giving novelistic form to his vast subject-matter, he has availed himself of every support, from *Angústia* and *Crime and Punishment* to cinematic super-productions.[6] If his universe is adjacent to the sensationalist and commercial imaginings of our period, it is quite opposite in spirit: anti-Manichean, anti-providentialist, anti-stereotypical. Its structuring themes are the miring of all intentions – Mané Galinha, gangster as sympathetic avenger, ends up as bad as his enemies – and the general dissolution of meaning within energies that become ungraspable. Which is to say: we are in the valid ambit of modern art, where there are no cheap consolations. So when, in epic scenes of collective action, interrupted and resumed to heighten suspense, police and gangsters head for a final, Hollywood-style showdown – nothing is resolved. Death always comes, but before the projected climax, from adventitious hands, for half-forgotten reasons, with no bearing on the act at sake. Salgueirinho, the best-hearted con-artist in the City of God, is run down by a reversing car. The worst *malandro* of all catches a bullet in the stomach – a meaningless death that does nothing to restore justices, to re-establish a balance in the world.

Behind this methodical discarding of conventions can be traced another, more subtle transition between stages of transgression, no less disconsoling. When Salgueirinho dies he is mourned by the *samba* schools, by his girlfriends, companions and disciples; and with him disappears the wisdom that people should only rob outsiders and not fight senselessly among themselves; that there are pickings enough for all. When Big Head – the hated police chief – dies, the *favela* is shaken up again, in a different way. But when the new-style gangsters die, the authentic sons of the *neo-favela* – nothing happens. The earlier forms of marginality were more sympathetic, perhaps, and less anti-social. In the

---

[5] Translator´s note: *Père Goriot*, 1835.
[6] Translator´s note: Graciliano Ramos, 1936; trans. *Anguish*, 1946.

months leading up to Carnival, the *malandros*, thieves and prostitutes would rob full steam ahead, to get funds for their local *samba* school. The crimes were no less but they could be said to be outweighed by a larger objective, of bringing good times to the city – as if there had been a certain homeostasis within the older inequality that made it bearable, up to a point; and that narco-traffic wars have destroyed. One of the book's most impressive achievements is to show how the liveliness of popular life and the splendour of the Rio landscape itself tend to disappear, as if in a nightmare, under the exigencies of their reign.

It has been said, in a perceptive phrase, that present-day society is creating more and more 'monetary subjects with no cash'.[7] Their world is our own. Far from representing anything backward, they are the product of progress – which, naturally, they qualify. Deep inside, the reader is at one with them – and with their regressive fantasy of simply seizing the glittering goods on display.

Translation by John Gledson

References

Candido, Antonio. 'Dialética da malandragem'. In: *Revista do Instituto de Estudos Brasileiros*. Universidade de São Paulo, (8), 67-89, 1970; *On Literature and Society*. Princeton, 1995, pp. 79-103.
Lins, Paulo. *Cidade de Deus*. São Paulo: Companhia das Letras, 1997.

---

[7] Translator´s note : Robert Kurz.*Der Kollaps der Modernisierung*. Frankfurt 1991: 225.

3. Writing the Script, Finding and Preparing the Actors
Fernando Meirelles

In 1998, I was 42 years old and my internal alarm went off frantically, warning me that my life as a commercial director was very comfortable, but not very satisfying. By chance, during this time, I read Paulo Lins´s *City of God* and decided to take on a new challenge: making a film based on this novel. I would be killing two birds with one stone: I would expose a view of my country that had shocked me when I read the book, and I would give my own life a boost.

My idea was to try to include as many of the stories and characters as possible. Cidade de Deus, a community with its own dynamics, would be the central character. Altman's *Nashville* or Pasolini's *A Thousand and One Nights* were the references for the structure of the story I was interested in making into a film. Multiple plots and many characters that are interconnected, and, in the end, what is left for the spectator is not the memory of an individual story, but the perception of the social, cultural, geographic, and even poetic context where the story really took place. The first impression of the script writer, Bráulio Mantovani, was that it would be almost impossible to produce a script from *City of God's* seven hundred pages and two hundred plus characters, yet he enthusiastically accepted the challenge. He quoted Artaud, and the quote ended up on his bulletin board where it stayed throughout the whole process: 'Since he did not know it was impossible, he did it'.

The Script

We held some preliminary meetings in which we tried to come up with a list of the characters and stories that interested us in the book. From the beginning, it occurred to me that Buscapé [Rocket], although of little importance in the book, could be the character who would guide the spectator to the end of the journey. Bráulio agreed that Buscapé's empathy would be enough to create some sort of identification with the spectator. Buscapé was then chosen as our narrator. Throughout the process, we even considered having other narrators simultaneously, but we gave up that idea. The film was already very fragmented. Bráulio started his work in an insane way. With the help of an assistant, he summed up the whole book passionately. The novel has exactly two hundred and forty-seven names of characters. He created a databank that allowed us to retrieve a summary and the page of each story in the book within seconds. If I said I liked a certain passage in which Cabelinho Calmo [Straight Hair] appears, we would immediately have in our hands all the details about that character. Even Paulo Lins would confuse the characters, and he relied on Bráulio to help him trace them in the book.

Once the basic lines had been defined, such as the structure with three periods, the mood for each of the parts and the main characters of our story, Bráulio jumped into the work eagerly. We had three months to hand in the first version to be able to participate in the Rio

Cine/Sundance Script Workshop, where well-known consultants would read and comment on each of the scripts. We were also in a hurry to enrol the script in the 1999 Audio-Visual Law Programme in order to start gathering funds, which in the end did not happen.

I detached myself from the script's development during this period because I became involved with the film production of *Domésticas* [*Maids*]. But, within record time, Bráulio completed the first draft of about one hundred and fifty-six pages, which unleashed an avalanche of events. The script grabbed me by the throat. It opens with a scene in which a cock is harassed by Zé Pequeno's [Li'l Zé] gang. The cock later turns into a chicken. The cock-baiting was a passage I already liked in the book, but I had never thought it could serve as the introduction to our story. However, this idea and the whole basis of what was to be filmed two years later was already in the script's first version.

This first draft had to be considerably shortened, but it did qualify us to participate in the Rio Cine/Sundance workshop, and later the script won the annual award for best international script from the Writer's Guild of America. Bráulio went to Los Angeles to receive the prize and was a guest at the home of script writer and director Alexander Payne [*About Schmidt*], who had been the most enthusiastic consultant at the workshop and consistently supported us. After this first draft, Bráulio and I started regularly exchanging ideas and comments about the script by e-mail. We would meet in person from time to time when there was too much to discuss or when there was a difficult issue to be resolved. Three more drafts were written during this intense exchange. Many characters from the first draft were left out in this phase. The fourth draft was already a reasonable size, one hundred and nineteen pages, and it was time for us to start thinking about the film.

During the rehearsals, during filming and for six months during the editing, my exchanges with Bráulio were continuous. Until the end, the script writer was there regularly to see the new version of the editing, to suggest inversions in the order of the scenes, and different arrangements for joining scenes. We rewrote almost all of Rocket's narratives many times. The script was finished only when there was definitely no time to change anything. What was interesting in this process, though, was that, in spite of all the countless adjustments along the way, as I said, the characters, the central plots, and the structure never changed from their original version. The ECA [School of Communication and Arts] library at USP [University of São Paulo] and the FAAP [Álvaro Penteado Foundation] library in São Paulo have a set of the various versions of the script, should anybody be interested in following such changes. There is a script for *City of God* published in book format, not the one Bráulio wrote, but actually the transcription of the final version – the thirteenth draft.

In July 2000, I gave up my career in advertising. I grew impatient waiting to see if we were going to receive financial support from the government's incentive programmes or from any other type of funding. I decided to invest my time and whatever money I had from directing ads in an actors' workshop. My attitude was, if anyone came up with some money, good, if not, all right. Nothing was going to stop me. And nothing stopped me indeed. Although not planning to, I ended up funding the whole film myself until it was ready, all set at the Avid editing system. Actually, to invest my life savings in a film about drug-trafficking, featuring unknown actors, filmed in the *favelas* was the dumbest thing I ever did in my life. It had all the ingredients of failure. It was the very face of defeat; it was obvious – so much so that we did not find investors for the first year. But at that moment, that did not matter. My internal alarm system was now blaring. Risk makes one keen. In the end, all came out right. My mother always says I was born lucky.

The Cast

On the day I bought the rights to Paulo Lins's book, *City of God*, I mentioned to Bráulio that the story was to be told by real people. While we were working on the script, we already had in mind the idea that we would have to make the film with non-professional actors. I wanted the audience to look at Li'l Zé and actually see the real Li'l Zé, and not an actor playing a role. The idea was to have these unknown actors in order to eliminate the filter, to let the spectator have a direct relationship with the character. All this, I thought, would bring out the truth I wanted to have in the film. Middle-class actors would not know how to interpret those characters. Besides, there were no young black or mulatto actors in Brazil. I would have to find the cast in the *favelas* of Rio. That would be the greatest challenge of the project. However, because of my experience, I did not think it was impossible to make a film with amateur actors; quite the contrary. In my 20 years as a director, I had worked with renowned actors only a few times. The major part of my work in advertising, TV, or even the film *Domésticas* [*Maids*], was done with amateur actors or actors who had no experience in the cinema. Also I was not in the least bit interested in having famous names just to guarantee a large audience. That definitely was not my motivation in this project.

Before I continue describing the process of preparing the protagonists, I want to redress an injustice or a misconception that occurred during the launch phase of the film *City of God*. I do not know if it was our fault, or if the press made a mistake, but a rumour was put around that the film had been made with a totally amateur cast. This is not true. The protagonists were, in fact, making their *debut* in the cinema world, but almost all the characters who were twenty-five years old or older were performed by professional actors. For example, let's begin in 1998 with Matheus Natchergalle, the first actor to be cast. Matheus, who was not yet a well-known person, was a good theatre actor. I thought he could be Li'l Zé if I did not find another unknown actor appropriate for the role. When I called him up, he accepted immediately. But two years later, when I prepared the script, we met in a restaurant and I said, 'Matheus, you have created a problem for me because you are famous now. I do not want well-known faces in the film. You have had roles in soap operas and feature films. You walk down the street and people ask for your autograph. You have spoiled my film'. But Matheus was nice, and turned the tables. He said, 'No. I know what you want. Leave it to me. It will be an excellent opportunity to do the work of a non-actor. I'll be in the film, and nobody will even notice. I'll disappear in the middle of the blokes. Don't you worry'. And then he fully followed his intuition. Other professional actors completed the team: Gero Camilo, playing Paraíba [Shorty], Graziela Moretto [a journalist], Charles Paraventi [Uncle Sam], Karina Falcão [Shorty's wife], Maurício Marques, playing Cabeção [Melonhead], Gustavo Engracia [photographer], and Guti Fraga [supermarket manager]. One of the bonuses from my having worked in advertising was dealing with hundreds of actors. Except for Matheus, I had already worked with all the others and knew exactly what to expect from each one.

The flair for dramatic interpretation is a gift. Some people are born with this software, and others are not. It is like an innate talent for drawing or music or sports. However, I knew I could find natural-born actors in Rio's *favelas*. The issue was how a guy such as myself, from São Paulo, who barely knew Rio, could get there. I needed a starting point. As luck would have it, in 1998, right after buying the book's rights, I read in a paper a full-page article about *Nós do Morro* [*Us from the Hill*], a theatrical group composed of people who lived in the *Morro do Vidigal*, a *favela* in the southern zone of Rio. I left this article on my bulletin board for two years because I knew that someday those blokes might serve as the starting point for the formation of my cast. Sometimes I would look at the pictures in that withered newspaper article to see if any of those faces looked like the characters Bráulio Mantovani and I were creating.

When we got to the fourth draft of the script, I decided to begin the preparation for the film. I invited Elisa Tolomelli to be my executive producer and I went to Rio. I told Elisa the first thing I wanted to do was set up an actors' workshop in Rio, work for six months with lots of kids, and only when I felt absolutely certain about the cast, would I say 'go' to the production. If we did not find the right actors, I would call the project off. It was risky. And that is the way it was done.

Elisa introduced me to Katia Lund, former assistant producer to Walter Salles. Besides her very good credits as an assistant, Katia had just finished co-directing with João Moreira Salles and Walter Salles the documentary *Notícias de Uma Guerra Particular* [*News from a Personal War*], about drug-trafficking in Rio. Because of the research she had done for the documentary, she had a lot to contribute to the project. But she happened to say no to our invitation to be co-director; she was beginning her career as a director. Nevertheless, she liked the script and the general idea, and she agreed to participate in the setting up of the workshop to train actors.

Our first step was to visit the *Nós do Morro* headquarters, where I finally met Guti Fraga, the actor who coordinated the group. Guti is one of the most extraordinary men I have ever met in my life. I was delighted and surprised when he accepted my invitation to direct the workshop. Because he believed in the project, Guti decided to stop his other activities and dedicate himself solely to the workshop for six months. As homage to him, I gave our new school the name *Nós do Cinema* [*We in Cinema*].

Lamartine Ferreira, dubbed the Lama, who later became the assistant to the film's director, was the last key-player in this process. He

16

coordinated the workshops. He has a charisma typical of *baianos*[1] like him, and so he centralised everything. He would scold with the same intensity he would welcome the lads. Within a short time, he was respected and loved. He was the element that kept the group united and focused on the job.

For our theatre workshop selection process, actors from *Nós do Morro* coordinated three teams. They would go out with video cameras to recruit interested participants from various communities. The workshop was free and offered travel expenses and snacks at the end of each class, besides granting a certificate at the end of the year. Because opportunities are scarce in these communities, two thousand lads showed interest and took our quick video test. The great turnout for the workshop was also due to Guti's reputation and to his highly regarded group, both associated with the workshop's invitation. After watching hours of video tests, we ultimately selected four hundred lads and invited them to come to our main office, at Foundation Progresso, in *Lapa*, a neighbourhood in central Rio.

Dividing them into groups of eight or ten, Guti organised a week of interpretation exercises, so that we could choose the best actors. We selected two-hundred pupils, aged nine to twenty-five, who were again divided into eight groups. Each group of twenty-five pupils had classes twice a week for five months. Lads from our waiting list replaced dropouts – but not many gave up. To the lads, Guti was the teacher, the Lama was the boss, and Katia and I were the assistants. That is how the Lama introduced us to the group. We did not tell anyone we were intending to make a film the following year.

In the second semester, I moved to Rio. For five months, I went straight to Foundation Progresso to follow the five classes, which went on from 9 a.m. to 9 p.m. After three months, when the lads found out we would be making a film, and I was going to be the director, the distance which might have existed in the beginning disappeared. I was just that simple barefoot chap in shorts, sitting on the floor among them, who sometimes offered hints while they rehearsed their daily presentations.

It was at these rehearsals that I evaluated the lads. There was never a formal test for the majority of the roles. Rather, during the rehearsals, I would ask for a change of attitude to see if I could count on a certain lad in a situation; I would ask another chap to interpret a dialogue from the script that he did not know, and thus I started seeing the birth of each character.

After class, my conversations with these young men put me in touch with their reality, the same reality of the film's characters. Everyday I would hear a different story. The brother who had been killed, the drunken father who had been found in Angra[2] and brought back home, the policeman who stole six *reais* from the money bag of one of them the previous day. This semester-long learning experience helped prepare me to understand the film I was going to make. Everything was

---

[1] Translator's note: *Baianos* are people from Bahia, a State of Brazil.
[2] Translator's note: Angra dos Reis, a famous beach resort in the State of Rio de Janeiro.

new. During my time spent in the workshop, I was always cheerful and happy. I had traded my neat clothes and my packed agenda of three hundred and fifty appointments for barefoot days, without a boss or a client, inventing scenes and exchanging ideas with blossoming young actors. Those six months opened my eyes and I saw a Brazil I thought I already knew.

In the first weeks of the workshop, Guti Fraga organised games to integrate the lads. Since they came from different places, he wanted to help them relax and feel part of a group. Actors from the *Nós do Morro,* already experienced in this process, were mingled with the group, and they dived headfirst into the exercises, showing the way to the others. Little by little, Guti conducted activities to integrate the participants and make the group more cohesive, while helping them understand they must have discipline and listen to a voice. It was funny when Guti would make these tough young men form a circle, hand in hand, and speak a little bit about the work. In the beginning, they felt a little uncomfortable holding hands. After two or three months, when the exercise was over, they were ready for the handholding part – it fostered a climate of mutual trust and they felt like friends.

Gradually, Guti started to propose scene improvisations. For example, one actor would play the role of a policeman, another would be a drug dealer, and they had to solve their conflict with sweet talk, not with force. We would give them time to create a story and rehearse it. At the end of the class, the groups presented their results and commented on each presentation. This entire preparation process is shown in an excellent documentary directed by Ana Braga (the mother of Alice Braga, who plays Rocket's girlfriend in the film), which is one of the extra features in the *City of God* DVD.

As soon as they grasped the mechanism of improvisation, we started to go through the scenes in the script, but without letting them know they were scenes of the film and without giving them dialogue. We would only tell them what the situation was, and they would develop it. I would keep a notepad in hand, jotting down the good ideas, interesting sentences and new situations created out of the proposed conflict. I would send these notes regularly to Bráulio, in São Paulo, and he would incorporate the new ideas and speeches in the text, until he came up with a new draft of the script. I would then ask the actors to improvise the new scenes and check their reactions. Sometimes they would complain about the dialogue or about the scenes themselves. 'This would not happen that way', they would say. In such cases, I would let Bráulio know and the dialogue or scene would be cut from the script, even if I liked them. Ultimately, the actors were the filters.

We started the school in August 2000, with the fourth draft of the script in our hands. Through this process, by December, we were already on the eighth draft. Four months later, when we started to film, we were on the twelfth version of the script. Always following the same process of sending the ideas to Bráulio, getting them back, checking the lads' reaction, and then sending them back to Bráulio. The team also participated actively in this process. Katia Lund and César Charlone contributed greatly to the story. For example, during the shooting of the

18

film, César told me he felt Li'l Zé was becoming too monotonic, because he was always violent. He was right. I then created the scene in which Bené [Benny] says he needs to find a girlfriend, and in the next scene, Li'l Zé invites Knockout's girl to dance but she turns him down. In that moment, we pity Li'l Zé – which was the missing trait in his character. That scene was created because César's comment gave the character a new dimension and altered the whole story. That is why when I say the film was real teamwork, I am not just praising the group – it is a fact.

Many people, during the process, would ask me if it was not crazy to work with two hundred amateur young actors. To which I would respond, 'But they have something that you cannot get from a professional actor, the highest degree of motivation'. Everyone was thrilled and really wanted to go for it.

The whole process of cast preparation was filmed – not so much for us to assess the actors, but to make them used to the presence of a camera to the point of ignoring it. The lads took turns operating the cameras during the rehearsals. This made them feel at ease with the equipment. Because of this process, we have four hundred VHS tapes, which no one has ever watched. After five months, I knew almost all two hundred boys by name, where they came from, and a little bit about their background. I already had actors in mind for each role. I just needed to test them in a situation more similar to a real film shooting.

Exactly at that point, Guel Arraes called and invited me to film an episode of *Brava Gente* [*Brave People*],[3] stories shown in a thirty-minute format aired on Globo network at the end of 2000. I told Guel I would shoot an episode if he let me test my cast and some options for the film I was preparing. I could never imagine Globo' network would want a story about drug-dealing, starring black, unknown actors as a Christmas special. But there is no one like Guel: he bought the idea on the spot and in the dark, allowing us to use the powerful Globo network as the sponsor for our rehearsal. For the episode, I passed along to Bráulio Guti Fraga's idea about two boys who had managed to get away from trafficking just through smooth talk and cunning. Bráulio mixed Fraga's idea with a passage from the novel *City of God* that had previously been taken out of the film script. Thus, the two characters Laranjinha and Acerola were born. Using *City of God's* prospective protagonists, we shot the short film *Palace II*.[4]

Shooting *Palace II*: A Rehearsal

Palace II was the closing event for the actors' workshop, and, at the same time, it was the rehearsal for the film *City of God*. To shoot *Palace II*, eventually, I called in the whole team that was to be involved in *City of God*. Each one was going to test his/her ideas a little: Tulé Peake as art director, Bia and Inês Salgado in costumes, Anna Van Steen in

---

[3] Translator's note: a weekly TV show that depicts typical Brazilians in their environment. The name comes from the Independence Anthem that contains the phrase 'Brava gente brasileira' [brave Brazilian people].
[4] Translator's note: This is the name of an apartment building in an elegant sector of Rio that collapsed in the end of 1998, killing about eight people.

makeup, César Charlone in photography, and Elisa Tolomelli in production. Even the location, the Cidade de Deus neighbourhood itself, was being tested as an option for the film. Since the work was being conceived in the daily tasks at the workshop, I invited Katia Lund to co-direct the short film with me, while Lamartine Ferreira was the assistant director.

Filming this episode was the best thing that could have happened in the process of making *City of God*. We fine-tuned our producing techniques, made the photographic decisions based on the tests, and we gained confidence in the cast. But best of all were the number of clashes we had with the local traffic, which ended up in a final grand collision on the fifth and last day of shooting. After that week, we realised it would be impossible to shoot *City of God* at Cidade de Deus. To do so would have been a mistake. I owe this finding to Guel.

At that time, Cidade de Deus was under the control of a few very young lads and teenagers are unstable. All the arrangements were verbal and mediated by third parties. We never knew for sure if the person who gave us permission was empowered to do so. One of our concerns was giving money to anyone in the gangs, so we agreed to pay for locations in donations to the community, such as truckloads of sand for the football field, and the like.

On the very first day of shooting, after several visits to the locations and production plans had been made, we were informed we could not shoot because the *favela* was mourning the death of a dealer from the previous day. We drove our lorries back home, without filming anything. The next day, when we arrived, they told us the 'owner' had changed his mind; he did not want us to film there because he had read the script and found it too violent (sic). The 'owner' said their lives were not a good example for youth and that the film should not be made. I was astonished.

Since the neighbourhood is divided into several areas, we moved without warning to the other side of the Yellow Line [*Linha Amarela*],[5] controlled by another gang, and we went on improvising locations, always under the sly supervision of the gang members.

'My friend, you cannot point the camera that way.'
'But my character comes down this street; I only want to show him coming...'
'But that building in the background cannot appear. Turn your camera to the other side.'
'Ok, we'll do that.'

The filming took five days. We were almost finished when, on our last night of work, two armed lads crossed the scene we were filming. Seconds later we began to hear shots. The people around us, watching the action, looked unruffled.

---

[5] Translator's note: *Linha Amarela* is a fast-track motorway that crosses the poorer northern neighbourhoods of Rio connecting the Red Line (city to the International Airport) to Barra da Tijuca.

'Cool down. What's going on is in the other block, not here'.

To prevent conflicts, we had made an agreement with the police not to go to that area while we were filming, but two policemen dressed in street-cleaners' overalls had entered the area and arrested a dealer who was watching our activities. The gang then blamed us for the arrest of their associate and closed the street with heavily armed folks.

'You said there would be no police, that's why we opened the area to you and we played the fool. But there were. Now, nobody leaves until he is set free.'

The makeup team was crying, while others were saying they would not work on the film. Meanwhile, we continued to film, making it look as if the disruption was no big deal. The production tried to speak to the policemen near the car parked two blocks from the site. We guessed it was the well-known *mineira* scheme. When the gangs do not pay their weekly amount, the police come and arrest someone and later ask for money not to take the prisoner to the station. Unashamedly they asked for ten thousand *reais* to free the bloke. Putting together all the money we had in our pockets, we barely had two thousand five hundred *reais.* And the police could not care less if there were children and a whole production team surrounded by a bunch of armed people.

'That's your problem, brother, you got yourself into it.'

Finally, at four in the morning, when the two policemen realised we really did not have any more money, they took the two thousand five-hundred and opened the back door of the police van for the bloke to get out. We stopped filming and left the *favela* in a convoy. Three months later, we learned the same drug dealers caught one of the policemen, sliced him, and burned him in the 'microwave', a pile of tires set ablaze. In *City of God,* I included a quick scene of a policeman receiving money for freeing a dealer, exactly as I saw happening there.

The TV special had a surprisingly large audience. In that same week, we were invited to make other episodes with the two characters, Laranjinha and Acerola. But we just could not. We agreed that as soon as we finished *City of God,* we would resume our negotiations.

Palace II was finalised for the cinema, as part of the tests, so we ended up showing it in festivals. It received several awards, among them the 2000 Berlin Festival Panorama for best short film. In the Brasília festival, the film provoked a debate over the treatment given to the images. Some critics said we were trying to misrepresent poverty. We were actually testing different lighting alternatives for *City of God*. There are scenes in which César did not use any lighting, only mixed sources of light of different colours, monochromatic and saturated scenes, scenes in which we tried to exaggerate the oil on the lads' skin to make it reflect light. Each sequence served as a specific test for César. And, in the end, it showed us the path to follow and what to be avoided in *City of God.*

We also tested a new process that consisted of shooting in 16 mm and 35 mm, which was transferred to high-definition video, and then, after editing, transferred back to regular film. This process is now much better known, but we were pioneers in 2000. Mega agreed to a partnership for final cutting, because they were also interested in developing the process. Together with César they made countless tests, of all kinds, until they learned the best way to pursue the long path between the 16 mm and the final copy that is shown in the cinemas.

City of God

In the first months of 2001, we dedicated ourselves to pre-production. By mere chance, we settled down in a studio which overlooked the Cidade de Deus *favela* at a distance. Tulé Peake covered the rooms and corridors with reference photographs and Bia and Inês Salgado set up a sort of clothes manufacturing shop on the upper floor, where they produced thousands of items of clothing, not only for the cast, but also for the extras. *City of God* is a film that takes place in three different decades, and for each period we had a concept that was very different from the other: lighter colours and home-made clothes for the first part, prints and stripes in the second phase, and monochromatic and darker clothes for the third part. Fashion changed over time, therefore, an astounding amount of clothes were made. Fátima Toledo, from São Paulo, prepared the actors. She worked with the cast in a large room, while the location producers travelled around looking for a place that resembled Cidade de Deus in the 1960s, and another for the 1970s.

The cast's enthusiasm was contagious. Preoccupied by all this excitement, I pretended to be unconcerned about two pressing issues: being away from home, which, for me, is being outside of my element, and the production's funding that still did not exist.

There was a verbal agreement with the American distributor, Miramax, and another with the French Wild Bunch. They would inject money into the film in exchange for the rights for the Americas and for the rest of the world, respectively. Lumière was involved in the negotiation, and I never knew what was going on. Whenever I asked when we would sign the contract, I got a vague reply: next month, in May, at the end of July. I lied to myself, pretending to believe it all. Three weeks before we started shooting, Maurício Ramos, a partner from VideoFilmes, informed me the contract with Miramax would not materialise in the coming months, much less the promised money. 'Pull the hand brake, Fernando. Stop everything and begin again next year,' Maurício warned me. At that moment, I pretended not to have heard what had been clearly stated. 'How much is due at the end of the month, Elisa?' I asked. 'X? That's all right. I will pay while we wait for a decision.' Self-deceiving, as Eduardo Gianetti[6] would say. So, every week, I would scrape up whatever amount I had in investments, until I realised I would finance the film until the end. I went straight on like one of tarot's arcanes, the one who looks aloft while walking towards a cliff. Enthusiasm

---

[6] Translator's note: Brazilian philosopher, economist, and professor who lives in Rio. He studied in Britain.

is a heavy dope.

There are some ingenuous directors who know exactly what they want in every department, who like to be the only voice heard on the set and who maintain a rigid hierarchy. Their teams are there to help them materialise a personal view. They tell the photographer how they want the lighting, and the art director how they want the scene, *etcetera*. Unfortunately, I was not born with this clairvoyance. I discover the film throughout the process of making it, so I depend on a team to help me create it. In general, my set is a mess; everybody gives hints, from the actors to the electricians. I stimulate participation and act like a filter in the process. *City of God* was made this way, through teamwork. Every film is teamwork, of course. But in this film, each contributor's creative participation, especially that of each department head, was more continuous. That's why I placed the names of this main group in the middle of the film's poster, and not at the bottom.

I had already been working with this team for a while. César Charlone, as I said before, was the person who introduced me to a 35-mm camera and has taught me much more than that during our fifteen years of partnership. As for Daniel Rezende, the opposite happened. I introduced him to editing work. He was my finishing assistant in advertising. He took care of client presentations and followed the whole delivery process of my films. One day I started asking him to try and improve details in the films that I myself had edited. His work surprised me and I started sharing the editing of some films with him, until he ended up doing it all himself, since his versions were better than mine. Although he had never edited a long production, I knew he had the sense to do it. And I was right.

I had worked with Bráulio Mantovani in the creation of *Telecurso 2000*,[7] and later as consultants in a series called *Oficinas Culturais* [*Cultural Workshops*], which he wrote and TV Cultura produced. *City of God* was also his first long script to be produced, but when I bought the rights to the book, I had no other name in mind to make the adaptation. Tulé Peake, the art director, was another partner with whom I had worked before. We had produced over forty commercials and the film *O Menino Maluquinho 2* [*The Nutty Boy*].[8] He is one of the most creative blokes I know. This freedom was what I was most interested in for the whole team. As we had all been working together for such a long time, we got along very well and everyone had the freedom to propose or dispute any idea, in any area.

Katia Lund was a later addition to the group, but she ended up getting totally involved in the project, and she played an important part in the preparation of the actors. She also participated in the definition of makeup and costumes. Her knowledge of the *favela*'s codes helped us tune the characters into the project and refine the script. We worked together in the television mini-series *Cidade dos Homens* [*City of Men*],

---

[7] Translator's note: An elementary and secondary school course taught through television.

[8] Translator's note: A film based on the book of the same name by Ziraldo, a contemporary Brazilian cartoonist and writer.

for the two following years.

The Game of Improvisation

City of God was filmed in eight and a half weeks, which was fast for a film that lasted three hours in its first version. We had to move fast, due to the costs, and to avoid filming too long in the same community. We managed to do so fast because of our good advance preparation. Besides the three months of exhaustive rehearsals in our headquarters, with or without the supervision of our cast trainer, Fátima Toledo, we would also rehearse each scene in the locations before filming. For these rehearsals, we had the presence of someone from each department, and we created the marks for the actors, that is, where he or she comes from, where to go, *etcetera*. With a small video camera, we would look for each position the camera would take. During the rehearsals there was much improvisation, but when it came to the real thing, we had to be objective because it was costing us more money. Therefore, the improvisation ended. At the end of each rehearsal, each one would know exactly what would happen on the set, and so all possible problems were solved or at least foreseen. Rehearsing on the locations saved us at least one week in the process. I adopted this method when I filmed *O Jardineiro Fiel* [*The Constant Gardener*], in 2004. Even when working with stars, I carried on rehearsals on almost all locations. Everyone approved of the idea.

The professional actors ran a great risk acting in a film with those lads. There is nothing worse than to notice an actor is acting, because side by side with the protagonists, any marked or technical gesture would stand out. They had to know how to enter the game of improvisation, to give life to their characters as naturally as possible, to be in tune with the cast. They had to do that, even though they had not had the same type of preparation. They did the exercise of 'non-interpretation', as Matheus said. Sometimes if we had a scene to film at five in the afternoon, and I would say, 'Oh, Matheus, do you want the car to fetch you only in the afternoon?' He would say, 'No, if the rest of the team is going at seven, I'm also going at seven'. He would stay from seven to five in the public seats, visiting people he had never met, who nevertheless invited him for a cup of coffee, or whatever. This way, little by little he became part of that world.

Filming started in the middle of June 2001 and was over at the end of August, without any incident. During that period, I set up the Avid editing system in Marcelo Tas's apartment, where I was staying, and Daniel Rezende would work right there, in the living-room. That way, I was able to follow the editing daily, after I came back from the shooting. When we finished filming, I rented a small and isolated apartment in São Paulo, and the editing was done there. It took us three more months to get down from the first cut of about three hours to two hours and twelve minutes. By then, Daniel and I could already quote every word spoken, we knew every gesture made by every actor, and we had already lost a little bit of the objectivity and the freshness we had seen in the film. At the end of this process, I started showing the cut to whomever was not present to see our daily chore. I showed the film to the directors of 02 Filmes first, and then to my family. Daniel Filho, one of the producers,

24

kindly spent some time with us at the editing desk, rigorously going through each scene, not as a producer, but as a friend who gives of his time and experience to someone who is just starting out. With little changes in the order of the scenes or dialogues, the film was polished until I considered it finished in the beginning of December 2001. Finally, it was time to try to sell the film that took up three and a half years of hard work and a large chunk of what I had made from other jobs over the preceding ten years.

Translation by Edson Martins Lopes

4. Shooting the Real: Boys from Brazil
Jean Oppenheimer

Since *Amores Perros* burst onto the international scene two years ago, Latin American cinema has been experiencing one of the most fertile periods in its history. Encompassing such works as Alfonso Cuarón's *Y Tu Mamá También* and Walter Salles's *Behind the Sun*, these frequently brutal portraits of life south of the border marry elements of Italian Neo-Realism with today's sophisticated film-making techniques to create an in-your-face realism of visceral and dazzling power. The latest example of this burgeoning body of work is *City of God* [*Cidade de Deus*], which premièred at the 2002 Cannes Film Festival and is Brazil's submission for this year's Academy Award for Best Foreign-Language Film.

This South American drama, shot by César Charlone and directed by Fernando Meirelles, conveys the chaos and violence that plague Rio de Janeiro's most notorious slum. A model housing project when the government built it in the 1960s, City of God fell victim to teenage drug dealers in the mid-1970s. Within 10 years, the situation had escalated into all-out war among rival street gangs. Murder was commonplace and few were untouched by violence.

The *favela*'s descent into bloodshed and chaos was chronicled in a 700-page novel by City of God native Paulo Lins. The film retains the book's structure but reduces the number of major characters. The story is told through the eyes of Buscapé [Rocket] who, in the film version, yearns to be a photographer (rather than the writer Lins became, partly because photography offered more cinematic possibilities).

'This is a story about losing control', declares Fernando Meirelles. 'In the 1960s, the state was there. People were brought to the *favela* to live. Then the drug dealers took over, the war began and the state totally lost control. It is still out of control today.'

It was the intense nature of the subject matter, as well as Meirelles's decision to make the picture with an almost completely amateur cast – actual kids from the ghetto, many of them homeless – that attracted cinematographer César Charlone, ABC, to the project. 'Our entire approach was dictated by whom we were dealing with', says Charlone, who spoke to *American Cinematographer* in Cannes. 'Most of these kids had never even seen a camera before. The conventions of "roll sound, roll camera" had nothing to do with their reality, and it was very important for us to respect that.'

A second guiding principle was to avoid glamorising the violence. Exploding bodies and slow-motion ballets of death, so common in Hollywood movies, were out. Instead, the film-makers wanted to suggest the casual nature of the violence that Lins describes in his novel; many of the killings are either shown indistinctly or kept out of frame.

Structurally, the film consists of three phases (corresponding to the three decades) and a prelude that is linked to the final phase. Each period had its own visual style, but rather than go with different film stocks the film-makers decided to give each segment a specific colour and shooting style. Charlone, who does not like using filters on the camera, intended to do all his corrections in the timing.

The cinematographer argued for a digital intermediate, not only to facilitate the extensive colour manipulation but also to facilitate the editing; he knew that Meirelles and the editor Daniel Rezende wanted to do a number of jump cuts and alter frame rates. Another consideration was that Charlone planned to shoot 40 percent of the film on Super 35mm (with an Aaton 35-III) and the rest on Super 16mm (with an Aaton XTRprod and Aaton A-Minima). He planned to shoot at 1.66:1 aspect ratio and then digitally reframe at 1.85:1; all of the cameras were fitted with 1.85:1 viewfinders. Scanning all of the film footage into the digital realm for colour correction made sense. The directors and producers agreed.

The 1960s phase of the film revolves around three friends known as the Tenderness Trio, one of whom is Rocket's older brother. The restless youths hold up delivery trucks and engage in other petty crimes, but they are not hardened criminals. The ghetto's younger kids, including eight-year-old Rocket (Luis Otávio) and his friends Bené (Michel de Souza Gomes) and Dadinho [Li'l Dice] (Douglas Silva), admire the older boys.

For this first section, Meirelles and Charlone wanted to suggest a sense of naïveté reminiscent of many old American Westerns. Sepia-toned or black-and-white footage seemed too obvious, so they instead went with a warm, yellow tint. 'Fernando and I watched a lot of Westerns,' recalls Charlone with a laugh. 'We wanted the assault on the gas truck to be like a stagecoach hold-up, with the boys and the camera running alongside the vehicle like gunmen on horseback. The boys even wore kerchiefs across their faces the way stage robbers did'.

'We used wide-open (Zeiss Superspeed) lenses – primarily 16mm and 24mm – because in this section of the film the city itself is the main character and we wanted to show the geography. It's the only time you really see wide shots of the *favela*. We favoured classical compositions and almost always set the camera on a tripod or dolly, although we also did some Steadicam work. Nothing in this section of the story was handheld, and because the younger kids looked at these guys as heroes, we frequently shot the trio from low angles to give them a slightly heroic air.'

The mid-1970s, when Rocket is in his early teens (played at this age by Alexandre Rodrigues), marked the beginning of the slum's psychedelic era. Everyone is smoking marijuana, and colour suddenly floods the screen. Blue and green, colours that were avoided in the first part of the film, come on strongly in the art direction and lighting.

The myriad colours suggest that this is a happy time for the kids. Rocket remains a sweet, rather shy youth who still dreams of buying a camera. Li'l Dice, rechristened Li'l Zé (Leandro Firmino da Hora), is well on his way to fulfilling his dream of becoming the most feared drug dealer in City of God. Bené (Phellipe Haagensen) is more laid back and well-liked by everybody.

The 1970s sequences were shot handheld; camera movements are freer but still respect cinematographic grammar. For these sequences, Charlone replaced the Zeiss Superspeeds with an Angenieux HR 7-81mm zoom. 'The Angenieux is a real beauty,' raves Charlone. 'We wanted this segment to be kind of nervous, filled with off-kilter framing'.

Things become even more urgent in the film's third section, when cocaine takes hold in the *favela* and drug wars break out among rival gangs. 'For this part of the story, we did not respect anything,' acknowledges Meirelles. 'The camera was shaking and frequently out of focus – not to be stylish, but because César would be in a room with seven or eight people, panning and zooming from speaker to speaker or capturing reaction shots. The mood at this point is cold, tense and monochromatic – like an opium trip'.

Whereas the first segment was fairly tightly scripted, the second and third parts were heavily improvised by the performers to allow the first-time actors greater flexibility; therefore, Charlone used the AatonCode sound system rather than a clapper. He explains, 'We could not afford to have a non-professional like Leandro da Hora [Li'l Zé] working himself up to the height of his anger and then suddenly have Fernando yell, "Okay, roll sound, clapper!" It would have killed the emotion.'

The same reasoning was behind Charlone's decision to shoot the bulk of the footage in Super 16. 'I did not want to be changing magazines every few minutes, particularly when we were working with the younger kids. We tended to do the wide shots on 35mm stock, when we wanted the ratio and the range, and then go tight with 16mm. I had learned during our tests that 16mm was very reliable for close-ups; it not only gave me a full 10 minutes on the mag, but it also offered a look that was comparable to 35mm. Even more importantly, the Aaton 16mm cameras are much quieter than the 35-III, so when I got in close I could get good direct sound.'

The 'tests' to which Charlone refers proved to be a godsend for the film-makers. Six months before production began, a TV station asked Meirelles to shoot a 20-minute short about the City of God. The four days the crew spent in the *favela* became a camera test for the longer film, *Golden Gate*, which used the same locations, performers and lighting situations. During this period, Charlone tried out 10 film stocks – five for each film format – using a variety of lenses, camera moves and lighting situations. The footage was then edited and digitally printed in both 16mm and 35mm. Some negatives were rejected as too grainy. In the end, Charlone chose Eastman EXR 50D 5245 and 7245 for sunny exteriors; Vision 250D 5246 and 7246 for low-light exteriors; Vision 200T 5274 and 7274 for interiors and scenes on stage or in controlled conditions; and Vision 500T 5279 and 7279 for night exteriors.

The cinematographer kept movie lights to a minimum, partially because they would have limited the young actors, who tended to improvise both action and dialogue. Natural light illuminated all day exteriors, while location interiors were lit with practicals augmented by a few Par 64s with 500-watt bulbs. To light Li'l Zé's apartment, the setting for about a dozen scenes, Charlone used small Par cans disguised as practicals. The largest units he used were 2.5Ks and 4Ks, which were placed on top of buildings to help illuminate the ghetto for night exteriors.

Charlone occasionally used grads to bring down the sky. All other contrast and continuity problems were taken care of in post. 'Rio de

Janeiro has very unstable weather – it can start out sunny and beautiful and change in an instant,' he notes. 'When the actors were ready, I could not afford to tell Fernando that a cloud was in the way and we had to wait. And putting lights up to simulate the sun limited the performers too much. With the digital intermediate, we could bring the contrast up a little bit in a flat image; or, if an actor suddenly entered a dark area, I could follow him, knowing that I could compensate in telecine.'

Another important lesson culled from doing the TV documentary was that it would be too dangerous to shoot a full-length feature in City of God. A couple of scenes were filmed there, but the majority of the feature was shot in two neighbouring and much safer *favelas*, Nova Sepetiba and Cidade Alta.

While shooting *Golden Gate*, Charlone also took hundreds of still photographs that he sent back to his postproduction assistant, Alessandra Casolari. 'We were looking for the correct colours to use for the three phases of the story, and I sent location photos to Alessandra in São Paulo, where our lab, Megacolor, is located. She processed them and worked with colour timer Sérgio Pasqualino in Telecine. They would send back the corrected pictures, and I would analyze them with Fernando and art director Tulé Peake.'

These tests had a significant impact on the colours used by the wardrobe and art departments. Three separate rooms – one for each decade – were set aside in the Rio production office, and all wardrobe and art-direction materials were kept there. Charlone hung corresponding stills on each door for quick reference.

When the costume department saw how yellow the 1960s phase would eventually look, they took a little yellow out of those costumes. Green proved problematic overall because it was difficult to take away in post, so that colour was used sparingly in clothing and set dressing.

Charlone says Casolari proved to be indispensable. 'She is five-star,' he declares emphatically. 'It was a privilege to work with her.' Regulars on his crew included gaffer Sérgio Isidoro ('my right hand in all lighting situations') and camera assistants Lula Carvalho ('a great focus puller') and Cristiano Conceição. He also praised Pasqualino, with whom he works frequently.

One unusual colour-timing situation occurred in the first phase of the story, when two members of the Tender Trio climb a tree to hide from the police. 'It had to be so dark that you could not see the boys in the tree or the policeman on the ground. I would have used a black screen and let the sound tell the story, but Fernando wanted to see the actors,' recounts Charlone with a laugh. The film-makers solved the dilemma by digitally separating the colours. 'Because the leaves were green, we painted the actors with red makeup – so red they looked ridiculous! – and then shot the scene day-for-night. If I had shot it day-for-night without the red makeup, the boys' dark skin tones would have gone way down. I had to find a way to bring them up. Makeup artist Ana Van Steen used the red makeup, and then in telecine I brought up what was red and took down what was green. We ended up with an appropriately dark forest, and the dark skin tones came up.'

Charlone comes by his feel for the image naturally. Raised in

Uruguay as the grandson of a noted art critic, he grew up in a house filled with paintings. A favourite pastime was stills photography and visiting museums. When he first became interested in stills photography at 15, his grandmother gave him darkroom equipment. 'I was always passionate about how much you could do with a picture after you took it', he recalls. 'My graduate thesis at film school was about colour timing – RGB, because digital did not exist back then. You can do such rich work on the image afterwards. I always leave a lot to do in post.'

Charlone and Meirelles have worked together on numerous commercials and television projects, but *City of God* is their first feature collaboration. Charlone's film credits include *O Homem da Capa Preta* [*The Man of the Black Coat*], *Feliz Ano Velho* [*Happy Old Year*] and *2 Billion Hearts*, which was the official World Cup film of 1994. The cameraman was also instrumental in establishing a film school in Cuba.

One concern for Charlone on *City of God* was how to light the performers, most of whom are black. After making the City of God documentary, Charlone decided to simply let light reflect off of their skin rather than lighting them directly. 'We visited the *favela* in January, when it was unbearably hot and everybody was sweating, and I noticed that this black kid's skin was very shiny. I took pictures of him while the sun was setting and his skin was like a mirror of the sunset.'

Later, Charlone happened to see a portrait of a black woman painted by Brazilian artist Di Cavalcanti. 'I think there was one piece of brown skin; the rest was green, blue and yellow,' he recalls excitedly. 'Sixty years earlier, Di Cavalcanti had captured exactly what I was seeing. The woman's skin was not all those colours, but it was a reflection of the colours that were around her. We went after that same thing throughout *City of God*.'

Although the production did not plan to shoot in January, the film-makers wanted to suggest the extreme heat of summer, so the makeup artists oiled the boys' skin. Charlone lit the objects around them and captured the reflections off their skin.

For a party scene in which Bené [Benny] is accidentally killed by Blacky, Charlone encountered an unusual problem. The scene, which features hundreds of extras gyrating on a dance floor, was lit by a single 2.5K strobe light hanging from the ceiling. As his nickname suggests, Blacky [Rubens Sabino] was one of the darkest-skinned actors in the film, and just trying to *find* him as he made his way through the crowd was difficult; against the pulsating strobe, it was close to impossible. Charlone preceded him, walking backward with the camera, trying to gauge where Sabino was going by watching his eyes.

To prolong the lit moments – even by just fractions of a second – Charlone shot this part of the scene at 15 frames per second. It was then telecined at 15 fps. The cinematographer says this was the only time during the entire shoot that he altered his frame rate in the camera.

Perhaps the most visually stunning sequence in the picture is the transition that links the five-minute prelude to the 1960s phase of the story. Although the audience does not realise it until later, the prelude takes place in the 1980s, when Buscapé and his friends are about eighteen. The transition effectively takes the story back to its beginnings, when the kids are only eight-years old.

City of God opens with a festive sequence in which the entire neighbourhood is preparing food for an outdoor barbecue. One of the chickens, sensing its fate, escapes down an alley, with 18-year-old Li'l Zé and his gang in hot pursuit, guns drawn. As they round a corner they come upon Rocket, who is walking down the street. Everyone yells at him to grab the chicken. As he tries to sneak up on it, he suddenly sees all the gang members freeze. He looks behind him and sees a line of policemen about to square off against Li'l Zé's gang. Rocket is caught between the two groups.

Charlone does a zigzag zoom in from a wide shot of the scene to a medium shot of Rocket while the camera does a quick half-circle dolly around him. The camera moves from left to right, and the zoom catches Rocket just as his head turns from right to left. Although Charlone filmed the shot at normal speed, it was speeded up in post, and it looks as though the background is whizzing by behind Rocket's head.

This swish-zoom/dolly shot is immediately repeated two more times. The third time, however, the camera keeps going so that it circles Rocket completely. While the camera is moving around him, the background dissolves from the 1980s street scene to a dusty scrap of land that the same characters used as a soccer field in the 1960s. (Inferno artists Marcelo Lepiani and André Pinto dissolved between the backgrounds using areas, rather than a one-time dissolve.) As the camera moves around the character full-circle, the older actor is replaced by the boy who plays Rocket at age eight. Suddenly we are in the 1960s, and the narrative takes off. Two hours later, when the 1980s segment rolls around, the shot of 18-year-old Rocket caught between Li'l Zé's gang and the cops is repeated. But this time, the story keeps going.

Charlone spent nine weeks grading *City of God* at Estudios Mega, a post facility located in São Paulo. José Augusto de Blasiis of Megacolor supervised the transfer of the film. The film was scanned via a Celco digital film recorder and graded on a C-Reality with a da Vinci 2K colour-corrector. The colour-corrected version was then recorded out to Kodak 5245, and Charlone force-developed the resultant internegative one stop. 'I wanted a thicker negative to print around 32 or 33, and the one I got out of the Celco came in around 25 or 26,' he explains. 'The lab did not want to change the settings, so I force-developed the IN to get darker blacks.'

Nearly a year after wrapping the film, Charlone remains enthusiastic about the experience. 'I'm so in love with this project,' he exclaims, speaking by phone from his home in São Paulo. 'I have shot eight other films, and this is the first one in which the main concern was being real, being believable. It goes back to the roots of Neo-Realism, but it's a new realism. We wanted to show this reality as faithfully as we could.'

5. Talking Bullets: The Language of Violence in *City of God*[1]
Lúcia Nagib

'Words fail. Bullets talk.'
Paulo Lins, *Cidade de Deus*

In both the book and the film *City of God* the degree of 'realism' is striking. It is impossible not to be impressed by the 'insider's point of view', as identified by Roberto Schwarz, through which an intellectual from the *favela* (shantytown) as well as the characters drawn from this location speak in their own voices, from both the page and the screen. This paper aims to identify the elements that give the novel and the film what I would term their 'realist aspect', thereby revealing the laborious process of its production. As I will endeavour to show, the creation of the apparent 'spontaneity' which predominates in both works requires a considerable dose of artifice.

Since its publication in 1997, the novel *City of God* has made its mark, raising its author, Paulo Lins, to the status of one of Brazil's greatest writers. It has given literary expression to an issue that is today central to Brazilian society and politics, namely the *favelisation* (spread of *favela* communities) and the war on drug traffic. This topic, as approached by Lins, has subsequently provided rich pickings for Brazilian cinema (within which, furthermore, the *favela* represents a traditional genre). Several films about *favelas* were made in the wake of this novel's publication, such as *Midnight* [*O Primeiro Dia*] (Walter Salles and Daniela Thomas, 1999) and *News from a Personal War* [*Notícias de uma Guerra Particular*] (João Moreira Salles, 1998), and some of them, like *Orfeu* [*Orpheus*] (Carlos Diegues, 1999), even called upon the skills of Paulo Lins when it came to writing the dialogues. Lins even co-directed music videos for the rap group 'O Rappa' on the same subject. But, naturally, adapting the novel itself for the screen was a far greater challenge in view of its extraordinary quality.

Nevertheless, it is fair to say that in various ways the film *City of God*, directed by Fernando Meirelles and co-directed by Katia Lund, proved to be a worthy match for the novel on which it is based. Consequently critics are faced with the difficult task of identifying, within the intersemiotic translation, the corresponding and equally successful techniques in both of the works. I would suggest that a good place to start such a study is the most original aspect of the book, that is to say, its use of language. One of the most immediate and striking aspects of *City of God* is the revelation that a vast number of Brazilians speak a language that not only differs from educated Portuguese, but that is totally unknown among the upper classes. The inventive use of slang, that verges on a dialect in its own right, results in an agile, precise, synthetic and quick-fire language, which is highly expressive of contemporary Brazil. The authentic language of the *favela* constitutes the

---

[1] This paper was first published in *Third Text*, vol. 18, issue 3, 2004, 239-250.

main source of the novel's realism, and, through indirect ways, the film as well.

Murdered Words

When someone refers to the 'insider's point of view' in relation to the novel *City of God*, you immediately think of the background of its author, who was born and brought up in a *favela*, managing against all odds to break out of the lifestyle predestined for him and to bridge the gulf between the social classes. His entrance into the world of literary fiction came about as a result of an ethnographical research project, coordinated by Alba Zaluar, entitled 'Crime and Criminality among the Popular Classes', which was intended to give a voice to a community that never appears in the media, unless through the mouthpiece of the ruling classes. But the origins of the author and his previous research do not adequately account for the realism of the novel. Lins's writing is far removed from the spontaneous testimony of popular writers, who, unfamiliar with erudite conventions, 'write like they speak'. It is true that the narrator of the novel insists on maintaining the narrow insider's vision of someone who is ignorant of 'life outside' and the causes of his misfortunes. However, the extreme linguistic sophistication, that is obvious from even the opening lines of the novel, leads us to reject the idea that Lins is using a direct register.

The Brazilian critic, Antonio Candido, in his famous essay 'Dialética da malandragem' ['A Dialectic of Trickery'], used the term 'structural reduction' to refer to how realist writers used to manipulate non-literary material in order to make it 'part of an aesthetic order ruled by its own rules, not the rules of nature, society or the individual'. However, according to Candido, 'nature, society and the individual seem to be present on every page' (1993: 9). Something similar happens with the manipulation of language in *City of God*, which seems to contain in its own structure the materiality extracted from the facts.

Let us take as an example the first ten pages of the book, written in a deliberately poetic way, full of alliterations, rhymes and figures of speech. The first paragraph contains a series of alliterations of the letter 'b': 'Barbantinho e Buscapé fumavam um baseado à beira rio, na altura do bosque de eucaliptos' [Stringy and Rocket were smoking a joint by the riverside, near the Eucalyptus wood]. This is a reference to two secondary characters, who in the present-day within the story live in a world dominated by a war between drug gangs, and are enjoying a moment of contemplation. Although they are still young, they are recalling their own childhood and what the City of God was like in the past, as if it were a far distant past. The soft consonant 'b' continues to feature, in the words *bagana* [joint], *braçadas* [strokes], *arrebentação* [surf], *boiando* [floating], and *brincar* [playing], words that introduce a description of a Golden Age, when City of God was still 'one big farm'. Before the encroachment, according to the narrator speaking in the third person, of that 'such a modern world', with its property speculation and factories, the characters enjoyed a rural childhood, when they used to buy fresh milk, dig up vegetables, pick fruit in the fields, ride horses on the hills, go fishing and hunting for rodents and sparrows to eat with manioc flour. In those days, herds of cattle passed by 'in the tranquillity of those unaware of death'.

That tranquil river, on the banks of which the characters recollect a past crushed underneath houses and the other buildings of a new *favela*, then begins to turn red, a colour that precedes the appearance of human bodies – corpses from the war that is now being waged. At that point, the narrator stops dead, in order to make a comment in the first person, the only time that he does so in the whole novel: 'Poetry, my benefactor, illuminate... the shades of my words,' he pleads, before plunging headlong into a prose that will have 'bullets flying into phonemes'. This abrupt cut occurs in a kind of mini-chapter of just 13 lines, that is entirely poetic in its format, containing metre, cadence and rhyme, and which ends with, two phrases that announce the nature of the prose that is to follow: 'Words fail. Bullets talk'.

From that point on, the narrator in the third person takes the reins of the plot, and we witness the evolution of a language that, through onomatopoeia, synthesis and aggression, attempts to materialise gunshots, the cut and death. The prose that follows is radically different from the opening pages of the novel, although it continues to draw on similar poetic techniques. The initial introspection gives way to action, leaving no room for description or reflection. The words themselves cease to be passive signifiers to become active referents. The initial softness of the letter 'b' is replaced by the percussive 'p' of *rapá* [man or bro], the obsessive vocative that marks the end of many of the conversation lines and punctuates the whole novel.

This noun *rapá* is a shortened form of the word *rapaz* [boy], derived from the term *rapace*, a word with a curious etymology: *rapace*, in Latin, means 'a person who steals' and, in the Middle Ages, it was used to refer to servants or lackeys. When transformed by the inhabitants of the *favela* into the form of *rapá*, an oxytone that eats up the resting end syllable of the usually paroxytone Portuguese words, the final *pá* produces an onomatopoeic effect that evokes the aggression of a gun shot. The 'ra', in turn, brings to mind the repetition of machine gun fire, or at the very least, repetitive percussion rhythms, as captured in the word 'rap', a music that articulates the protests of American blacks as well as other marginalised groups throughout the world. Thus you could say that the single word *rapá* encapsulates the essence of the entire novel, since it single-handedly evokes virility, bullets, high speed and abrupt halt, which is death.

This technique, which dictated the choice of the words used throughout the novel, gives language an almost absolute power, enhanced by the sense of speed, repetition, accumulation and massification. Writer Guimarães Rosa, who elevated the uneducated language of Brazil's backlands to the status of erudite literature, unearthed from it a universalising ethics charged with mythical power. Paulo Lins's achievement, although similar, has the peculiarity of showing the appropriateness of the language spoken by deglamorised criminals, children who are enslaved by a logic that they neither know of nor can control, and which ultimately annihilates them. In Lins's hands this quick-fire language, of shortened words and phrases, acquires an interesting poetic quality, like a poem that before attaining philosophical status comes to an abrupt halt, as the 'bullets penetrate the phonemes', and that ends up being nothing more than a collection of clichés and prejudices. The characters tend to express themselves in proverbial forms, but because these are not preceded by any explanatory discourse, the result is often nonsense or black humour, as in these examples: 'When one Brazilian pees, all the others pee', or 'The blond child was the son of God, the white one God brought up, the dark child was his bastard son and the black one was shit by the Devil'.

The language of *City of God* is so authoritarian that it manipulates the very characters who speak it. A clear example of poverty's hierarchy is visible in the characters' names; practically all of them are known by nicknames that sum up their life and confine them to rigid characteristics succinctly captured by one or two words. There is no shortage of examples: the name 'Cabeção' [Melonhead] that is given to a policeman, instantly reveals that he is from Brazil's Northeast, where people supposedly have 'flat heads', and also reflects the prejudice against Northeasterners, which he also suffers from and which, to a certain extent, justifies his violent and vindictive behaviour towards blacks. The 'good guy' is called Mané Galinha [Knockout Ned], from which we deduce that, despite being black, he is 'Mané', an abbreviation of the name 'Manuel', a very common name in the Portuguese community and which became in Brazil a synonym of unintelligent. (The Portuguese have traditionally been the butt of jokes in Brazil for their legendary stupidity.) *Galinha*, on the other hand, refers to this character's ability to attract women.

Thus the language of the novel reveals the prejudiced nature of a culture that has neither time nor space for reflection. In this land of tough guys who kill and die like flies, life is described in ready-made phrases that are loaded with conservative morality, such as the following: 'Women are like dogs. They soon get used to new owners'. Such discrimination is directed at gays, the Portuguese, blacks, Northeasterners, whites, in a word, all the characters who, in the narrative, are slaves to their linguistic labels.

In the novel *City of God*, words also die young – like the characters, who are children turned into adults and then die before they are 20 years old. Given this context, pre-formed ideas are not only natural but also essential, since there is no time to hesitate or to choose. In gang warfare, whenever a character is about to 'unwrap an idea' his interlocutor kills him, or he kills the latter before any dialogue can take place. Repentance is also offset by more deaths with the result that everything is reduced to the indifference of mass production or, to put it more accurately, mass annihilation. The speed of the bullets interrupts and remedies the slow pace of the speech.

In order to guarantee some kind of existence, however ephemeral, nouns need to be concise and radical, reducing, for example, workers to idiots (*otário* or sucker/mug) and criminals to animals (*bicho-solto* [wild beast]), qualifications that often correspond to their death sentences. The murdered phoneme is also a murderer, in a world dominated by speed and by the ephemeral. In fact, the verb *matar* [to kill], among the gang members, is replaced with *passar* [to pass or waste]. 'Pass him, pass him!' shouts over and over again Li'l Zé, the most prolific and quick-working criminal, who does not sleep or relax, but compulsively snorts cocaine, which keeps him both desensitised and yet alert enough to 'waste' anyone who crosses his path. Death is just an incidental occurrence in the vicious circle of life.

Concentration

Unlike the novel, the film adaptation was not tied to words, and could rework the linguistic devices into other aspects of the film, such as the performance of the actors, the photography, the editing, the dialogues, the music and so on. Not to mention the script, written by Bráulio Mantovani, who brilliantly performed the arduous task of eliminating countless characters and incidents, as well as merging many others. As far as the realism is concerned, what perhaps stands out most of all is the cast. The 'authenticity' of the children and teenagers whose faces bear witness to their own origins, as well as those of the characters they are portraying, namely the *favela*, have fascinated audiences in Brazil and all over the world. The appearance on screen of real-life *favela* inhabitants, with their varying shades of dark skin, their frequently semi-naked, raw beauty, seems to emphasise the characters' veracity and restore the reality that gave rise to this fictitious story. Without a shadow of a doubt, the film has the revelatory quality of a 'hidden reality' that previously characterised neo-realist films, which depicted the ravages of war, or the films of the Brazilian *Cinema Novo* movement, that depicted the misery of the Brazilian backlands. However, given that the film is not a documentary, and that the actors are not nor could they ever be the gangsters they portray, its realist aspect is clearly not due to a mere attempt at copying reality.

We know from press releases and interviews given by the film-making team that the casting was a laborious and costly process, which took a whole year to complete. In several *favelas* (or communities, to use the team's politically correct terminology), amateur theatre schools and young people's associations, two thousand people were interviewed, from whom 400 youngsters were chosen to take part in a theatre workshop. The workshop, which concentrated on improvisation exercises, was directed by Guti Fraga, the founder of the *Nós do Morro* [*Us from the Hill*] group, an acclaimed amateur theatre group composed of *favela* inhabitants. As a result of these improvisation exercises that were observed and reported on by the directors and other members of the team, the 60 main actors and 150 supporting cast of the film were selected.

But the training given to the cast was still not over. Each actor was then coached by Fátima Toledo, and a short film was made, entitled *Palace II*, which acted as a screen test, but also as a run-through for the directing, set design, camera work and editing of the feature film *City of God*. During this process radical changes were made to the script, the dialogues and the performances, all with the intention of 'naturalising' what is believed to be the 'reality' of the *favela*. It was via this intense and prolonged period of coaching that the film-makers managed to achieve shockingly and almost unbearably realistic scenes, such as the one featuring the two children tortured by Li'l Zé, who end up shot, one of them lying dead. Given the energy that was channelled into achieving this level of technical mastery, it is clearly inadequate to attribute the film's realist aspect simply to the physical appearance and origins of the cast. The film's realism must, therefore, stem from its form.

Let us take as an example the opening scene of the film. It adapts the poetic style of the first pages of Paulo Lins's novel, combining it with an incident when a chicken is chased through the *favela*, which takes place almost at the end of the book. The images and the editing aim to create a visual rhyme, in the style of Eisenstein. The film opens with the preparation of food for a meal, adopting the metaphor of the knife (you could say that at the beginning of the film 'knives do the talking') and other cutting objects: the blade being sharpened alternates with the beak of a live chicken, the claws on the feet of other dead chickens and a close-up of the protruding, snarling teeth of Li'l Zé (the most feared gangster in the *favela*, as we subsequently discover). The sound of the knife being sharpened on the stone disrupts the *samba* rhythm – a forewarning of the violence that will bring an end to the Golden Age of the community, which is described in the following scenes to the sound of old *samba* songs. Then we hear the first phrase shouted by Li'l Zé, which ends with the synthetic word *rapá*: 'Grab the chicken, *rapá*!' Both the escaped chicken and the people who are chasing it are in danger of taking a bullet.

In this brief prologue, the virile nature of the story is established – a story that is composed essentially of male characters (a story of *rapazes* [boys]), and that is conveniently full of phallic imagery: the chicken (the 'cock'), the knife, the carrot being peeled, and the gun itself. Here it is worth remarking the visual/linguistic pun with 'chicken' and 'carrot', words used as nicknames of Li'l Zé's two enemies whom he wants to kill and eat, as he jokingly says later in the film. In this sequence, the personality of Li'l Zé is also established, as is his relationship with the other residents of the *favela*, and the spatial and temporal setting of the film, all scanned by the fast pace of a diegetic *samba* percussion. This is how cinema can translate the rules of synthesis, metre and rhyme, incorporating into its form the features of its subject matter. The violence of the language used here becomes as palpable as, or even more so than, the violence of the action on screen. Incidentally, it is important to remember that explicit scenes of violence are rare in the film. Virtually no blood is shown, and you do not see the customary severed limbs of Hollywood thrillers. The violence is contained in the form of the film, especially in the editing, and for this reason is all the more powerful.

But now we are touching on a more complex question. Eisenstein defined his montage of attractions by the degree of aggression contained in the images and by their capacity to elicit an emotional response from the audience. In the film *City of God* the aggression is conveyed not only via the imagery and signs of cutting and death, but also by the abrupt cuts in the editing. Cuts, as we know, are traditionally seen as contravening the conventions of realist cinema. The great theorist of film realism, André Bazin, writing after the Great War and appalled by violence, defended the sequence-shot and the deep focus cinematography, techniques that, according to him, respected the integrity of the time and space of phenomenological reality. Eisenstein, in his revolutionary combative films – rejected by Bazin – championed cuts, aggression and shock treatment.

Obviously, the film *City of God* is also in tune with the precepts of classic editing, the objective of which is not to achieve realism but a 'reality effect'. The violence, whether contained in the plot or the language, cannot fail to produce the same effect desired by American commercial cinema, namely, the illusionistic catharsis. The frenetic rhythm of the novel is translated into the quick-fire cuts of the digital editing, in the style of an advertisement or music video. In truth, the film could easily have gone down the route of the post-modern language of a cinema of citation, such as that of Tarantino, who only 'surfs' on the surface of reality. The film could equally have reproduced the easy gimmick of contemporary American cinema, infinitely repeating attractions that relegate the narrative to a secondary place.[2] But the film, just like the novel, avoids such schemes via the importance it gives to the narrative. Paulo Lins's great achievement was precisely to find a language with which to portray the encounter between the most violent modernity and the narrative potential of the myth. As a consequence of the bullets and the brusque cuts, the tale is not fragmented but rather is shrunk and condensed.

One line in the film, adapted from the novel, exemplifies this process. The words are spoken by a boy of just eight years of age, called Steak n' Fries, who works as a look-out for Li'l Zé's gang. The following is how he responds when Knockout Ned dismisses him as a 'child': 'who are you calling a child? I smoke, I sniff, I've killed, I've robbed. I'm a man'. During his brief existence so far, this character, who considers himself an adult, has not missed any stage of his life, but
radically shortened all of them. Already an experienced man of the world, this eight-year-old adult is not only ready to kill but also ready to die, which is predictably what happens to him soon after.

The Weight of History

The three-part structure of both the book and the film reflects the desire to create a sense of balance and completeness. The novel is deliberately divided into three 'stories':1) Shaggy's story: 2) Benny's story: 3) Li'l Zé's story. The emphasis placed on the word 'story' (*história*, in Portuguese, means both 'story' and 'history') is not incidental or unwitting: on the contrary, it indicates that the life stories of these criminals – who in real life are only known for their crimes – are urgently crying out to be told. By foregrounding story and history the novel continually reinforces the importance of its connection with reality.

The same is true of the film, the three-part structure of which hinges on the characters of Shaggy, Benny and Knockout Ned (three

---

[2] See Linda Williams, 'Discipline and fun: *Psycho* and postmodern cinema' (2000:351-378).

'good' gangsters) and on three different time frames: the end of the 1960s, the 1970s, and the beginning of the 1980s, each with their respective costumes, fashions and music. The development of the mythical structure is made even more apparent, with the references to 'Paradise', 'Purgatory' and 'Hell' in relation to the three different phases in the history of the City of God *favela*. In the novel, the passage from one phase (or story) to the next is marked by a speeding up of the narrative, which in the final part ends up summarising entire life destinies (invariably tragic) in just a few, frantically paced lines. In the film, the editing gives this sense of increasing speed, together with the lighting and sound effects, use of colour and camera work.

In the first part of the film, that I referred to earlier as the Golden Age of the community, we are conveniently confronted with golden sunlight and the orange hues of the unpaved roads of the City of God *favela*. Exterior shots from a static camera predominate, as well as long dialogues. In the second part of the film the number of interior and night-time shots increases. As the number of dead bodies piles up, the camera frees itself from the tripod and when Benny is murdered the images become confused due to the unprivileged position of the camera and the fragmentation caused by the strobe lighting at the disco where the scene takes place. The final part of the film, that deals with Knockout Ned's revenge on Li'l Zé, who raped the former's girlfriend and killed members of his family, is the darkest. The camera, frequently hand-held, becomes unsteady as it goes in search of objects that hide in badly lit locations. The cuts become ultra-fast and abrupt. The close of the film, as in the novel, shows the Runts (a group of very young delinquent children) taking the place of Li'l Zé and planning a series of murders. Thus their own premature deaths and the even shorter lives of future generations are implicitly predicted.

This structure, that begins in paradise and ends in hell, suggests a romantic nostalgia for the past. As we know, the myth of the Golden Age or of Paradise Lost differs from the Utopian myth. The former consists of a past that is lost and now unattainable, whereas Utopia, the ideal place conceived of not by the gods but by man, shapes up the *telos*, reaffirming faith in reason and the possibility of a better future.[3] Nostalgia, more easily identified in the novel than in the film, refers to a vision of the *favela*. Utopian thoughts were possible. In particular, some of the films that deal with *favelas*, like the previously mentioned *News from a Personal War*, *Midnight* and *Orfeu* (all of which tellingly involved Katia Lund and/or Paulo Lins), attest to the changes caused by the appearance of guns, which marks a dividing line between two separate historical periods. Cacá Diegues, when he conceived of his film *Orfeu*, was also convinced of the radical changes that drug dealing and firearms brought with them to *favela* communities. He divides the *favela* history into three phases: 1) the phase of the lyrical *samba*, up to the end of the 1950s, when 'those who lived up on the hill were near to heaven', to quote from a *samba* by Herivelto Martins; 2) the 'plaintive' phase, which

---

[3] See chapter 'A *Utopia* de Thomas Morus', especially p. 151, in Afonso Arinos de Melo Franco (1976).

started with the waves of chaotic migration that brought overcrowding and criminality to the *favelas*, making them closer to hell; 3) the phase of the pride of being a *favela* inhabitant, despite all its adversities.[4]

In the film *City of God* the lyrical *samba* of the time when the *favela* was synonymous with being close to heaven is used to recreate the mood of what I referred to as the community's Golden Age. This first part of the film opens to the strains of the *samba* 'Alvorada' ['Dawn'] by Cartola and Carlos Cachaça, which goes:

> Dawn up there on the hill
> How beautiful!
> Nobody is crying, there's no sadness
> Nobody is unhappy
> The colourful sun is so pretty, so pretty

Another *samba* by Cartola, 'Let Me Go', brings this section of the film to a close, accompanying the death of Benny:

> Let me go, I need to leave
> I'm off to try
> To laugh so as not to cry[5]

During this Golden Age, it is also worth noting that the criminals of the *favela* were still a kind of social bandit, who shared the fruits of their robberies amongst the poor population, such as when they held up the gas delivery truck. The emergence of drug dealing, particularly involving cocaine, marks the transition to crime on an industrial scale that ceases to have a social function, and is motivated by purely personal issues of rivalry and revenge. As Ismail Xavier has stated in an excellent essay, recent Brazilian cinema is full of characters whose discomfort stems from the fact that they are stuck in the past and obsessed with the desire for revenge (2003: 56). Now that the political motivations that previously inspired social bandits, as portrayed in *Cinema Novo*, have been exhausted, the criminals in new Brazilian cinema only act out of resentment and their aggressive behaviour is turned against their own kind, when not against themselves.

An Interrupted Utopia

Aggression for trivial reasons, that is typical of Li'l Zé and the other gang members in *City of God*, who kill someone because 'he's a pain in the ass', interrupts the Utopian trajectory, which was beginning to emerge in several different ways: via religion, work and studying. However, it does not hinder the full development of the several short stories that make up the narrative of *City of God*. In another paper I considered the Utopia of the sea in Brazilian cinema, which from Glauber Rocha's films onwards has promised the poor a share in the wealth of the

---

[4] See *Press Book* of *Orfeu*, pp. 22-23.
[5] Fernando Meirelles told me an interesting detail about this song: it was composed on the death of the composer's daughter, who was a cocaine addict.

coast (2001-2002: 148-58). In *City of God* the picture-postcard Rio de Janeiro, with its coastline and beautiful scenery, remains a privilege of the rich, attainable only as a 'vision' for the inhabitants of the *favela* (as in the case of the character Clipper who, after having a 'vision', chooses religion as his way out). As an image, the beautiful Rio is merely a hazy silhouette on the horizon in the film. The sea is only attainable for Rocket, the social climber who has to get close to the 'groovies', that is, the white inhabitants of City of God.

Rio de Janeiro is thus presented as a divided city, to use Zuenir Ventura's term (1997), containing, on the one hand, the sea of the rich and, on the other, the *favela* of the poor. However, this division, that interrupts the Utopia and destroys young lives, does not lead to an 'interrupted spectacle', to use Robert Stam's term with regard to anti-illusionistic techniques. Consequently, none of the self-reflexive techniques used in the film create a distancing effect, the most obvious one being the alter-ego of the film-maker personified by the character Rocket, the omniscient narrator of the film. Devised as a middleman, with access to the middle classes, he is also the film's conscience, suggesting an identification with the editor himself sitting at his editing table. Behaving as the truth keeper, he organises, with his voice over, the facts that make up the narrative, dictating at whim the freeze-frames, flashbacks and fast forwards, zooms and long shots, thus exposing the mechanics of digital editing.

Several times, after a flashback, the story, under the control of the narrator's voice-over, returns to the same point, showing the identical scene from a different point of view. This is the case, for example, when Li'l Zé takes Blacky's 'mouth' (drug-dealing turf). Explaining the story of each of the characters involved, Rocket's commentary takes the narrative back to the beginning three times, as if the editor were testing the different points of view offered by three different cameras. At no time, however, is the story called into question, and thus the repetition of the scene from different angles does not ultimately discredit the narrator, unlike, for example, in Sérgio Bianchi's film *Chronically Unfeasible* [*Cronicamente Inviável*] (1999), which uses a similar technique.

Rocket can still be interpreted as a reference to film-makers/photographers of the past, when he takes a photograph of Li'l Zé and his gang, just as in the 1930s the famous Benjamin Abraão photographed and filmed the bandit Lampião and his followers, unwittingly leading to his capture and subsequent death. This subject has been repeatedly exploited by film-makers in Brazil as a form of self-reflexive commentary, in such works as *Memories of Banditry* [*Memórias do Cangaço*] (Paulo Gil Soares, 1965), *Corisco and Dadá* [*Corisco e Dadá*] Rosemberg Cariry, 1996) and *Perfumed Ball* [*Baile Perfumado*] (Paulo Caldas and Lírio Ferreira, 1997). Likewise in *City of God* the publication of the photograph of Zé and his gang on the front page of the *Jornal do Brasil* newspaper prompts the police to begin to hunt them down. The police do not kill Li'l Zé but they force him into an extortion racket and take his money, making him vulnerable to the gang of Runts, who shoot him dead in a 'Soviet attack'. Thus, indirectly, the camera becomes the murderer of the object that it captures, analogous to a gun, as has been extensively studied in film theory.[6]

Rocket's self-reflexive position is what guarantees the realist quality of the actors' performances. Indeed, the highly polished, exquisite dialogues in the film, which draw on the very best of the novel, would not be possible if the narrator did not take on the didactic function of presenting and explaining the characters and their stories. Stripped to the bare essentials, the speech has none of the superfluous information common in film dialogues that is intended to contextualise the speakers. Rocket, who, unlike the other characters, is not in a hurry, has all the time in the world to explain, in voice-overs, how drug dealing is organised in the *favela*, even providing a glossary of the hierarchy of the drug business, from the 'look out' to the 'manager'. This is an example of didactic, ironic and good-humoured self-reflexivity, as created by Jorge Furtado, in his short film *Island of Flowers* [*Ilha das Flores*] (1989), which led to an entire school and today is regularly used in TV series, such as *City of Men* [*Cidade dos Homens*], inspired by the film *City of God*.

The essential speech of the characters, resulting from their ignorance of educated norms and the creative lack of awareness with which they express prejudices and clichés, brings to the fore the childlike innocence of these serial murderers, rapists and mutilators. This for me is the most moving reality that emanates from *City of God*. The extreme skill of linguistic devices in the novel, and cinematic techniques in the film, are directed at avoiding the idea that the interruption of the Utopia will put an end to history. Although aimless, these armed children, who were born to kill and die young, are the essence of Brazil's contemporary history, and probably that of many other countries.

Translation by Lisa Shaw

References

Candido, Antonio. *O discurso e a cidade.* São Paulo: Duas Cidades, 1993.
Melo Franco, Afonso Arinos de. 'A *Utopia* de Thomas Morus'. In *O índio brasileiro e a Revolução Francesa.* Rio de Janeiro: Topbooks, 1976. pp. 151 ff.
Nagib, Lúcia. 'Imagens do mar – visões do paraíso no cinema brasileiro de ontem e de hoje'. *Revista USP* 52, Dez-Fev 2001-2002, 148-58.
Nagib, Lúcia. 'Death on the beach – the recycled utopia of *Midnight*'. in Nagib, Lúcia (ed.), *The New Brazilian Cinema*. I.B. London and New York: Tauris, 2003, pp. 157-72.
Oliveira, Jane Souto de; Marcier Maria Hortense. 'A palavra é: *favela*'. In Zaluar, Alba and Alvito, Marcos (eds.), *Um século de favela*. Rio de Janeiro: Fundação Getúlio Vargas, 1998, pp. 90 ff.
Schwarz, Roberto. 'City of God', in *New Left Review* 12, Nov-Dec 2001, 102-112.
Ventura, Zuenir. *Cidade partida*. São Paulo: Companhia das Letras, 1997.
Virilio, Paul. *Guerre et cinéma.* Paris: L'Etoile/Cahiers du Cinéma, 1984.
Xavier, Ismail. 'Brazilian Cinema in the 1990s: the unexpected encounter and the resentful character'. In Nagib, Lúcia (ed.), *The New Brazilian*

---

[6] See, for example, Paul Virilio, *Guerre et cinéma*.

Cinema. London and New York: I.B. Tauris, 2003, pp. 39-63.

Williams, Linda. 'Discipline and fun: *Psycho* and postmodern cinema'. In Christine Gledhill & Linda Williams (eds.), *Reinventing Film Studies*. London: Arnold, 2000, pp. 351-378.

6. *City of God*: A Landmark in Brazilian Film Language
André Gatti

The advent of a film like *City of God* is an unparalleled phenomenon in the history of Brazilian cinema. The film raises cinema production to an unequalled standard and breaks with a certain naivety and tradition in the Brazilian film industry. The scope of *City of God* creatively and uniquely intertwines the aesthetic and the artistic, the ideological and the economic, the cultural and the anthropological. Such distinctiveness may be why *City of God* has become the most controversial film of the recent era that has conventionally been called the 'Recovery of Brazilian Cinema'.

Fernando Meirelles: Independent Production and the Professionalisation of the Film-Maker

As the primary mentor and investor on the project, Meirelles is a new breed of film-maker in the field of national audio-visual production. Such a description may be attributed to the film-maker's unique way of inserting himself within contemporary independent production. Meirelles's career path breaks away from that of the traditional Brazilian film-maker, as he pursues a trajectory uncharted by other national cinema authors.

His professional trajectory towards film-making begins in the pioneer video-producing firm Olhar Eletrônico [Electronic Eye], as he recounts:

> Since I already had a camera and wanted to make films, four of us got together, each one put in 8,000 dollars, and I went back to Japan and bought an editing suite. With this equipment at our disposal, we founded Olhar Eletrônico (now with Paulo Morelli, Marcelo Machado, Dário Vizeu, and Beto Salatini we were five). We called the front room Production, since the suite was assembled there; we lived in the bedrooms. We gave screen tests for advertising agencies, made some promotional videos, and experimented with video, always with the objective of making film or television (in Saraiva e Cannito, 2002: 40).

This was the beginning of the 1980s, when the U-Matic video equipment Olhar Eletrônico used was cutting-edge technology. Simultaneously, São Paulo was undergoing a singular cultural unrest due to the emergence of the independent music and alternative literature movements. For a number of reasons, experimentation in the arts was the agenda of the time; therefore, audio-visual arts were also absorbed into this conceptual whirlpool. Since Olhar Eletrônico had the capacity to produce creative and inexpensive videos, they soon came to be a powerful local resource.

Olhar Eletrônico quickly grew and it soon interfered with open television programming in an unprecedented way. This is to be understood as the participation of an independent producer of images in the most important segment of Brazil's audio-visual industry, that is, television. The insertion of Olhar Eletrônico was the work of journalist Goulart de Andrade, who shared part of his time at TV Gazeta Station with Olhar Eletrônico, which ended up creating its own programme, *Antenas*.

Later, due to problems with the sponsor, Olhar Eletrônico would lose that space for good. However, it did not stay behind the scenes for very long, because it managed to get back on air with the production of a programme called *Crig-Rá*, made in association with Abril Video, and which aired successfully for nearly six months. The result of these two television experiences comprised about a year of practically uninterrupted activity. Besides these programmes, in 1988 Meirelles also worked on TV Gazeta's *TV Mix* programme. He describes this period of his life thus:

> Audience ratings were very low, but as a laboratory, *TV Mix* was excellent. We managed to introduce many good people to the world of TV. Serginho Groissman, for example, had a radio programme. We insisted that he come to television [...]. Later on, when MTV was installed, they called Marcelo Machado to direct it and he took with him the whole group that starred in *TV Mix*, including Astrid, the clip programmer, Rogério Gallo, the technicians, editors, among others. It was a bunch of guys who would feel uncomfortable at TV Gazeta. The first generation of MTV came basically from *TV Mix* (in Saraiva e Cannito, 2002: 43).

However, one could say that the great professional breakthrough for Meirelles would come in 1989, when he was hired to work on the children's serial *Rá-Tim-Bum*, at TV Cultura, where he directed 180 episodes. *Rá-Tim-Bum* was the most successful children's series ever produced outside the large television networks with record-breaking audience ratings.

In the early 1990s, already very experienced and reasonably well-known in Brazilian television, Meirelles and part of the group from Olhar Eletrônico decided to found the production company O2 (October 1991), with the goal of working in the advertising market. The advertising agency DPZ hired O2 to work on a marketing campaign for TELESP (a phone company), using the actor Marcelo Tas to play the character Ernesto Varela. O2's fees were so low that they soon had lots of clients and became a fad. When they noticed that they could make more with commercials, money started coming in, and the face of the firm changed – so much so that after 10 years in business, O2 enjoyed a reasonably comfortable situation. Not only was O2 the largest firm in Brazil in its sector, but also it was twice as big as the second firm. In 2002, O2 produced 416 television commercials. Nowadays, one cannot watch television for half an hour without seeing at least one commercial produced by O2.

The growth of O2 demonstrates how an experiment – considered a bit 'crazy', due to its unconventional ways – could become a prestigious and financially successful enterprise. To maintain its dominant position, today O2 has, by Brazilian standards, a large infrastructure, with three small and three big studios, three full cameras, a generator, non-linear editing and finishing equipment and plenty of lighting. In addition, because the work done with the actors was responsible for O2's high profile in the advertising market, it maintains a staff of 16 people in charge of screen tests. One can imagine the dimension of this work by the size of the cast. In 2002, O2 had about 6,000 professional actors registered on its books. This kind of experience can be easily traced in the preparation of the cast in *City of God*.

Meirelles and his partners' strategy was to use their existing infrastructure so that the directors could devote time to new projects and their dream of making films for the cinema. Actually O2 comprises three production companies: one is called O2 Shorts, which belongs to Meirelles. Paulo Morelli owns O2 Films. There is also O2 Produções, which is managed by Andrea Barata Ribeiro and has 10 staff directors. When Meirelles makes a film, he earns through his firm, and the same is true for Morelli. In the last eight years, however, they have both invested their profits in O2 Produções. And this has been possible because of the arrangement described above.

The O2 partners began to turn their dream of film-making into a reality around 1998, when they made their first short films. Later came the experiences with feature films. Fernando Meirelles's own filmography starts with *Menino Maluquinho 2* [*The Nutty Boy 2*] (1996), followed by *E no Meio Passa um Trem* [*And in the Middle a Train Passes*] (1998), *Domésticas* [*Maids*] (2001), *Palace II* (*Golden Gate*) and *Cidade de Deus* [*City of God*] (2002), thus making up two short films and three feature ones. *Nutty Boy 2*, directed by Fabrícia Alves Pinto, was Meirelles's debut in feature films, and it proved his ability to work within this format. The first feature which originated at the very heart of O2, *Maids*, co-directed by Nando Olival, allowed Meirelles to more freely exercise his techniques as a director with greater originality.

Strategy of the *City of God* Project

Two films show a certain maturity of some Brazilian film-makers to tune into the contemporary international project of circulation of audio-visual material: *Central do Brasil* [*Central Station*] and *City of God*. If the strategy for creating *Central Station* was an individual's intelligence, the making of *City of God* as a team project can be interpreted as a meaningful move forward in contemporary Brazilian cinema. The elements involved in a film production such as *City of God* should actually become living models for the building of an audio-visual industry in Brazil synchronised with industrial and commercial planning in the most professional way possible, capable of facing up to international competition and globalised production for the broadcasting systems. Hegemonic and emerging film industries, all showing a similar appetite, battle fiercely for market niches.

In the production planning of a film of the scope of *City of God*, a good script, among other things, is foremost. The script of the film went through twelve drafts in the hands of Bráulio Mantovani, who had Meirelles himself as his closest support. Therefore, it can be said that the process of gestation of the film was marked by an extra care not common

46

in local productions. One must bear in mind that Meirelles was pressed for time, since he wanted to apply for audio-visual production law incentives funding and the deadline was imminent. To everybody's amazement, the script, which was believed to be only a draft, was chosen for the Sundance-Rio Film Laboratory and was awarded prizes by the Motion Picture Association and by the Writers' Guild of America. We now know that the first draft was not exactly rudimentary, as all those involved in the project had thought. Eleven other versions were written, and afterwards parts of the narration were rewritten during the shooting of the film.

A very solid craftsmanship marked out the weaving of the cinematography of *City of God* from the very beginning. It originated from Paulo Lins's book by the same name (1997), which was a bestseller and has since been translated into several languages. Thus, from the start the film relied on a very powerful argument, in turn derived from the original conception of the text. According to its author, in 1982, he had recorded interviews with people directly or indirectly connected to crime in *Cidade de Deus* for a project called *Crime e Criminalidade nas Classes Populares* [*Crime and Criminality in the Popular Classes*], directed by the anthropologist Alba Zaluar. Then, he wrote a poem that was published in an academic magazine called *Novos Estudos Cebrap*, with the support of Roberto Schwarz, who, at that time, encouraged him to write a novel. Lins started writing the book *City of God* in 1986, and some ten years later it was ready. A work of fiction based on social-anthropological research is very unusual in Brazilian literature. From another perspective, Lins further attests to the fact that, from its very conception, the book project already contemplated a cinematographic horizon:

> While I wrote, I imagined that some day that story could be made into a film. I have always liked the cinema; I even participated in the *Cidade de Deus* cinema club from 1980 to 1987. The club used to show political films, such as *Braços Cruzados, Máquinas Paradas* [*Arms Crossed, Machines Stopped*] and *Eles Não Usam Black-tie* [*They Don't Wear Black-tie*]. I then imagined that [if] *City of God* became a film, many more people could participate in the discussion of this reality (2002).

This may have been a factor that pushed Lins into greater participation in the making of the film. He was also very excited because of Fernando Meirelles's enthusiasm when the film-maker presented the first ideas for the development of his project, which was the main reason why Lins sold the book rights in 1997. Two years later, Lins worked again as a consultant, this time at the invitation of Katia Lund, with whom he had worked on the documentary *Notícias de uma Guerra Particular* [*News from a Personal War*] and in the clip *Minha Alma* [*My Soul*], with the Rappa group. The invitation came when Katia Lund tried to go deeper into the characters' profiles in preparation for the actors' workshop that the film producers had begun to set up in Rio de Janeiro.

The cast of *City of God,* comprising approximately 110 boys, required special consideration. To deal with so many people, directors Meirelles and Lund created a performance workshop to train non-professional actors from several communities in Rio de Janeiro in the eight months before the shooting of the film.[1] The workshop that was created at *Morro do Vidigal*, a *favela* in Rio, was called *Nós do Cinema* [*We in Cinema*]. It relied on the contribution of a professional specialised in the development of actors for specific purposes, Fátima Toledo.

The distinctively innovative film-making strategy of *City of God* was teamwork. Meirelles describes the process thus:

> This film involved six partnerships in the several phases of the process throughout which we all had a lot of room for creativity. [...] I worked with Bráulio Mantovani, the screenplay writer, for two years. Then Katia came in. She was involved in the whole process of formation and preparation of the cast; she also helped us to continue elaborating the script. In the pre-production stage, César Charlone came in and, together, we organised the script and thought up the cinematography. Tulé Peake, the art director, followed this process very closely all the time. I invited my editor, Daniel Rezende, to do his first work in the cinema [...] I was absolutely right. These partners are creative co-authors of *City of God* (in Leal, 2002: 18). The division of tasks in film-making is a major factor that must be considered ever more carefully for any audio-visual product that is intended to become competitive in the current marketing phase.

The 'Non-Photography'

The making of *Golden Gate* [*Palace II*], a kind of photographic laboratory, was precisely the formula that would later become a hit in *City of God*. An important debate took place at the *Associação Brasileira de Cinematografia* [ABC – Brazilian Association of Cinematography], in the Cinemateca (São Paulo, 2002), that gathered together the main technicians involved in the making of *City of God*.[2] Four different types of film emulsion were used to test the reactions of the negatives, the several shooting situations, and their results in the finishing process (Kodak's 5245 50D; 5246 250D; 5279 500T, and 5289 800T), besides two different cinematographic gauges (16 mm and 35 mm). This transformed the short film, as the photographer said, 'into a patchwork, both of light and of cameras, sometimes on a tripod, sometimes handheld, as well as different negatives and textures'. The result was that, in the shooting of *City of God*, negative 5289 800T was rejected, while negative 5274 200T was used instead. According to Charlone, the latter had produced a better response.[3]

---

[1] Editor's note: See Fernando Meirelles in this volume.
[2] The information about the debate on the technical aspects of the film was later made available at ABC's website by André Moncaio, under the title 'GT Projeção' (2002).
[3] Editor's note: See Oppenheimer for a detailed discussion of *City of God*'s cinematography.

In order to make the work more manageable, the film was divided into three distinct phases, so that each one would have its own period reconstruction, direction, and photography.[4] Charlone pointed out during the debate that *City of God* would be a film totally different from any others ever made in Brazil. If it bore any resemblance at all, it would be to the documentaries that were made in the beginning of the 1980s. He adds that from the experience with documentaries came the tradition of the handheld camera, trying to prevent even the minimum interference with reality. The camera itself was allowed to suggest the framing and even the light (or maybe the 'non-light'). The aesthetic project was to do what was described above without many technical details; however, there are moments when plans of highly creative elaboration are found, with a certain flavour of an advertising film. On the other hand, the film ends up finding its own cinematographic language in the uses of camera, light, interpretation, and location. The final project was dubbed 'non-photography' by the team.

Due to the factors so far described, I posit that *City of God*, at least the way it is, could hardly have been made by more traditional film-makers. The team's competent experimentalism was derived from their experience in producing commercials and their exploration into the infinite possibilities of the digital post-production technology. This coupled with the 'tense' handheld camera, alternating with takes on a tripod, in the creation of a visual language that is very different from that of the average contemporary Brazilian cinematographic productions. Also, at the same time, it brings Brazilian production up-to-date with cutting-edge film-making technology. This type of cinematographic upgrade, I believe, will point the way for Brazilian productions from now on, especially for those film-makers who are interested in participating and competing in the international and national markets of moving pictures. This may be the only way to create a place for Brazilian cinematographic production in local and international markets.

The film's so-called realistic project had as a basis two main locations: the development known as Conjunto Habitacional de Sepetiba (a set of humble houses built by the government in a municipality outside Rio de Janeiro), and outside the alleys of Morro Santa Marta (a *favela*), where the sequences of battles between the gangs and the chases were shot. Even so, the production team always needed to have an alternative filming plan. After all, such spots are known to be ruled by a parallel power, organised crime, or drug dealers.

In the *Notas sobre a produção* [*Notes on the Production*], the team members reveal that 'fiction and reality got mixed up in the set.' The interior scenes were shot in studios, except for the sequences in bars and the sequences of Dadinho's [Li'l Dice] ritual of initiation into the gang. He later becomes known as the famous outlaw Zé Pequeno [Li'l Zé], in the motel robbery (one of the strongest and most revealing scenes), all filmed on location.

---

[4] Editor's note: See Oppenheimer in this volume.

The Controversy in Brazil around *City of God*

Such innovative techniques and strategies combined with its ideological and economical policies are, in my opinion, what provoked diverse opinions and controversies around the film. However, the extremes of criticism only happened in Brazil, because overseas the criticisms were, in general, very favourable. An article published in the newspaper *O Estado de São Paulo*, which said the following, generated great contention around the film:

> Never before has there been in Brazil so much circulation and consumption of images of poverty and violent images, pictures of outcasts, of the so-called 'deviating' or 'abnormal' behaviours. Violence and the denunciation of crime have become lately almost a journalistic genre. That could even be interesting, if these figures did not usually come out of context, spontaneously generated, without any relationship with the economy and social injustices, and were not treated as a spectacle, a breathtaking event, a type of television tabloid or reality show that can be consumed with extreme pleasure. The so-called modern New Cinema, something like 'thou shalt not take pleasure in another's misery', that has created an aesthetics and an ethics of the intolerable in order to deal with the problems of poverty has been displaced by the incorporation of local themes [trafficking, *favelas, sertão*[5]], a new transnational aesthetics, a post-MTV language, a new Latin-American realism and brutality that has as its source high dosages of adrenaline, reactions per second created by the assemblage and total immersion in the images. In other words, the bases of pleasure and of efficacy in North American action films, in which violence and sensorial stimuli reach the level of hallucination, an imperative and sovereign delight of seeing, causing, and suffering violence (Bentes, I, 2002, p. D-1).

I gather that the analysis of the film's structure proposed by the author is appropriate and corresponds to the project of a product, of a commodity, of a symbolic merchandise that intends to reach a broad spectrum of the public and of the market with the aim of finding its place in the present stage of the economy and of the world. In this sense, understanding the producer's and the creator's positions is a very complex task. The project of a film like *City of God* must be understood under these conditions, that is, of the international circulation of images in the contemporary world and, consequently, of its market-based organisation.

The critic and theorist Paulo Emílio Salles Gomes, author of the celebrated *Cinema*: *trajetória no subdesenvolvimento* [*Cinema*: *Trajectory of Underdevelopment*], may be still resonant for an understanding of the tensions generated by this project. The model of

---

[5] Translator's note: *Sertão* is an untranslatable Brazilian word that means the faraway and inhospitable lands of the country.

interpretation of the development of Brazilian cinema that Gomes devised is based on the dichotomy 'cinema of the occupier' versus 'cinema of the occupied.' This model relates to the prominent dependency theory in the 1970s. If we translate 'occupier' into today's 'imported', one may say that today, practically, nothing is foreign, borrowing Gomes's words:

> This mass of films that overtake us, that we understand little of, is nothing more, after all, than a meaningless vice. The products that are thrown at us by the foreign cinema industry in reality do not say anything to us, because any living communication implies the notion of a dialogue. Films talk to us; we must answer them, but doing so is useless; the eventual counterpart speakers are out of reach. Their voice is strong, because we import it, but when it comes to our turn, we talk to no one, or to ourselves, wearing out our muscles to move on the surface of a culture that has nothing to do with us (1986: 262).

In *City of God*, Meirelles goes against those who believe that foreign cinema has nothing to tell us. His position is that of a direct negotiation, without hierarchies, with the tradition of the cinema of the 'occupier' to the detriment of an exclusive dialogue with the Brazilian film tradition. This specific reference to *Cinema Novo* was used by some to express their antagonistic views towards the film, notably by the critic Ivana Bentes. Despite such reservations, the Brazilian public continued to flock into the theatre houses.

We may come to understand that the relationship between a product's content and the aesthetics of a commodity with the market tends to become a variable that cannot be underestimated any more. From all this arises a situation in which all injunctions tend to intermingle in an undeniable way. The cinematographic artist works with a mass culture and with the market procedures specific to the cultural industry. Because he understands this, Meirelles has been criticised sometimes in a distempered way; strangely enough, this did not happen to Walter Salles in *Central Station*. After all, Meirelles and Salles are two film-makers who share the same ideological and economical type of project for the Brazilian cinema.

The making of a film like *City of God* is one of those events that cause abrupt transformations in the production of entertainment films in Brazil. *City of God* was able to put together distinct elements around a coherent aesthetic project whose results have not yet been completely assessed by modern historiography and criticism. This situation defines the original position occupied by *City of God* in the national and international cinematographic fields.

Translation by Edson Martins Lopes

References
Almeida, Paulo S. *Quem é quem no cinema.* Rio de Janeiro: Espaço Z, 2003.
Bentes, Ivana. 'Da estética da fome à cosmética da fome', in *O Estado de S. Paulo,* 31 de agosto de 2002, p. D-1.

Calil, Carlos A. (org). *Paulo Emílio, um intelectual na linha de frente*. São Paulo: Brasiliense, 1986.

Leal, Hermes. 'Chegou a sua vez'. Interview with Fernando Meirelles in *Revista de Cinema*, September 2002, 13-18.

Lins, Paulo, 2002. In www.cidadedeus.com/notasdaprodução (last accessed September 28th 2002).

Moncaio, André. 'GT Projeção'. In www.abc.com.br/seminario/ (last accessed October 10th 2002)

Saraiva, Leandro, & Cannito, Newton. Entrevista com Fernando Meirelles. *Sinopse*, no. 7, 40-46, 2002.

www.abc.com.br/seminario/ (last accessed October 10th 2002)

www.cidadededeus.com (last accessed Sept. 28th 2002)

7. *City of God*: Mastery and Contradiction
Leandro Rocha Saraiva

Cidade de Deus [*City of God*] challenges some of the ideas which are becoming established in the so-called 'Recovery' of Brazilian cinema. First, the film breaks with the circle of psychologism and moral crisis that, according to Ismail Xavier, has characterised Brazil's recent production (2000: 97-138). Meirelles boldly confronts the most perverse aspect of the country's apartheid: drug-trafficking, marginalised people's horizon of horror, which emerged to counteract the failure of development.

Paulo Lins's book, which is the basis for the film adaptation, has already, in the words of Roberto Schwarz, been 'hailed as an event'. The explosive nature of its themes, the scope and difficulty of its ambition and its unprecedented form of internal narration', all this contributes to uncommon artistic adventure' (1997).

As if all this interest were insufficient, there is the unusual nature of the production. Meirelles, owner of Brazil's most successful advertising firm, O2, personally invested almost three million dollars in the film, which he has since recovered with lucrative international sales. The costly production was organised as a lengthy series of workshops for actors recruited from the drug-ravaged *favelas*. Thus, he juxtaposed the costly and sophisticated knowledge of Brazil's audio-visual industry (advertising) with a long neglected participation of poor popular segments in an artistic creation, a process long neglected.

The film, on one hand, suggests a kind of 'bourgeois revolution' in Brazilian cinema, the glimmer of a possible upswing in the industry, under the leadership of directors/producers who come from the advertising industry. On the other hand, the feature-length film is the result of an effort to incorporate the book's 'insider's point of view'. Besides being a resident of Cidade de Deus, Lins, the book's author, was a research assistant of anthropologist Alba Zaluar (1985) and an assistant in the youth workshops.

Is this something new, a pace-setting film, or is it the most exquisite class imposture, the incorporation of the bitter experience of people as the raw material for a spectacle that dissolves and pasteurises that experience? The most promising way to approach the question is to suspend *a priori* judgements, or judgements extrinsic to film, and even to put aside any questioning of the film's documentary value – which compares, point-by-point, details on the screen with facts of reality. Let us pay attention instead to the mode of the film's composition, its formalisation of the social material it intends to represent.

A 'Very Cool' Narrator

In the first place, there is the choice of Buscapé [Rocket] as narrator. Ironically, this fellow, who tries to keep out of the way of the drug traffic, is our guide through the world of organised crime and the evolution of Zé Pequeno [Li'l Zé]. Told in flashbacks, the narrative, with its distancing in relation to the narrated facts, makes it possible to reflect upon what has transpired through the decades. This structural feature of

Cidade de Deus at once suggests a reference to Scorsese, who in *Casino* and especially in *Goodfellas* used crime as a reflection of society.

And yet, the connection with Scorsese cannot be taken much further. The presence of a narrator does not lead to an epic composition, as in the didactic *Casino*. *Goodfellas* is rather closer, not only in its criminal theme, but in its realistic, more continuous tone, which the narrator does not break but only summarises and makes more 'tremulous'. We are, however, far from the modes of Meirelles's film. Scorsese's film is finally shown to be a courtroom drama, in which the narrator gives testimony about a crime as a repressed truth, a negative image of American society: onto the movie *Mafiosi* are projected the desires that drive everyone. But this never abolishes the distinction between law and crime.

The difference of *Cidade de Deus* is in the absence of moral judgment on Buscapé's part. There is not in him or in any other character even an attitude of moral confrontation, of an individual struggling against a hostile environment, as, for example, in Ken Loach's *My Name is Joe*. No one questions the drug dealers in moral terms; there is an infernal logic in the action, which is only evaluated in practical terms. In Buscapé's judgement, people are divided into those who are, and those who are not, 'very cool', those who recognise 'someone' in the other (in him, Buscapé). For this reason, Bené [Benny], the last *malandro*, the familiar rogue who depends on his wits rather than violence, adapted to the cruel times of the drug traffic, is 'very cool', while Zé Pequeno, who dominates the area by terror, and not 'by authority', is an 'asshole' and a 'son of a bitch'.

Buscapé, without moralising dramatisation, oscillates between a legal and a criminal existence. His attempts at crime fail because he cannot succeed in taking his 'victims' as such (they are, after all, 'very cool'). His efforts as a 'sucker' (worker) also fail, and the camera, which will be his pass to a normal life, comes from the game of banditry. Could this be seen as a weakness in the film? After all, Buscapé is a character who is, let us say, weak, who does not move the plot (he is more of an observer) and who does not gather round him a picture of moral drama or the existential experience of living amid the inferno of drug dealers.

Conversely, the 'minor key' of the narrator may be what differentiates *Cidade de Deus's* composition from that of other international violent crime thrillers. Buscapé's mediation provides *Cidade de Deus* with what Antonio Candido (1998) refers to as a 'dialectic between order and disorder', which shows that the film cannot be classified simply, as some critics have already done, as a film in a foreign genre transposed to Brazil. In Cidade de Deus, 'if you run, you get caught, if you stand still, you get eaten'. So it becomes necessary to live, in the life of the *malandro*, with no moralising outlets – which helps avoid 'moral dilemmas' (different from Ken Loach's film, which, in the relationship between Joe and his girlfriend, builds the conflict in order to show it as socially dislocated).

Contradictions

But this lucky break on the part of the narrator does not inform the film as a whole. An important part of the set of characters and their relationships, as well as the development of the plot, aims at another side, more in tune with classical dramatic principles. The script, adapted from the novel by Bráulio Mantovani, shows control in its pace (pulsation between tension and explosion, a chain of small events producing enormous effects, the effective use of ellipses, flashbacks, and narrative summaries) and in the reduction of a large set of literary characters to a tightly-knit group of film characters. The direction works on the same scale of effective concentration – in the realistic and precise gestures and speech, at moments of virtuoso editing (as in the opening 'cinematographic drumming') or in the sustained intensity of scenes like Filé com Fritas's [Steak and Fries] first murder. The film thus achieves narrative fluidity and tension, obtaining as a result the spectator's involvement through identification, which ensures the film's popular success.

And perhaps it is here, in the contradiction between Buscapé's dialectics of order and disorder and the choices it promises, and in the film's effective presentation of the history of crime and what it ensures, that we can expose the contradictions that already insinuate themselves into an effort belonging both to the film industry and anthropology.

The 'Annoying' Things about the Film

Buscapé's point of view goes against the tendency towards a dramatic film, with nuances from the thriller, which confronts characters reduced to action. It is well to remember that the theme allows for this approach: the violence of crime certainly lends itself to a spectacle of confrontation. But it is also true that, for the sake of effectiveness, there was a decrease in the potential for a wider vision of the ambiguities of the lives of people who live out the events and experiences of life in chronic precariousness, on the margins of society, in this terrible zone in which the drug traffic concentrates.

It is not a question, of course, of demanding fidelity of adaptation, but of recalling how Lins's novel can help us perceive the narrative decisions made in the writing of the script. The book, both in its narrated episodes and in its incorporated social languages, carries with it a naturalism redolent of anthropology. In the book, Cidade de Deus is an immense social fabric, which extends beyond the reach of literary chronicling, within which the rise of criminality takes place in a multiplicity of violence that, by statistical proportions, trivialises and generalises death, making mortality material for general reflection rather than an ending of personal histories.

In the first section of the film, especially, one feels the lack of this wider dimension. The petty criminals of the Trio Ternura are the result of a time when crime was still far from the organised, businesslike specialisation that would come with the drug traffic. This wide, grey area is there, for example, in the distribution of kitchen gas, but does not go very deep in generalising this relative moral disorder against the grain of bourgeois morality. For already in this beginning, it is necessary for the sake of narrative fluidity to concentrate on the scenes of criminal activity and their protagonists – even because these characters will be either present, as older, in what follows, or will have strong ties to those to come, always according to the rules of good drama. The general result, in the absence of a strong, comprehensive conflict involving the Trio, reveals a certain looseness (the social material refuses to fill in the dramatic form).

In the transition to the central section of the film, there is an episode – the 'baptism' scene of Dadinho [Li'l Dice] as Zé Pequeno by a *pai-de-santo* [*Candomblé* 'priest'] – that is frankly unfavourable to the efforts of dialectisation represented by the scenes that have their basis in Buscapé. This baptism exposes an attempt at linearity in the story, a spectacularised impression that (so far from the frequently existential mixture of faith and life in Lins's book) has its most unfortunate moment. In the same style of maximum spectacular visual concentration there is also the 'transcendental drop' of the conversion of Alicate (curiously, the reductionism of the image-synthesis is more obvious in these religious scenes, where the invisible is more important than the visible – as Eduardo Coutinho's *Santo Forte* has taught us).

The dramatisation gathers strength in the central section, where Zé Pequeno divides and disputes with Bené the control of the drug traffic. Here we have a real dramatic shock: domination by terror or by the 'new roguery' of Bené? Here are concentrated the best moments of the film, perhaps because it is a matter of a conflict, let us say, of the 'second power', where Zé Pequeno, who 'only thinks about work' (as Buscapé says), tries to organise everything as a function of his 'character program' (being in command of Cidade de Deus, conquering the world), and Bené confronts his dramatic adversary-friend in criminality, inserting the drug traffic and its actions into the malevolent fabric of life in Cidade de Deus.

Finally, the last section, the gang war, tries to conciliate the dizzying spectacle of violence with the permanence of ambiguity for those who are directly involved in it; Buscapé hovers between death and a permanent job, in the readings of the images that he makes as apprentice photographer. And again we are led along with narrative assurance, but the impression remains that something, between the frantic killing and Buscapé's chance to make it, escapes us, something like the experience suggested by the man himself, waking up at night from one more shootout, saying that life in the *favela* has gone from purgatory to hell.

To sum up, though not as a conclusion, one ought to say clearly that *Cidade de Deus*'s problems, even contradictions, are the result of its boldness of execution – a boldness that has as its impulse the need to throw light on a serious blind spot of contemporary Brazilian cinema, worked out with all available aesthetic resources. The result is a 'very cool' film, which opens up new paths, one of them taken by the very makers of *Cidade de Deus*, now working for television.[1]

Translation by Thomas Laborie Burns

---

[1] Editor's note: The new path referred to is the TV series *Cidade dos Homens/City of Men* (in this volume).

References

Candido, Antonio. 'Dialética da malandragem'. In: *O discurso e a cidade.* São Paulo: Duas Cidades, 1998.

Schwarz, Roberto. 'Cidade de Deus'. Originally published in the *Folha de São Paulo*, Caderno Mais!, September 7, 1997, republished in Schwarz, Roberto. *Sequências Brasileiras.* São Paulo: Cia das Letras, 1999, and in England, in the *New Left Review*, No. 12, Nov/Dec, 2001.

Xavier, Ismail. 'O cinema brasileiro dos anos 90'. *Revista Praga*, no. 9. São Paulo, Ed. Hucitec, 2000. pp. 97-138.

Zaluar, Alba. A máquina e a revolta: as organizações populares e o significado da pobreza. São Paulo: Ed. Brasiliense, 1985.

8. The Brazilian *Goodfellas*: *City of God* as a Gangster Film?[2]
Miranda Shaw

The international success of Fernando Meirelles's *City of God* has put Brazilian film more firmly on the international map. It is undoubtedly positive for the country's film industry which, although having a rich and important history, has never really been high profile or obtained the kind of mass audiences which *City of God* has gained. Its success involves many factors. One of them is the aesthetics of the film, which consists of an exciting pop soundtrack, bravura editing and a humorous script. Another reason for its success abroad is its acquisition by Miramax in the United States, which has warranted its worldwide distribution and publicity. Further to this, the reviews in the American and British press have appealed to the public by revelling in its violence and concentrating on what they call its 'pop aesthetics'. However, according to the director Fernando Meirelles, the film was not originally intended for an international audience.

Probing further into this phenomenal international success, this paper thus concentrates on how the reviewers and critics prepared international audiences for a film which is deeply rooted in Brazilian reality. An analysis of an archive compiled from 27 of the most relevant reviews of *City of God* in the United States and the United Kingdom during the period December 2002 to October 2003, has revealed a recurrent categorisation of the film as a gangster film, possibly to make it accessible or appealing to American and English spectators who would otherwise dismiss it in favour of a potential Hollywood blockbuster. The most frequent comparison is made with *Goodfellas* (Martin Scorsese, 1990), but others such as *Pulp Fiction* (Quentin Tarantino, 1995), *Casino* (Martin Scorsese, 1995) or *Reservoir Dogs* (Quentin Tarantino, 1991) are also mentioned. Phrases such as 'The Brazilian *Goodfellas*' (Clarke, 2003: 16), 'a kind of Boyz in the Brazilian hood' (Backstein, 2003: 39) or 'Gangs of Rio de Janeiro' (Holden, 2003) are also typical of the way in which the film is reviewed. In sharp contrast, an archive of 24 reviews from Brazil during the period August 2002 to February 2003, and already existing critical material on the film by scholars, as well as interviews with the director himself, have stressed the film's social agenda and its connection with, or the revitalisation of *Cinema Novo*.

In light of these differences, this paper also investigates how *City of God* connects both to the gangster genre and to the film language of *Cinema Novo* that it is said to revitalise. Even though both the gangster genre and *City of God* are related to contexts of economic difficulties (depression in the United States, deepening recession in Brazil) and the consequent development of new currencies (bootlegging and drug

[2] This piece arises out of work I did as a student at the Department of Hispanic Studies, Queen Mary, University of London. I would like to thank Fernando Meirelles for granting me an interview on his visit to the Brazilian Embassy in London on the 11th February 2004.

trafficking, respectively), the settings, the treatment of the themes and sub-themes, the characters and the cast, reveal some areas of convergence but predominantly of crucial differences in their objectives. Thus the gangster film is linked both to moral doctrine and entertainment within the context of depression and prohibition America whilst *City of God* concerns itself with the development of political awareness in the pursuit of social reform in Brazil.

My overall thesis therefore is this: whilst the categorisation of *City of God* as a gangster film may have enabled it to be recognised by a non-Brazilian audience, this can be particularly misleading in some respects. It has made the film into an international commodity, and this has led to the neglect of some of its most important aspects. These are: its national relevance, its social agenda, and its link to the historically politicised Brazilian cinematic tradition. Such categorisation may also give those already unwilling to look at Brazil's social problems a further excuse to misunderstand the country and fall into the paternalistic trap of the First World's image of violence and social problems in the Third World. The article concludes by commenting on what may be perceived as the ignorance or relative irresponsibility of the reviewers in the United States and United Kingdom who have placed the film within the cognitive framework of an English speaking audience and therefore away from the film's national specificity and its key social and political objectives.

The Contexts of the Gangster Film and of *City of God*

The gangster is a character steeped so deeply in the social reality of the United States that, in my view, it seems hard to reconcile him and the characters in *City of God* as being within the same tradition. This becomes even harder when we delve into Brazilian social reality and the film tradition of which *City of God* is a fundamental part. Of course the gangster genre developed both inside and outside the United States, and no text develops within a vacuum. However, the Hollywood films that critics use to categorise *City of God* retain their fundamental link to an American film tradition, which was born with the classic gangster films of the early twentieth century. It is a genre which 'has played an important role in both forming and reflecting the American imagination' (Shadoian, 1977: 1). Indeed, this examination of Americanism would be hard to attach to *City of God*, which has a national relevance of its own.

The decision by the United States government to prohibit 'the manufacture, sale and transportation of alcoholic drinks' during the years 1919-33 and the 1929 stock market crash, which led to the Depression and which caused 'worldwide economic collapse and precipitated commercial failure and mass-unemployment' (Hayward, 2000: 153), were catalysts for a massive increase in organised crime in American cities. De-mobbed soldiers and victims of the economic crisis found their way into organised criminal gangs who took advantage of the economic crisis and found themselves with an exceptionally lucrative business opportunity. With this came the growth in fame of individual, notorious criminals such as Al Capone and Arnold Rothstein, who, through racketeering, took over entire cities and dominated the American newspapers (Baxter, 1970: 9). These characters, whom the press sensationalised, captured the imagination of the public and consequently of the big studios, typically Warner Brothers.

The gangster in film was born with *The Musketeers of Pig Alley* (1912) and gained momentum with *Little Caesar* (1930) and *The Public Enemy* (1931). It reached full speed with *Scarface* (1932), establishing and 'laying down the bases for future developments' within the genre (Shadoian, 1977: 19). The gangster, and the collection of films which developed from his fame, epitomised the life of Americans at that moment: their horror and fascination with the social ills within their own country, the contradictions of capitalism and the inversion of the American Dream. Susan Hayward suggests that the Depression exposed the myth of the American Dream, as it revealed that, despite the constitution which promised success to all, American society was nevertheless a hierarchy of those who had wealth and those who did not. Therefore the gangster, who embodied the proletariat in American society, could only gain the wealth and individual success he deserved as an American, by stealing or through illegal activity (Hayward, 2000: 154).

The gangster exemplifies the basic flaws of capitalism: he obtains success, in the form of wealth, through individual endeavour and ambition only by breaking the law. He may run a successful business and obtain affluence, but only through covert operations: ultimately he fails because having broken the law he must die. The gangster's demise was something the early films were always careful to include so as not to show up the contradictions of the Dream. Later in the 1930s, the Hays Code required the toning down of glamorous gangsters amidst a wave of moral panic. So, whilst you are free to pursue the American dream you must proceed with caution (Hayward, 2000: 154-56). No such lesson is shown in *Cidade de Deus* and we are not morally guided in any way. The 'gangsters' die because Brazilian society cannot provide for them. In the United States, the government was keen to protect itself from such judgements.

The gangster was, and still is, a figure with which all Americans can identify; he is an embodiment of their frustrations, their desires, their failures and their successes. Jack Warshow stresses that 'in ways that we do not easily or willingly define, the gangster speaks for us, expressing that part of the American psyche which rejects the qualities and demands of modern life, which rejects "Americanism" itself' (2001: 100).

In his book *Dreams and Dead Ends*, Jack Shadoian explores some common traits which are universal to most gangster films and which we can indeed identify within *City of God*. Most pertinently, he describes the setting of the gangster film: 'the majority of gangster/crime films make implicit commentary on the nature and power of cities. The city rarely plays a neutral role; it is generally seen as a virulent environment [...] the city is the broadest icon of the gangster/crime film, and it is a death-trap [...] the seat of large-scale crime and death [...] the city is a prison' (1977: 6-7). The fundamental difference is that *City of God* is a city within a city. It is indeed a prison but it is much more prison-like than the city of the American gangster. Although we know that the *favela*, where the action takes place, is part of the urban structure and ultimately part of the city, it is basically a ghetto. In the film we only ever see the inside of the *favela*, not the outside or the rest of the city within which it is contained. In fact in the film, the *favela* city and the city proper become almost mutually exclusive, as the occupants of neither are able to penetrate the others' space. The American gangster becomes fully integrated into his city. Even though it can be a hostile environment he is able to retain a productive relationship with it. He utilises it for his business exchanges and in turn its shadowy buildings hide and protect him.

When considering more recent developments within the gangster genre, Scorsese's *Goodfellas*, with which *City of God* is most often compared, is perhaps a good point of reference. In *Goodfellas*, the protagonist Henry and the other characters retain a façade of living within legitimate society, inhabiting the suburbs, visiting bars, cafés and restaurants; living as if they were 'normal' citizens, whilst conducting their illegal activities. They use and abuse the services of the city, its people and institutions, whilst it protects and absorbs them into its milieu. Until the police arrest him, Henry's domestic life seems conventional. He has a wife, a house, children and a social support network. His wife describes how all the mobster families gather for birthdays and christenings whilst the viewer sees shots of parties, food and material wealth. The Brazilian *favelados* [dwellers of the slum] are excluded from the real city, pushed to its edges and the city proper serves them no purpose other than to highlight their social exclusion. In *City of God*, the only character who manages to penetrate the city is Buscapé [Rocket], when he is in the office of the *Jornal do Brasil*. Even then he is seen imprisoned in its buildings, unable to become a true part of it: his only view permitted through the slits in the blinds. Furthermore, when he tries his hardest to stay on the right side of the law by working in a supermarket, he loses his job because he is seen talking to children who come from Cidade de Deus, a place for no-hopers, the city on the edge. His *favelado* status lets him down and he cannot blend in. In contrast, Henry describes how he is treated well by others: he jumps the queue in the bakery and people carry his mother's groceries 'out of respect'. This cannot be said of the inhabitants of Cidade de Deus, who are the epitome of the marginalised. Their place of residence, as well as their appearance and position within the social spectrum, deny them a place in the life of the city. This also fits in with Shadoian's idea of a 'versus' within the gangster film. That is, the idea of 'a man, a woman or a group in opposition to society.' Both those in *Goodfellas* and *City of God* are in opposition to society; however, the difference is that those in *Goodfellas* can use society to hide themselves. In addition, both look at 'a world that is opposed to legitimate society', which 'makes us see things that would otherwise be hard to see' (Shadoian, 1977: 3-4). In *Goodfellas* we see the inside workings and effects of cocaine trafficking within the city. However, in *City of God* we see cocaine trafficking inside the *favela*. Therefore the exposition of the clandestine world is manifold. We not only see the gangster business but we see it unfold within a context which we would not normally see: the inside of the *favela*. The *favela*, unlike the city, is a denied reality and therefore one opposed to legitimate reality. Although its presence is glaringly obvious, clinging to the hills of Rio de Janeiro with rich tourists sunbathing in its shadow, it is a reality which the Brazilian middle classes deny. No one could enter a *favela* ordinarily, it is far too dangerous, but Meirelles shows it to us.

The films also share with other gangster pictures the genre's iconography, for example the prevalence of guns and drugs as the staples of the illegitimate business. However, the trafficking of drugs in the modern American gangster film seems very much an activity connected not only to survival but also to the flip side of the capitalist coin, illegal profit making. Such profits ensure that gangsters in film enjoy the privileges of the wealthy. In fact, in *Goodfellas* involvement in a criminal lifestyle reaps not only social rewards as we have seen, but also many material rewards. For Henry the lifestyle has many benefits and he earns a great deal of money from his criminal activities. At one point the camera pans over a row of different coloured suits and shoes and we see that Henry's wardrobe is full. At his wedding he is given hundreds of envelopes full of money to 'help him get started'. When he starts dealing in cocaine he trades his suburban house for a larger one, and furnishes it with expensive leather sofas and a decadent electronically controlled audio-visual set up.

For the characters in *City of God*, drug-trafficking brings no comforts other than, at best survival, at worst death. Even when the cocaine business is at its height (in *City of God*), the characters are confined to the *favela*, condemned to poverty. The only things they buy are basic items such as new T-shirts and hair dye. Buscapé's only material want is a camera. He finally manages to acquire one but 'como todo pobre, tive que começar por baixo e comprar a câmara mais vagabunda do mundo' [like all poor people I had to start at the bottom and buy the lousiest camera in the world]. Although Henry's family life is deeply disturbed by the criminal underworld, there is no theme of poverty in *Goodfellas*. All the characters can acquire material possessions at will and money is no object. Although the cocaine dealers are the highest earners in the *favela*, it is never enough to raise them above the poverty line and achieve a place in legitimate society.

Another key difference between the two films is illustrated by Henry as he embarks on his story. He begins: 'as far back as I can remember I always wanted to be a gangster'. Indeed, Henry gets a job in one of gang leader Paul Cicero's businesses and leaves school. He makes a calculated decision to get involved with the gang because he likes the lifestyle. He describes himself as 'the luckiest kid in the world' who could 'go anywhere' and 'do anything'. This element of choice is in stark contrast to the children in *City of God*, who have no such choice and whose involvement in gang warfare is a way of surviving in an otherwise inhospitable environment. They get involved in the gang as there are no other opportunities. In *Goodfellas*, staying the right side of the law is alluded to in the narrative, but Henry can choose to disregard it. He describes it as a life for people who have 'no balls' or who are 'suckers', that is to say, to choose the gangster lifestyle is to take a risk but is also to choose money and glamour. In *City of God* even basic necessities are denied to the residents. As Buscapé describes, when they first arrive in the *favela*, 'não tinha luz, não tinha ônibus' [it had no electricity, it had no buses]. They have no hope of achieving the affluence finally reached by Henry.

I believe the analogy between this genre and *City of God* shows a disputable responsibility by critics (who presumably have a duty as writers to research and examine all aspects of a film's background). This is damaging to both *City of God* and the gangster film and only serves to reintroduce the debate on cultural dependence (to which I return), which for decades Brazilians have been fighting so hard to counter.

The Theme of Violence Contrasted

The issue of violence is also a staple of the American gangster film and is clearly seen in *Goodfellas* as well as being a key theme in *Cidade de Deus*. Furthermore it is something with which we (the American/European cinema-going public) have a morbid fascination and this becomes even more intense when the violence permeates from the Other, in this case, the Third World, when we further imbue it with paternalism and false understanding. By linking the two films, and more specifically by terming *City of God* 'the Brazilian *Goodfellas*', press reviews capitalise on this fascination with violence and we are immediately drawn to the film, because it seems to exemplify a recognisable genre within an 'exotic' context. This, however, is misleading as the violence we see in *City of God* is more intense, more pervasive and in no way analogous with the violence seen in *Goodfellas*.

In *Goodfellas*, Henry is 13 the first time he sees someone shot, whereas in *City of God* neglected children are shot before their teens, and are corrupted by violent crime from an even earlier age. This is illustrated when a young child of about 10 years of age asks to be allowed to join in the war which has started between rival gangs for control of the trafficking territory. When accused of being only a kid, he proclaims, 'Eu cheiro, já roubei, já matei, sou sujeito homem' [I sniff, I've killed, I've robbed, I'm a man]. This disturbing level of criminal precociousness is what makes *City of God* tragic. In *Goodfellas* it seems exciting that Henry wants to leave school to get involved with the gang, or at least we feel it has been his decision and in many ways he will be looked after by his fellow gang members. The child who is imprisoned in the *favela* is offered little alternative for survival other than to give in to the criminal lifestyle.

The violence in *City of God*, indeed the whole film itself, has a national relevance which I will discuss later in more depth, but for now it seems appropriate to exemplify this by using Ivana Bentes' point when she talks of seminal Brazilian cineaste Glauber Rocha's *An Esthetic of Hunger* in her paper 'Terra de fome e sonho: o paraíso de Glauber Rocha' ['Land of Hunger and Dream: Glauber Rocha's Paradise']. She explains: 'Para compreender a fome, dentro ou fora da América Latina, seria necessário violentar a percepção, os sentidos e o pensamento' [In order to comprehend the hunger inside or outside of Latin America, it would be necessary to violate perception, feelings and thought] (Bentes, 2002: 3). This idea of the violation of all of one's senses is at the centre of the *mise en scène* in *City of God.* During the film every one of our senses is assaulted. In contrast, the violence in *Goodfellas*, although explicit (we see people beaten, shot, stabbed and intimidated), is purely superficial and only penetrates one level of our consciousness. It is not gratuitous, being clearly a major part of the criminal underworld; however, it is different from the violence in Meirelles's film. Here too we see people shot, beaten and intimidated in graphic detail, but the violence is more profound. The whole film shows a strong thread of violence woven into its fabric which is both explicit and implicit. There is a violent attack on all of our senses, and it is this (type of all pervasive) violence which makes us realise this film is not just a narrative on celluloid, but a visual expression of deeply ingrained social injustice. The violence manifests itself in many ways other than through the portrayal of bodily harm. There is violence in the surroundings; the tattered clothes of the small children who run around the streets, the dilapidated buildings, the piercing slang of the characters and the grating satanic tone of Zé Pequeno's [Li'l Zé] drawl. There is violence in the form and content of the film. The montage, the split screens and the stills are pasted together in a kind of horrific pastiche. All the cinematic techniques Meirelles utilised are not purely for show, as some would have us believe, but to make us aware of the intrinsic violence in Brazilian society.

In some aspects *Goodfellas* can be seen to be stylistically similar, but *City of God* is more complex. The film is multi-layered, its tiers overlapping and interlocking. In contrast to Scorsese, Meirelles uses a wider range of cinematic tools in order to create the violence of his characters and their situations. For example, the character of Zé Pequeno is often photographed from a low angle in order to emphasise his control and callousness. The use of colour to differentiate the three different eras which exist in the story adds a further layer to the narrative, beginning with warm earthy colours in order to suggest the relative calm of the initial phase and ending with dark film noir hues when the drug war is in full swing in the 1980s. The camera is more mobile and versatile and thus comments on the volatility and instability that exists in these characters' lives. When we are told the story of the flat that Zé Pequeno takes over in order to run his drug racket, we have split screens so we are able to see two narratives simultaneously and voice-over narration which links shots in a fluid and continuous way. It is a kind of visual chaos and a cinematic manifestation of a violent society.

The opening of the film probably best illustrates this visual assault on the viewer. The first thing we hear is a knife being sharpened, then we see it, then a black out. Next, we are given the image again, then black. Subsequently we begin to hear the hypnotic polyphonic sound of a *samba* beat and begin to see flashes of a meal being prepared. We hear the guitar, the drums and other musical instruments as shot and sound are united. We see hands, then a chicken being plucked and prepared, followed by a medium shot of a plate onto which the slaughtered chicken's blood has been dripped. The next chicken to be slaughtered has an air of almost human fear about it as it works itself lose from its rope. All these are separate shots interspersed with black. We see a fire, peeling and chopping, limes being crushed and squeezed until the narrative finally takes off as the live chicken escapes and Zé Pequeno's gang all rush off down the street in hot pursuit. The speed, complexity and visual sharpness of the opening of the film, and its attack on our senses, foregrounds the rest of the film and its tone of intrinsic violence. This multi-faceted violent chaos in the film further links it to Brazilian cineaste Glauber Rocha's thoughts. Although Ivana Bentes denies the validity of Meirelles's cinematic techniques, in my opinion, her views on Rocha's theories can equally be applied to *City of God*:

> Glauber's *An Esthetic of Violence* should result in images of unbearable power to the viewer. They have nothing to do with the aestheticised, explicit violence of action movies, instead they are charged with symbolic violence which leads to trance and crisis at all levels…he moves away from critical realism and classical narrative, creating a kind of aesthetic apocalypse (Bentes, 2003: 123).

I think the 'aesthetic apocalypse' of which Bentes speaks, as seen in Rocha's *Deus e o Diabo na Terra do Sol* [*Black God White Devil*] and *Terra em Transe* [*Land in Anguish*], is manifested in the multi-layered chaos of *City of God*, all the elements which make the film a piece of total cinema. Discontinuity in the editing, first seen as the film begins, like the montage veteran Kuleshov planned, awakens our senses and encourages us to 'reflect on the meaning of the image' (Hayward, 2000: 339). This makes us immediately more socially aware and invites us to concentrate not only on physical assaults but also on all the other types of violence that affect those in the film. No such invitation for introspection on national reality through violence is offered in *Goodfellas*.

A Tribute to the American Tradition?

As we have seen, the establishment of the gangster genre and its consequent development is inextricably linked to the national reality of the United States. Similarly *City of God* is inextricably linked to Brazilian national reality, therefore not a gangster film, much less a Brazilian *Goodfellas*. To illustrate further, a discussion on the cinema of Brazil, a reference to its cinematic history and a look into its most important cinematic/social movement, *Cinema Novo*, is required. The movement grew up in the late 1950s and early 1960s (with film-makers such as Glauber Rocha, Nelson Pereira dos Santos and Carlos Diegues) out of a perceived need to explore social problems in Brazil through cinema. It was part of the wider debate raging in Latin America during the 1960s on cultural dependence, which denounced the imposition of European and American cultural and economic models on the continent. In Brazil this imposition culminated in the military coup of 1964, which later plunged the country into an overnight economic 'miracle' paid for with foreign loans and reinforced by multinational business. *Cinema Novo* was thus a reaction to the metaphorical and actual colonisation of Brazil and her social institutions by the United States and Europe, and in terms of film, more specifically, Hollywood. It was an attempt to reassert a Brazilian national reality in the face of neo-colonialist paternalistic views of Third World poverty, which had previously been explored through piteous and melodramatic techniques. It aimed to politically mobilise the spectator through film and inspire people to act on social ills through showing them their own socially dispossessed. Its principles were primarily Marxist, although in practice it became mostly the domain of a left-wing intellectual elite. Glauber Rocha, one of the most, if not the most, important veterans of *Cinema Novo*, theorised the movement's aims and beliefs in his manifesto, *Por uma Estética da Fome* [*An Esthetic of Hunger*] (1965) using the metaphors of hunger and violence to criticise the paternalistic attitude of foreign audiences towards the third world. Rocha states, '*Cinema Novo* reveals that violence is normal behaviour for the starving. The violence of a starving man is not a sign of a primitive mentality […]. *Cinema Novo* teaches that the aesthetics of violence are revolutionary' (Johnson, 1984: 95).

I believe Meirelles's film contributes to the social ideology of Rocha's *An Esthetic of Hunger* and violence. In an interview with the *Daily Telegraph* he explained, 'this film is about people who are not considered; invisible people who want to be recognised. Sometimes they have to get a gun to say "Hey, I exist" ' (Said, 2002: 15). Furthermore, Meirelles has been faithful to his commitment to 'think about the book' on which the film is based, when creating the picture. Paulo Lins's semi-autobiographical book is based on 'a vast and highly relevant social research project' entitled 'Crime and Criminality in Rio de Janeiro', conducted by Alba Zaluar of the State University of Rio de Janeiro (Schwarz, 2001: 109). This is evidence of the strong social ethos present in the work. When talking about the book *City of God* Roberto Schwarz states, 'It becomes immediately comprehensible, for example, why young children should start out by mugging pregnant women and the elderly. It is perfectly rational to beat up the disabled and steal what they have got. It is quite understandable why prostitutes should pull knives when they cannot find clients' (2001: 108). Why is this understandable, we may ask? It is because, like the protagonists in Rocha's films, these people are starving metaphorically as well as literally and violence gives them a voice. In a speech given at the Brazilian Embassy on 11th February 2004, Fernando Meirelles said he hoped that the film would encourage people to 'act on the issues' presented in the film. He was trying to mobilise them through film. In this way we can surely reconcile the film with the principles of *Cinema Novo*.

Furthermore, the casting, acting and shooting of *City of God* are all facilitated by methods similar to those employed by *Cinema Novo*, which, as part of the commitment to social realism and as a reaction against using the American model, wanted to subvert the artifice of Hollywood cinema. *City of God* uses a cast of mostly non-professional actors. These are children, taken from the *favelas* of Rio de Janeiro and trained through a social theatre project, *Nós do Cinema* [*We in Cinema*], Meirelles and co-director Katia Lund ran and organised (*Folha Online*, 2002). We must remember, when thinking of the gangster comparison, that *Goodfellas* is a Hollywood production and as such uses actors from a well-established star system. The film has some of the most famous and experienced Hollywood actors at its disposal. In addition, the actors are genre actors, Robert De Niro and Joe Pesci being amongst some of the more famed Italian-American stars who have appeared in many other contemporary gangster/crime films such as *Casino* (Martin Scorsese,

1995), *Once Upon a Time in America* (Sergio Leone, 1984), *Taxi Driver* (Martin Scorsese, 1976) and others. This is in stark contrast to the amateur child actors of the *favelas* of Rio. *Cinema Novo* also favoured shooting on location as a direct reaction to the studio set-up of Hollywood, which Rocha believed, demonstrated only exploitation and falsification (Johnson, 1984: 103). The film, although not shot in the eponymous Cidade de Deus, where the crew were denied access, was shot in a Rio *favela*. Additionally, the use of improvisation in the acting as well as in the script was the preferred model both in *Cinema Novo* and in *City of God*, along with the use of the handheld camera. Although Meirelles himself has never shown any intention of mimicking the ideology of *Cinema Novo* directly, the employment of many of its methods in the making of the film ties it more tightly into the history of Brazilian cinema, thus distancing it further from the American genre.

The setting of *City of God* is also a fundamentally Brazilian locus. In fact, the *favela* is a common theme in Brazilian cinema. It is the place where the dwellers of the *sertão* (the dry infertile land of the Northeast where the poor work for the *latifundium* owners), have flocked, and has been a theme in Brazilian film since the late 1950s, that Glauber Rocha and others have heavily utilised. The *favela* is symbolic of all who are dispossessed in Brazilian society, those who have been forced off their dry land and have been sent to the *sertão* within the city, which is as infertile and unforgiving as ever. The *favela* is the last place of humanity, where people are forgotten, hidden and forced to create their own underworld as a reaction to a world that has forgotten them. Cidade de Deus is just one more of these *favelas* in the history of Brazilian cinema which is home to the dispossessed.

Clearly, *City of God* viewed as the Brazilian *Goodfellas* becomes, not a tool with which to explore the Brazilian contribution to social film as it should be, but a tribute to the American cinema, only recognisable 'pela dívida e pela imitação' [as a debt and as imitation] (Santiago, 1978: 20-21). In his seminal text, *Uma literatura nos trópicos* [*A Literature in the Tropics*], Silviano Santiago problematises this in terms of Latin American literary texts. Particularly in the essay, 'O entre-lugar do discurso latino-americano' ['The inbetweenness of Latin American discourse'], he explores and condemns the type of criticism which finds value in texts from colonised countries only by seeing them either as indebted to, or imitative of, texts from the colonising country. He views this kind of criticism thus: 'Tal discurso reduz a criação dos artistas latino-americanos à condição de obra parasita, uma obra que se nutre de uma outra sem nunca lhe acrescentar algo de próprio; uma obra cuja vida é limitada e precária, aprisionada que se encontra pelo brilho e pelo prestígio da fonte' [Such a discourse reduces the creations of Latin American artists to the status of parasitical works. A work which feeds off another without ever adding anything of its own; a work whose life is limited and precarious, imprisoned, which finds itself through the brilliance and prestige of the source] (Santiago, 1978: 20). *City of God*, as a gangster film, worryingly illustrates that this debate on cultural dependence, rife since the 1920s and Oswald de Andrade's *Anthropophagous Manifesto*, is still as pertinent as ever. Potentially, the effect of this is that the major social contribution of the film is obliterated in the face of a kind of cultural neo-colonialism, facilitated by negligent reviewers and critics.

Undoubtedly *City of God* and *Goodfellas* share some stylistic similarities. For example, the various cinematic distancing techniques employed: freeze-frames followed by non-diegetic inserts over the top as well as either a song or a voice-over from the narrator. Additionally, both films follow a non-chronological narrative and both contain fast editing and intertitles in order to break up the narrative, as well as popular music soundtracks serving as temporal markers. Also, as is characteristic of gangster films, both use nicknames for the main characters. In *City of God* we have Cenoura [Carrot], Mané Galinha [Knockout Ned], Cabeleira [Shaggy], and in *Goodfellas* we have Fat Andy, Freddie No-Nose and Pete 'The Killer'. However, fundamentally *City of God* has clearly been made with an undeniable sense of Brazilian national consciousness, which is completely irreconcilable with the American gangster genre. Maybe the point here then is this: why should Meirelles have to justify himself and somehow prove the film is not a gangster film or the Brazilian *Goodfellas* when he himself says he never intended it for an international audience? He claims that if he had been planning the film for an international audience he would not have included so many dialogues. He also points out how there are images in the film which an international audience would not understand. For example the inclusion of *Candomblé*: the syncretic religion popular in Brazil. Furthermore he points out that much of the humour and spontaneity of the language is lost through translation and the subtitles do not do the language justice. Most pointedly is that, when asked about the categorisation of the film as a gangster film, he agreed that it was a misleading description and that to label it as such achieved nothing. He was keen to reiterate that he made the film for Brazil and that it is about 'our culture [...] about our neighbours, a local film'. The director's statement further disconnects the film from the gangster genre which originated in the socially troubled United States in the early 1920s.

The international success of *City of God* has clearly been facilitated by the slant Miramax has taken on marketing it and has been carried along on the wave of criticism discussed above. It has probably contributed towards making the work the most successful Brazilian filmic export of all time. This is a long-awaited and welcome achievement, the value and success of which cannot and should not be denied. However, the categorisation of the film as 'The Brazilian *Goodfellas*' also serves to obscure its important social message. It seems like a deliberate piece of marketing by Miramax, taking advantage of the fact that 'what matters is that the experience of the gangster as an experience of art is universal to Americans. There is almost nothing we understand better or react to more readily or with quicker intelligence' (Warshow, 2001: 100). In this way the distributors are manipulating the film to fit in with an America mentality, thus gaining bigger audiences and more profits.

Furthermore, it is also important to recognise why such marketing may be culturally damaging and we should react against this colonial appropriation and misrepresentation. Aside from the fact that the film is more closely comparable to *Cinema Novo* than to the American gangster genre, we must not forget that *City of God* can stand alone as a piece of Brazilian cinema in its own right, as a visually stimulating, well written and superbly directed study of the social apartheid in Brazil. In her examination Ivana Bentes has highlighted a question that she believes is still to be resolved by Brazilian cinema, that of 'how to show suffering, and represent territories of poverty and the excluded, without falling into folklore, paternalism, and conformist and lachrymose humanism [...] how to create a new means of expression, comprehension and representation of the phenomena related to territories of poverty, how to lead the viewer to experience the radicalness of hunger, the effects of poverty and exclusion, inside or outside of Latin America' (2003: 122-123). I believe that by neither being totally complicit to the gangster genre nor by falling into the trap of aestheticising poverty, but by creating a new film language that combines effective cinematic techniques with a strong social ethos, Fernando Meirelles has provided an answer to this question.

References
Books and Periodicals
Baxter, John. *The Gangster Film*. London: A. Zwemmer, 1970.
Bentes, Ivana. 'The *sertão* and the *favela* in contemporary Brazilian film'. In *The New Brazilian Cinema*, ed. Lucia Nagib. London: I.B. Tauris, 2003. pp. 120-137.
Bentes, Ivana. 'Terra de fome e sonho: o paraíso de Glauber Rocha'. *Biblioteca on-line de Ciências da Comunicação*. 2002. www.bocc.ubi.pt. (Accessed 02 January 2005).
Hayward, Susan. *Cinema Studies: The Key Concepts*. London and New York: Routledge, 2000.
Johnson, Randal. 'Brazilian *Cinema Novo*', in *Bulletin of Latin American Research*, 2: 95-106, 1984.
Rocha, Glauber. 'An esthetic of hunger', in *Brazilian Cinema*, ed. Randal Johnson, Robert Stam. New York: Columbia University Press. 1995. pp. 68-71.
Santiago, Silviano. *Uma Literatura nos Trópicos*. São Paulo: Editora Perspectiva, 1978.
Schwarz, Roberto. 'City of God', in *The New Left Review* 12: 101-113, 2001.
Shadoian, Jack. *Dreams and Dead Ends: The American Gangster Crime Film*. Cambridge, Mass; London: M.I.T Press, 1977.
Warshow, Robert. *The Immediate Experience, Movies, Comics, Theatre and Other Aspects of Popular Culture*. Cambridge: Massachusetts and London, 2001.
Review articles
'Atores vem dos morros e pasaram por oficina de atuação', *Folha Online* [online newspaper], http://www1.folha.uol.com.br/folha/especial/2002/cidadededeus/personagens.shtml, Accessed 20 October 2003.
Backstein, Karen. 'City of God', *Cineaste* vol.XXVIII no. 3: 39-49, 2003.
Clarke, Roger. 'Cinema: The Best Films', *Independent*, 30 January 2003, p. 16.
Holden, Stephen 'Gangs of Rio de Janeiro', *New York Times*, 17 January 2003,

www.nytimes.com/2003/01/17/movies/17CITY.html, Accessed 04 January 2005.

Said, S. F. 'The word from the Streets', *Daily Telegraph*, 30 December 2002,
p. 15.

Films

Cidade de Deus, Dir. Fernando Meirelles, Brazil, 2002.

Goodfellas. Dir. Martin Scorsese, United States, 1990.

9. Trajectories of *Malandragem* in *City of God*
Juliet Line

City of God (Fernando Meirelles, 2002) opens with an image of one swift stroke of a blade being sharpened on a stone. The image alerts the viewer to what they are about to see: a double-edged sword. The film looks like a Brazilian social drama. From another angle, it looks like Hollywood.

For the film-makers, one of the primary objectives was to present an alternative depiction of a social reality to those the media generally offers. Specifically, they sought to convey a more accurate depiction of the role of the criminal within the internal logic of the Brazilian *favela*. Committing itself to a high level of realism, *City of God* updates *Cinema Novo*'s ethos of using the cinema as a tool by which to aggressively confront Brazil's citizens, seeking to force them to face up to the unspoken but not unseen horrors of their own society. Yet unlike the Marxist inspired *Cinema Novo*, *City of God* was not specifically intended to be received by the disenfranchised masses as a call to arms, but by the middle classes who it was hoped would be so inspired by the content of the film that they would use their privileged positions to bring about positive changes in society.

The film uses highly original methods in order to ensure a remarkable verisimilitude. Most notable perhaps is the cast, which comprises amateur actors, most of whom live in *favelas* similar to Cidade de Deus. Their performances, in which they frequently bring their own improvisations to the script, are so convincing that many viewers have found it difficult to distinguish the fictional film from the social reality in which it finds inspiration. Drawing on Paulo Lins's novel of the same name and a real event that occurred in the 1980s, the film explores the ways in which criminal practices and attitudes towards these practices changed over a period of three decades.

As distinct from *Cinema Novo*, the film departs from the idea that social issues should necessarily be presented using a low budget, low-tech aesthetics. The social subject matter and the involvement of some of Brazil's most economically deprived citizens are interwoven with the technical expertise and cinematographic virtuosity of high-level media production. Equally, the nationalist discourse of *Cinema Novo* is notably absent in the film, as is evident from its use of the practical involvement of a US distributor (Miramax) and an American scriptwriting advisor. Alexander Payne (*About Schmidt*, *Election*) closely guided Bráulio Mantovani in his work, also arranging for him to attend a Screenwriters Guild of America workshop. The published version of the script tells us Alexander was present right up to the world première in Cannes (Meirelles in Mantovani, 2003: 11).

The influence of Hollywood is also evident in the film's adoption of certain conventional dramatic techniques and narrative formulae. The most notable of these is the reduction of the complex social dynamics of the
favela to a typically Hollywood-esque dramatic conflict between good and

evil. From a classical cinematic point of view, the sophisticated set of interwoven symbols used to embellish the drama reveals an impressive attention to detail and remarkable artistic virtuosity. However, instances of a simplified use of a conventional Christian symbolism undermine the film-makers' explicit objectives of realism and a possible demystification of crime. Via a discussion of the film's portrayal of the evolution of criminality in the *favela*, this paper will consider the ideological implications, in the context of a social critique, of the emergence of sub-texts usually associated with a conformist cinema. It will go on to propose that, by drawing on extreme characteristics of both Brazilian social realism and Hollywood's dramatic expertise, *City of God* speaks both to wide national and international audiences but pays the price, at times, of sitting uncomfortably between these two cinematic traditions.

The *Malandro*

The critic Leandro Rocha Saraiva notes in his text '*Cidade de Deus*: maestria e contradições' (English version in this volume) that the difference between this film and the North American gangster films and thrillers to which it has (sometimes pejoratively) been compared lies in the absence of a moral stance on the part of the narrator/protagonist Buscapé [Rocket]: 'Então é preciso conviver, na malandragem, sem acessos moralizantes' ['So it is necessary to live together amongst the *malandragem* without a moralistic approach'] (Saraiva, 2002: 13). The practice of *malandragem*, an untranslatable and constantly shifting Brazilian concept that has been explored at length in Brazilian literature, music, film and critical discourse, has been understood in many different ways throughout contemporary history. In *City of God* we see examples of it in the socially conscious *pé de chinelo* [amateur] bandits who appear in the 1960s stage, and later in the more subtle modern-day *malandragem* of the narrator/protagonist Buscapé, who in fact commits no actual crime. His mediatory role between the worlds of legality and illegality appears rooted in Antonio Candido's model of 'Dialética da malandragem' ['A Dialectic of Trickery']; the landmark essay that proposed that Brazilian society hinges on a dialectical relationship between the abstract spaces of order and disorder, between formality and informality, and between distinct (yet negotiable) social classes. The essential quality of the *malandro* as understood in these terms is his capacity to exist *in-between* these structures, as he neither opposes nor submits to the demands of either.

The *malandro* (one who practises *malandragem*) is, by definition, ambiguous. The word itself finds its roots in the Latin word for 'bad' [*malus*] and the Greek for 'man' [*andros*]. Yet the ambiguity inherent in the ethos of *malandragem* ensures that it escapes accurate definition, rendering distant the *malandro's* original limiting classification as a 'bad man'. Throughout Brazilian cultural history, frequent identifications have been made between the *malandro* and the social type named by Eric Hobsbawm as the 'social bandit', implicitly calling into question this 'badness'. However, Hobsbawm himself never referred specifically to the *malandro*, concentrating instead on Brazil's rural social bandits, the *cangaceiros*. These famous outlaws of the *sertão*, the country's

Northeastern back lands, sought by violent means to bring about the justice that the establishment denied them. Their role was overtly subversive and dissenting; that of the *malandro* is necessarily more uncertain.

The Fall of the *Malandro*

For its discussion of the evolution of criminal behaviour, the film takes as its starting point three examples of archetypal 'good *malandros*' of old times, the Trio Ternura [Tenderness Trio]. When Alicate [Clipper], Cabeleira [Shaggy] and Marreco [Goose] hold up a gas truck that is passing through the *favela*, they announce its arrival to their neighbours so that they might come and help themselves to its cargo. Having robbed the driver of his money they throw banknotes to the air, instructing a group of nearby children to buy some new footballs. Marreco reveals a concern for his family, making a point of giving some money to his brother to pass on to their father. The intimacy and sense of urgency created in this scene via the actors' performances, the close-up camera work and the careful control of rhythm in the editing result in a character/spectator identification that effectively prevents judgement from being passed on their actions. As Cabeleira says 'Tá afim de tomar um tiro pelo dinheiro do patrão?' [You wanna die for your boss's damn money?], he emphasises the relative unimportance of rich people's money compared with their mission to 'spread the wealth'.

The hero of the lower classes is a recurring motif that appears within Brazilian culture on several levels. The *cangaceiro* in particular was often used as a symbol for popular resistance in the political allegories of the 1960s *Cinema Novo*. Similarly in music the *malandro* appears, for example, in Jorge Ben's *Charles, Anjo 45*, in which the *malandro* protagonist is referred to as 'protetor dos fracos e dos oprimidos/ Robin Hood dos morros, rei da malandragem' [protector of the weak and of the oppressed/Robin Hood of the hillsides, king of the *malandragem*]. In the *sambas* of the early thirties the *malandro's* bohemian and idle lifestyle came to represent an alternative model to the Vargas regime's enforced ideals of work, compliance and family values. Songs containing references to *malandragem* and its surrounding lifestyle were either censored or banned, regarded as a threat to the political order (although several artists managed to subvert this by way of ironic acquiescence and parody). Contrastingly, the 'social bandits' in *City of God* do not possess symbolic political significance, nor do they pose a threat to the social order. Instead the film seeks a portrayal of this social type that is realistic (or, compared with the revolutionary optimism of *Cinema Novo*, pessimistic) in order to chart the disappearance of social banditry in contemporary society.

This disappearance seems to coincide with the gradual urbanisation of the *favela*. *Favelas* tend to share certain characteristics with the *sertão*, since they are often largely populated by rural immigrants who move to the city in search of a better life. The whole of the first section of *City of God* is characterised by an atmosphere evocative of this rural lifestyle. The *favela* described in Paulo Lins's novel as 'ainda uma grande fazenda' [still a big farm] is evoked here by a predominance of outdoor shots in which people are seen relaxing in a spacious setting of trees and open landscapes. Classical filming techniques including a warm colour scheme, medium length, rhythmically edited shots and the gentle *samba* tune of Cartola's *Alvorada* are used in this section to create a sense of nostalgia that distinguishes it from the brutally realistic style of later scenes. Hobsbawm tells us 'The fundamental pattern of banditry [...] is almost universally found in certain conditions. It is rural, not urban. The peasant societies in which it occurs know rich and poor, powerful and weak, rulers and ruled but remain profoundly and tenaciously traditional and pre-capitalist in structure (Hobsbawm, 1959: 23). Thus, the drama that ensues as the narrative of *City of God* progresses can perhaps be understood as a discussion of what happens when social banditry, or in this case *malandragem*, meets modernity.

The impending shift in criminal behaviour is punctuated by a conversation between Dadinho [Li'l Dice] and Alicate that reveals the contrast between the older boys' attitude and that of their young protégé: Alicate proposes that their next plan should be to rob a rich person's house. Dadinho contradicts him, saying 'Acerta nada, rapaz... o negócio é fazer o que tô bolando aqui'. [Hell no. What you need is to follow my plan]. The crime that immediately follows is the motel robbery, in which Dadinho is given the job of lookout. Whilst the Trio had intended to do a simple robbery in which they would take some money and leave no casualties, Dadinho enters the building afterwards and murders all those inside; his only apparent motivation is to satisfy a thirst for killing.

At the end of the film's first section, Cabeleira decides to flee from the *favela* to the countryside with his girlfriend to escape from his life of crime. This retreat may be understood as the social bandit's attempt to recapture a mythical rural environment, as it is the mirror image of a trajectory that Cabeleira's ancestors possibly made. By this stage, Dadinho has already killed one of the other members of the Trio and the other has abandoned the criminal lifestyle in favour of the church. Cabeleira's plan to leave town goes wrong when the driver of the car he has hijacked pretends that it will not start and Cabeleira gets out to push. As he runs along beside the car, which by this time is speeding away with his girlfriend, he is shot by the local policemen who are still mistakenly in pursuit of him for the motel massacre. A travelling shot of Cabeleira taken from inside the runaway car shows the *malandro* being overtaken by the machine, the primary symbol of the industrial, capitalist society that is responsible for having rendered his social type an anachronism. Cabeleira's death marks the end of the first chapter and the demise of the social bandit in the *favela*.

In the wake of the socially conscious but disorganised amateur banditry of the 1960s phase, a new style of distinctly antisocial organised criminal emerges. With the help of his sidekick Bené [Benny], Dadinho decides to begin an ambitious project to remove the existing hierarchy of drug dealers (who are now responsible for this organised crime) and take over as the *dono da favela* ['owner' of the *favela*]. He suggests, 'A gente mata esses otários e fica com a boca deles' [We'll kill these suckers and take over their business]. Despite the obvious disparity between him and the now extinct 'social' *malandros* of the previous chapter, the calculating Dadinho is nevertheless aware of the fact that notions of social crime and other values associated with a traditional rural culture continue to inform the mentalities of the residents of *Cidade de Deus*. Thus, as the film traces and laments the disappearance of the social bandit, it also considers the way in which a popular attachment to the myth of 'honourable crime' can be used as a tool for manipulation and exploitation.

When the group of young renegades called the Caixa Baixa [the Runts] begins to disrespect the 'rules' of the community by stealing from residents and shopkeepers inside the *favela*, Dadinho, who is now called Zé Pequeno [Li'l Zé], is quick to put a stop to their activities, assuming the role of 'community peacekeeper' and proclaiming vehemently that in his *favela* no-one robs or rapes. The residents are grateful to him for having re-established a state of order, as they are shown greeting him and thanking him for his apparent good work. Buscapé, speaking in retrospect, is able to appreciate the tactical nature of Zé Pequeno's actions as, in response to the criminal's widespread popularity, he says, 'O pior é que, com o Zé Pequeno, a Cidade de Deus virou um lugar mais seguro para os moradores. Quase que não tinha mais assalto nenhum. [...] Era só falar com Zé Pequeno.' [The worst thing about it was that with Zé Pequeno around the *favela* turned into a safer place for the residents. There were hardly any more robberies at all. All you had to do was talk to Zé Pequeno].

Despite Zé Pequeno's concern with maintaining order, a disagreement over a girl eventually sparks a battle between him and the once pacifistic Mané Galinha [Knockout Ned] that soon escalates into full-scale gang warfare in the *favela*. A montage, in which different young boys consecutively appear on the screen, individually expressing their motivations for wanting to join in the battle, illustrates the arbitrary nature of the fighting that then ensues.

> Zé Pequeno: 'O que que você quer, moleque?'
> Boy 1: 'O moleque do Cenoura me deu uma tapa na cara'.
> Yuri: 'O soldado do Pequeno me deu um chute no cu'.
> Cenoura: 'Vai lá. Um 22 ai pra tu'.
> Robson: 'O filho da puta que "estrupou" a minha irmã tá na boca do Cenoura'.
> Eucledes: 'É pra assaltar, matar e ser respeitado'.
> Boy 2: 'O cara expulsou a minha familia da favela'.
> Boy 3: 'Tô desempregado há tres anos'.
> Othon: 'Quero me vingar do assassino que matou meu pai'.

[Zé Pequeno: What do you want, kid?/Boy 1: Cenoura's kid gave me a slap in the face./Yuri: Pequeno's soldier kicked me in the ass./Cenoura: There you go. A 22 for you./Robson: The bastard who raped my sister is with Cenoura./Eucledes: It's all about assaulting, killing and being respected./Boy 2: The guy sent my family out of the *favela*./ Boy 3: I've been unemployed for three years./Othon: I want to get revenge on the murderer who killed my father.]

Again, values evocative of the distant culture of the *cangaço* have been given new meaning, this time in the form of an excessive and premature preoccupation with principles of revenge, manhood and honour. This theme recurs frequently throughout the film, particularly in one of the most emotionally disturbing scenes. Zé Pequeno implicitly asks a 12-year-old boy to prove his value as 'a man' by forcing him to choose one of his peers to shoot dead. Shortly after this 'initiation ceremony' the same boy announces: 'Eu fumo, eu cheiro. Já matei e já roubei. Eu sou sujeito homen' [I smoke, I snort. I've killed, I've robbed. I'm a man]. This statement of self-affirmation echoes Dadinho's similar proclamation earlier in the film, as he insists to the Trio Ternura 'I'm a gangster too'.

The *Malandro* Crosses National Frontiers

Whilst *City of God* expresses the way in which the characters' lives can be informed by recontextualised archaic values, it also draws attention to the influence of the more modern brand of misinformation that is generated by a global mass media. The film updates a principle that was central to *Cinema Novo*, in that it uses its very form as a vehicle for its critique. Fast editing, extreme camera angles and the evocative use of music combine in an aesthetics that draws unmistakeably on the language of advertising. Yet as the images that appear are brutal rather than glamorous or seductive, an uncomfortable juxtaposition is created that prevents the viewer from deriving voyeuristic pleasure from them.

The influence of the branch of the media that is Hollywood film is evident in the characters' own language; Buscapé compares the situation in the *favela* to living in Vietnam, the Caixa Baixa children announce an 'Soviet attack' – an attack from above – and the film suggestively names the arms dealer Tio Sam [Uncle Sam]. All of these can be seen as modern manifestations of the lingering vestiges of outdated conflicts. This notion is explored in the novel, *City of God* (Lins, 1997, 2002) in which the word '*alemão*' [German] reappears frequently in reference to foreigners, strangers or indeed anyone who is disliked. By transferring the language of other people's wars (often media inventions anyway) to their own situations, the young 'soldiers' attempt linguistically to lend meaning to their otherwise pointless fighting. Using such military-infused language, which is actually used in real life contemporary *favela* vernacular, the film and the novel draw attention to the potency of the cultural and ideological influence of North America in the *favela*. Paulo Lins cites himself in a radio broadcast that he made to the people of Cidade de Deus on their own radio station at the time of the gang war in the 1980s: 'Ô, meu amigo, pára com a Guerra, essa coisa de que alemão é inimigo é coisa de americano, alemão não é inimigo, não tem mais nada disso' [Oh, my friend, stop this war. This idea that Germans are enemies is an American thing, this does not exist anymore] (Lins, 2003: 36). Here, he explicitly warns the residents of the *favela* of the destructive potential of misplaced foreign nationalistic concepts in their vocabularies and collective imaginaries.

Despite its implicit critique of migrating Hollywood mythologies, a closer look at some of the film's subtexts reveals that it too depends on an adherence to a number of ideologically loaded structures, themselves characteristic of the North American cinematic tradition. During the final gun battle between Zé Pequeno and Mané Galinha a second gas truck appears, which Zé hijacks and uses as a platform from which to kill the young Othon. This visual motif draws a narrative juxtaposition between this scene and the earlier one starring the Trio Ternura: here, the truck's cargo is ignored. By this stage the gang war takes precedent over any material need on the part of the community that the contents of the truck might have satisfied. The clear distinction that the film draws between the crime of the past and that of modern times via the use of social types and archetypes is engaging from a narrative point of view. However, the opposition constructed here provides little real insight into the highly complex and problematic issue that is the relationship between the modern drug dealers who control the *favela* and their communities.

This 'good *malandro*/bad organised criminal' binary is particularly apparent in almost all of Zé Pequeno's interactions with Bené. Zé's partner in crime is essentially a *bon viveur*: good looking, well dressed, respected by the community, and despite moving in the lower echelons of society with the likes of Zé Pequeno, he is able to seduce a girl from another social circle. He represents the reincarnation of the figure of the *malandro* as expressed in the *sambas* of the 1930s, possessing all the qualities of this classic icon. Yet unlike the Trio Ternura, he does not seem to be a relic from the past. Enjoying the things that modern mainstream consumer culture has to offer him whilst maintaining a thinly veiled lifestyle of crime, he has been described by Leandro Rocha Saraiva as performing a type of *neo-malandragem* (Saraiva, 2002: 15) that functions in direct opposition in the film to the tyrannical behaviour of Zé Pequeno, the film's 'false *malandro*'. From an early age Dadinho/Zé Pequeno derives immense pleasure from killing, as is evident from his menacing laugh that accompanies every murder that he commits. Techniques such as extreme low angle camera shots and close-ups on Dadinho's face are used here in a classical manner to establish and emphasise the power relationships on-screen. Significantly, every time that Zé tries to kill someone, Bené is always right behind him urging him to spare the victim.

Paulo Lins has described Zé Pequeno's character as 'meio lombrosiano' [a bit 'Lombrosian']. Lins's point is based on his observation that the character appears to correspond with the 19th century criminologist Cesare Lombroso's 'Sociological Theories of Deviance', which attributed criminal behaviour to hereditary rather than social factors. A tendency towards such notions necessarily undermines a discourse that tries to propose that crime is a *social* problem. Lins in fact intervened in the script over a line by Buscapé that proposed that some people seem to have predisposition to evil. Lins vetoed the line and it was removed (Leal, 2002: 14). The inherent implication that people can be 'born bad' inevitably conflicts with Meirelles's explicit wish to dispel conventional media myths associated with drug and gun crime. In an interview with the *Estadão*, the director draws attention to the decontextualised nature of such sensationalist depictions. He notes people's misguided desire to 'do away with' criminals and stresses that, contrary to what the media would have us believe, criminals do not 'just appear', and it is therefore not possible to 'do away with' them (Leal, 2002: 14). However, despite these intentions, and although the controversial statement identified by Lins was removed from the film, the contradiction remains. The official promotional website upholds the 'Lombrosian' stance, maintaining unequivocally 'Zé Pequeno's wicked nature is clear from the start'.[1]

The 'inherently bad' antagonist is a classical cinematic character type that is used to enhance dramatic impact, particularly as it has a tendency to carry religious connotations. *City of God* exploits the verbal and visual language of religion in order to develop its characters and situations in certain ways. Since the film's website has told us the camera will be Buscapé's 'redemption', the specifically religious connotations of this terminology become clear in the scene of Bené's farewell. Bené, like Cabeleira before him, had been jaded by the apparent futility of the urban criminal world. He too attempts to seek a meaningful existence in the countryside with a girl. At the dance, Bené acquires a stolen camera and, knowing of Buscapé's love of photography, gives it to him as a gift. Overcome with jealousy for Bené's attention, Zé Pequeno grabs the camera from Buscapé's hands, insisting he hand it over. The ensuing confrontation that occurs between Bené and Zé results in Bené mistakenly being shot dead by a bullet that had been intended for Zé. In the silent and empty dance hall, Bené lies on the ground, legs together and arms outstretched in the shape of a cross. The strobe lights continue to flash, highlighting both the sense of divine drama and the edges of his blond Afro, making it resemble a halo. As he gives up his life for his (undeserving) best friend whilst also fighting for the object that would define the fate of the film's protagonist, Bené becomes a martyr. The conflict between him and Zé over the camera can thus be interpreted as a battle between good (*bene/bom*) and evil.

In distinct contrast to the positive Christian imagery surrounding Bené's character, Zé Pequeno is presented as a product of African Brazilian culture in a resolutely negative way. In an extremely stylised scene, about half way though the film, he visits a *pai de santo* (a *Candomblé* priest) and undergoes the ritual transformation in which he changes from Dadinho to Zé Pequeno. He is presented with an amulet and the instructions: 'Suncê quer poder. Suncê tá certo, menino. Deixa eu dar o que vai dar poder pra suncê. Ó, ó, e pra mudar a sorte de suncê, eu vou te dar o meu protetor, menino. Mas suncê não pode furunfar com a guia... Porque senão suncê vai morrer' [You want power. I have something that will give it to you. To change your fate I give you my protector, boy. But you mustn't fornicate with the amulet otherwise you'll die]. Later, in the scene where Zé rapes Mané Galinha's girlfriend, a momentary close up reveals that the amulet is still around his neck. Just before he dies it is seen again in another fleeting shot. The implied association between African Brazilian religious practices and notions of 'the malign' adds a highly problematic Christian/pagan dimension to the good/evil binary that has already been constructed.

Of all the characters in the film, Zé Pequeno's most direct antithesis is Buscapé. Zé terrorises him from an early age, initially by

---

[1] See www.cidadededeus.globo.com

killing his brother and later by bringing about the death of Bené, his guardian angel. Buscapé expresses his attitude toward his future very early in the film, stating that when he grows up he wants to be neither a criminal nor a policeman. He sees himself neither in the dangerous world of disorder (crime) nor the supposedly 'orderly' world represented by the police force, instead representing yet another example of the ethos of *malandragem*. At an early age, Buscapé is fascinated by the work of a newspaper photographer at the scene of a murder. However a lack of resources and opportunities means that he is not immediately able to pursue this career path. In the meantime, he tries his hand at both the 'Vida de Otário' [A Sucker's Life], in this case represented by a job in a supermarket, and subsequently attempts a life of crime. Finding himself ill-disposed to both extremes, by a stroke of luck he eventually acquires a stolen camera that allows him to explore his natural talent for the art of photography. Having already been the 'official photographer' for the groovy crowd, he then goes on to play the same role for Zé Pequeno's gang. Eventually, a mix-up with some photographic films results in the images of Zé's gang being printed on the front page of the newspaper for which he is working as a delivery boy. This 'lucky mistake' secures his destiny since as a result he fulfils his dream and is offered a job as a photographer.

Buscapé is the ultimate career *malandro*. His ability to straddle two worlds will be the secret of his professional success as a photographer: he is valued by Zé Pequeno and his gang who vainly revel in seeing their faces in the newspaper, and equally his allegiance to the criminals gives him access to an illicit world that is forbidden territory to the journalists. His creativity and determination allow him to reject both the demeaning world of manual labour and the risky one of crime. The film's message can be linked to its actual making, since Buscapé comes to represent an ideal example of the integration principles of the social project and drama workshop from which the cast was selected. As identified by Xavier, 'The film's production became part of the very process it takes as its theme' (Xavier, 2002: 29).

Buscapé: Success through *Malandragem*

Despite Buscapé's embodiment of these Brazilian ideals, his character also corresponds accurately with Hollywood's 'success hero' model. His ambitious plight forms the central thread of the narrative and (as described above) the means by which he achieves his goal can be seen as an allegory for the film's ultimate message. Like most of the other characters in the film, Buscapé is participating in a battle. His weapon, however, is not a gun but a camera. In the last few minutes of the film the views through the camera lens and the gun's sights become confused, creating an ambiguity that adds to the metaphorical impact of the substitution. Again, *City of God* revives the discourse of *Cinema Novo*, before proceeding to reject it. In marked contrast with the revolutionary projections of the *Cinema Novo* directors, whose mission was to uncompromisingly oppose the structures of industrial culture and the media by attacking them from the outside, Buscapé's camera work for the newspaper relies on a *participation* in these structures. Indeed, the character spells out his limitations as an artist:

> Se eu entregar essa foto do bandido, eu consigo trabalho. Com essa aqui, eu garanto pagamento todo dia dez. Aluguel, cerveja e cinema com a namorada. Com essa daqui, eu fico famoso. Vai sair até em capa de revista. O Pequeno nunca mais vai me encher o saco. Mas e a polícia? [If I submit this photo of the gangster I'll get work. With this one I'm guaranteed monthly pay. Rent, beer and cinema with the girlfriend. With this one I'll get famous. It'll even go out on the front cover of magazines. Pequeno's never going to bother me again. But the police?]

The photographs that follow on the front page of the newspaper reveal that rather than risk his safety and his job as a photographer by publishing the more controversial photographs of the police, he has opted instead for the more visually spectacular but less revealing shots of the dead gangster. Xavier again draws a parallel between Buscapé's situation and that of the film's directors. He writes 'City of God too has had to adjust its viewpoint and tone in order to play to a mass audience, setting aside a balanced picture of the community and a clear sense of context' (Xavier, 2002: 30).

During the course of City of God, as the drama intensifies, the focus gradually shifts from a social issue (of poverty) to a moral one (of drug dealers). The film offers a 'good' but archaic social bandit and, through a process of exoticisation and demonisation, constructs a cultural Other of the organised criminal. His death offers diversion and catharsis to the viewer, and the reassurance that in the end good will inevitably triumph over evil. However, this reassurance is achieved at the expense of a deepening of the understanding of modern criminality in favelas that the film might have delivered. As a result, reality remains, for most viewers, remote:

> In their spirit of independence and self reliance, success heroes exhibit their kinship with the frontiersmen, that archetypal individualist of American myth, whose self-transformation takes the form of mastering the savage in the name of civilisation (Traube, 1994: 56).

Some of the final images of the film feature Buscapé repeatedly 'shooting' his nemesis Zé Pequeno with his camera as he lies dead on the floor. Corresponding with the above description of the success hero model, Buscapé's defeat of the implied favelado 'savage', Zé Pequeno, indeed coincides with his own self-transformation. He implicitly adopts a conventional identity to achieve success and has the last word, telling the viewer: 'Aí, esqueci de dizer. Ninguém mais me chama de Buscapé. Agora eu sou Wilson Rodrigues, fotógrafo' [I forgot to say. No one calls me Buscapé anymore. Now I'm Wilson Rodrigues, photographer].

Like the photographer in the film, the makers of City of God have been both malandros and success heroes. Defying conventional classification, they have masqueraded in Hollywood's carnival in order to perform their social drama to a worldwide public. Yet the *malandro*'s gift is ultimately his ability to *negotiate* rather than challenge the social boundaries that would otherwise limit and define him. Therefore, whilst artfully adopting the identity of the Other, *City of God* and Wilson Rodrigues alike must respect the implications of such a tactical metamorphosis.

References

Hobsbawm, Eric. *Primitive Rebels*: *Studies in Archaic Forms of Social Movement in the 19th and 20th Centuries*. New York: Norton Library, 1959.

Leal, Hermes. 'Chegou a sua vez'. Interview with Fernando Meirelles in *Revista de Cinema*, September 2002, 13-18.

Lins, Paulo. *Cidade de Deus*. São Paulo: Companhia das Letras, 2003.

Lins, Paulo. 'Sem medo de ser'. Interview in *Caros Amigos*, São Paulo: May 2003, 30-35.

Mantovani, Braúlio; Meirelles, Fernando; Müller, Ana Luiza. *Cidade de Deus*: *o roteiro do filme.* Rio de Janeiro: Editora Objetiva, 2003.

Saraiva, Leandro Rocha. 'Cidade de Deus: maestria e contradições', in *Sinopse*, v.4, n.9, São Paulo: CinUSP, 2002, 12-15.

Traube, Elizabeth G. 'Secrets of Success in Postmodern Society', in *Culture/Power/History*: *A reader in Contemporary Social Thought*. Edited by Nicholas B. Dirks, Geoff Eley, and Sherry B. Ortner. New Jersey: Princeton University Press, 1994, pp.587-584.

Xavier, Ismail. 'Angels with dirty faces', *Sight and Sound*. January 2003, 28-30.

www.cidadededeus.globo.com (accessed 15/01/05).

10. The Aesthetics of Violence in Brazilian Film [1]
Ivana Bentes

Never before in Brazil has there been so much circulation and consumption of images of poverty and violence, images of the outcasts, of the so-called 'deviating' or 'abnormal' behaviours. Violence and the denouncement of crimes have become lately almost a journalistic genre. This could even be interesting, if these images did not usually come out of context, spontaneously generated, without any relationship with the economy and social injustices, and were not treated as a spectacle, a breathtaking event, a type of television tabloid or reality show that can be consumed with extreme enjoyment.

Dramatic television news shows such as *Linha Direta* [*Hot Line*], *Cidade Alerta* [*City Warning*], *Ratinho* (the newscaster's nickname, meaning little rat), among others, that thrive on condemnation and accusations, always focusing on the poorer environments, breed diffuse fear and insecurity that, instead of fostering a discourse of change and integration, reinforce, in a conformist way, the social distance between the groups. The phenomenon of incrimination of funk culture in Rio de Janeiro was at first one of the symptoms of the fear of the social and cultural ascension of lower-class youth groups that conquered the music market, thus influencing fashion and the behaviour of other social groups. The success of these funk and hip-hop movements ended up reinforcing the naive and out-of-context relationship constantly publicised between crime, poverty, and violence.[2] Their cultural product was associated with drug-trafficking and with the violence that the funk dances manifested.

The most perceptible outcomes of this discourse of 'fear' are: more indifference to the origins of poverty and to other structural injustices; more private security; more repression; demand for the confinement of the populations of the *favelas*, so that they do not leave their ghettos without suitable surveillance, as well as the setting up of more security cameras to protect private property. The 'descriptive' discourses about poverty (on television and newspapers) tend to function as mere reinforcement of stereotypes in which the poor are shown as 'bearers' of risks and social threat.

Within this context, Brazilian music and cinema will point at other discourses less marked by the idea of a 'risk of poverty', and other expressions that emerge already laden with ambiguities. It must be stressed, however, that the ethical and aesthetic issues that involve the experiences of violence in art, in film, on TV, or in videogames have been

---

[1] This article is part of an ongoing research project forthcoming in book form. A previous part, on the representations of *favelas* in earlier Brazilian cinema, has been published as The *Sertão* and the *Favela* in Contemporary Brazilian Film', in Nagib, Lúcia. *The New Brazilian Cinema*. Oxford: University of Oxford Centre for Brazilian Studies, I.B Tauris & Company, Limited, 2003, pp. 121-137.
[2] References to music and to hip-hop in this articles are based on Micael Herschmann's research *O funk e o hip hop invadem a cena* and the co-authored article 'O Espetáculo do Contradiscurso' published in the *Mais!* Supplement of *Folha de São Paulo*, August 18th, 2002.

thematised for a long time, even in the Brazilian context. But it is only now that the levels of this experience have become epidemic, or better still, a transnational and constant perception of global insecurity which has been rendered explicit and more visible after September 11th, the invasion of Iraq, the continued global wars, and the state of political exception.

An Esthetic of Hunger and of Violence

In Brazil, political and aesthetic meditations on violence experienced a privileged moment and were particularly meaningful in the 1960s, within the movement called *Cinema Novo* [*New Cinema*]. We shall find here different uses of violence and an original proposal in two manifestos by film-maker Glauber Rocha: *Estética da Fome* [*An Esthetic of Hunger*] and *Estética da Violência* [*An Esthetic of Violence*], which are worth re-visiting.

We may notice a type of modernist 'interdict' in *Cinema Novo*, something like 'thou shalt not take pleasure in the other's misery' which created an aesthetics and an ethics of the intolerable in order to deal with the difficulties of poverty. This was in a context in which the outcasts were seen positively as 'primitive rebels', bearers of a revolutionary wrath, while cinema set out to deconstruct European pathetic paternalism and exoticism and to create an aesthetics of hunger and an aesthetics of violence. This was the possibility of treating poverty and the difficulties of destitution without turning them into a product for immediate consumption, as mere entertainment or folklore. In this text, written by Glauber Rocha to be presented at a conference in Genoa, Italy, he made a radical turn. He relinquished the political-sociological discourse of condemnation and victimisation in the face of poverty, current in the 1960s and 1970s, in order to give an affirmative and transforming sense to the phenomena connected to Latin-American hunger, poverty, and misery. He attempted to transform 'maximum self-destructive forces' into a creative, mythic, and oniric impulse.

We find in Rocha one of the most laudable efforts at thoughts and political intervention in modern Brazilian cinema. In *An Esthetic of Hunger*, Rocha focused with anxiety and virulence on European paternalism towards the Third World. He analysed the 'discourse of tears and mute suffering' of humanism, a political discourse and an aesthetics that was unable to express the brutality of poverty, transforming hunger into 'folklore' and a mitigated weeping. It is a bold text against a certain pious humanism, against the cliché images of poverty that still today feed the international information circuit. Rocha raises a question that, in my view, has not been answered or resolved by the Brazilian cinema, by television, or by the international cinema, and that is still on the agenda. The ethical issue is how to show suffering, how to depict the territories of poverty, the disinherited, the excluded without falling into folklore, into paternalism, or into a conformist and lachrymose humanism.

The aesthetic issue is: how to create a new mode of expression, understanding, and representation of the phenomena connected to the *sertão* and the *favela* as sites of poverty, and to their characters and dramas? How can one make the spectator 'understand' and experience the violence of hunger and the appalling effects of poverty and exclusion, within and without Latin America? These are complementary issues, to which Rocha provides the political, ethical, and aesthetic response that was viable at that moment: through an aesthetics of violence. It was in the sociological, political or behavioural clichés that the perception, the feelings, and the thoughts of the spectator would be assaulted in order to destroy the clichés surrounding poverty.

Rocha proposes an aesthetics of violence, capable of creating an unbearable and intolerable atmosphere before such images. It is not the aestheticised or explicit violence of action films. It presents rather a symbolic violence that brings about the trance and the crisis at all levels. That is what happens in *Deus e o Diabo na Terra do Sol* [*Black God White Devil*], *Terra em Transe* [*Land in Anguish*], and in *A Idade da Terra* [*The Age of the Earth*], as well as in all of his films. Departing from critical realism and from classical narration, he restores a type of aesthetic apocalypse that stirs the spectator out of their immobility.

This proposal, which gave birth to classic films such as *Deus e o Diabo na Terra do Sol*, *Vidas Secas* [*Barren Lives*], *Rio 40 Graus* [*Rio 40 Degrees*], and *Os Fuzis* [*The Guns*], has been displaced by local themes (drug traffic, *favelas* and *sertão*) forming a transnational aesthetics, a post-MTV language, the new realism, that has as a basis high discharges of adrenaline, per second reactions created by editing and full immersion in the images. This means the same bases of pleasure and efficacy as that of the North-American action movies in which violence and its sensorial stimuli are almost hallucinatory, an imperative and sovereign pleasure in seeing, causing and suffering violence.

The idea, rejected in such films, of expressing suffering and the intolerable within a beautiful landscape, or of glamorising poverty, reappears in some contemporary films in which classical language and photography would transform the *sertão* into an exotic garden or museum to be 'rescued' by the great spectacle. This is what we find in films such as Sérgio Rezende's *Guerra de Canudos* [*The Battle of Canudos*], in Aníbal Massaini's *O Cangaceiro* [*The Bandit*] and, more recently, in Walter Salles's films or still in Fernando Meirelles's *Cidade de Deus* [*City of God*].

We shift from the 'aesthetics' to the 'cosmetics of hunger', from an idea in the head and a camera in the hand (a struggle with the real) to the steadicam, the camera that surfs through reality, a sign of a discourse that valorises 'beauty' and the 'quality' of the image, or still, the mastery of the classical technique and narrative; an 'international popular' or 'globalised' cinema whose formula would be that of a local theme, whether historical or traditional, and an 'international' aesthetics.

World-Folklore

The 'cosmetics of hunger', the parodic term for Glauber Rocha's *An Esthetic of Hunger*, that we propose, can be thought of in different contexts, from Sebastião Salgado's photography that 'glamorises' poverty, as the essayist Susan Sontag has pointed out, to the cinema and publicity that increasingly produce fashion commercials with super models in an ambience of exotic poverty, in a perverse contrast. This is a trend that is not new, to deal with complex and difficult themes, such as the representation of *favelas*, of poverty, of social violence, using for that purpose the language of entertainment films, the folkloric and *cliché* images of advertisements, as well as a kind of narrative based on action and what is spectacular. Commercial cinema can be very sophisticated, so can be the language of television and advertising. The problem is that a modish treatment of images, when confronted with social themes, tends to create a 'package' that neutralises any potential to disturb and the ethical issues that involve the themes of misery, poverty, annihilation of the other, leaving only the sensorial impact. The same applies to many action films that 'jeer' at the other's suffering and death or that transform this into a mere exotic background, a 'tropical surrealism', as Glauber Rocha said back in 1965.

How could these images of poverty thus produce an ethical shock, a thought, another sensibility? Would Brazilian contemporary cinema be a counterpoint to television images? Is there a current Brazilian cinematographic thought that would problematise this 'other' and these images of exclusion? We are experiencing a moment of fascination with this social 'other' in which the discourses of the marginalised start to gain a place in the market: in literature (writers Paulo Lins and Férrez)[3], in music (funk, hip-hop), in politics (Zero Hunger, a governmental program to eliminate hunger in Brazil), discourses that reveal the daily lives of *favela* dwellers, unemployed or underemployed people, convicts, drug addicts, a 'diffuse' mass of castaways who have managed to appear in the media, and that are shown in this same media in an ambiguous way. It is poverty and violence that have acquired a niche in the market because they are themes of an urgent now.

Eduardo Coutinho's ethical cinema, as in *Santo Forte* [*The Mighty Spirit*] and *Babilônia 2000*, signalled a different path when it placed on the screen characters that discuss their own lives, without demonising or glamorising the figures and territories of misery. Films such as Tata Amaral's *Um Céu de Estrelas* [*A Starry Sky*], Murillo Salles's *Como Nascem os Anjos* [*How Angels are Born*], and Beto Brant's *O Invasor* [*The Trespasser*] manage to deal with brutality in a very disturbing way; the documentary *Notícias de Uma Guerra Particular* [*News from a Personal War*], by João Moreira Salles, succeeds in drawing a new map of these characters and issues. In video-art, an artist such as Arthur Omar will present installations and videos whose theme comprises aesthetic and sensorial violence in a singular way, and also social violence (*Ressurreição*, *Atos do Diamante*, *Massaker*, *Sonhos e Histórias de Fantasmas*). However, we are still treading on difficult, unstable ground.

Poverty and Violence in Contemporary Brazilian Cinema

Beyond the mediating discourse of diffuse fear and demand for repression, we find still other ways of 'consuming' poverty, such as in the

---

[3] Editor's note: Férrez is the pen name of the marginal writer Reginaldo Ferreira da Silva (1975), a resident of the Capão Redondo, a violent area in São Paulo. He is equivalent to Paulo Lins with reference to Cidade de Deus, both places contributing to a prominent creative artistic trend in Brazil over the last two decades.

areas of tourism and cultural exchange. The less perverse, and, at the same time the oldest, makes us think of poverty and misery as a kind of 'museum of humankind', in which *favelas* are protected and preserved by the government (an urban tendency, since the idea of population relocation is more and more repudiated every day); they are tourist attractions in their exotic primitivism, their multicultural and 'nearly-extinct' way of life. The scene is common in Copacabana: a huge olive-green jeep, full of tourists dressed as if they were going on an African safari, crosses Atlântica Avenue leaving the Copacabana Palace Hotel. The Jeep Tour takes people of all nationalities to see 'on location' or from the top of the jeep the 'habitat' of the poor, ironically incorporated into the tourist and folkloric image of Rio de Janeiro.

Favela Chic is the name of a hot-spot Brazilian bar in Paris, a paradoxical and subtly cynical image. It is the image of a multicultural and peripheral society in which poverty and social confrontation, within and without cinema, can be seen at the same time as intolerable and 'charming', and as a famous brand name. The *favela* is a controversial postcard, a kind of museum of misery, a not yet overcome historical stage of capitalism. And the poor, who should have started becoming extinct through the production of wealth in the world, are part of this strange 'reservoir', 'preserved', but likely to fall outside the grip of the government and blow up, thus 'threatening' the city.

It is in this context, of a culture that is capable of relating to poverty and violence with pride, fascination, and terror, that we can analyse contemporary Brazilian films on this theme. Such films – perplexed narratives – rarely intend to 'explain' any context, do not risk judgements, and present themselves as 'mirrors' and 'confirmation' of a *status quo*. They represent the demise of a modern political discourse for the brutal post-MTV narratives and video-clips, a 'new' Latin-American 'realism' that would include films from *Amores Perros* [*Love's a* Bitch] to *O Invasor* [*The Trespasser*], in both cases dealing with irony and black humour *vis-à-vis* the ruins of peripheral metropolises. A biting cinema that differs from the mere pleasure for violence, as is seen frequently in *City of God*, a film that is a synthesis of several of these issues and, as we shall see, points to new impasses.

Actually, we stand before very distinct proposals and narratives that must be analysed in their peculiarities. *Como Nascem os Anjos*, by Murilo Salles, Beto Brant's *O Invasor* and *O Matador* [*Belly Up*], and Tata Amaral's *Um Céu de Estrelas* are films that describe an exploded social context where violence is frequently associated with very specific social groups: the poor, the lower-middle class, the destitute, and the young. With the exception of *O Invasor* and *O Matador*, the majority of the films do not relate violence or poverty with the elites, the businessmen, the bankers, the merchants, the middle class, and besides they point to a recurring theme: the spectacle of extermination in which the poor kill themselves. Violence appears also as a new urban folklore, stories of crimes, massacres, horrors. In this brutish show, one may discover that none of these films works with the idea of complicity or mercy. They are films of confrontation.

This random violence, lacking any meaning, will produce pure

86

spectacles, and will also be a hallmark of contemporary audio-visual production. In the last 90 years, fiction cinema has presented scarce scenarios of reconciliation or integration between the *favela* and the rest of the city; it is a context of confrontation and complicity only as far as crime is concerned, and this context is more and more categorical every day. One also notices the absence of any political discourse to explain poverty and violence, as was common in the films about the *favelas* in the 1960s. It is through violent images that the new outcasts hurt and assault the world that has rejected them; it is through images that they are also demonised by the media, but it is also through images that they take possession of the media and its resources: seduction, glamour, performance, and spectacles, for them to exist socially.

The Collector and *The Trespasser*: Violence and Hedonism

The entrepreneurial and marketing relationship between violence and drug trafficking, the rapacious entrepreneurial philosophy, and the corrupt State only very recently made their debut on the screen. An important reference is the literature of Rubem Fonseca that has only now become 'popular', and reached the cinema screens and influenced the audio-visual culture. When it surfaces, it brings out the brutality of the underworld in a rough and inexorable language. In Fonseca's *O Cobrador* [*The Collector*] (1979), the criminal is a proletarian who hates anyone that owes him ('I keep watching the telly only to see my hatred grow'). He discovers a meaning in exercising his hatred, and he goes about charging society, killing and murdering selectively those who owe him: 'Everybody owes me! They owe me food, fannies, blankets, shoes, a house, an automobile, a watch, teeth, they owe me.'

In Beto Brant's *O Invasor* (2002), we start to see this complex traffic of shared values between a 'good old criminal' who loves comfort and commodities and who dares to share music, drugs, sex, and 'attitude' with the adolescent daughter of his victim (a businessman he was hired to kill), and the entrepreneurial culture of São Paulo. For this new 'collector' and 'invader' it is not enough to kill those that owe him something; he wants to take possession of their world, he wants to be part of the bourgeoisie, to ascend socially, to join parties and 'raves',[4] take ecstasy, and dance the whole night in a night club at the Jardins.[5] For him, expanding his symbolic capital is more important than making money. By the same token, businessmen and entrepreneurs do not mind becoming criminals, if that increases their capital.

Rubem Fonseca's criminal-collector, who wanted to destroy his oppressors, starts to channel his hatred towards a possible classical political confrontation, but disappears. He watches TV to feed his ambitions: cars, night clubs, a house with a swimming-pool, fashion, attitude, drugs, all types of hedonism are sold to him, and he only wants to be 'part of this fantasy'. He does not hate the businessmen (two

---

[4] Translator's note: Raves are parties among high-class individuals that are well known for their excesses of all types.
[5] Translator's note: Jardins is a high-class neighbourhood in the city of São Paulo where there are expensive restaurants and night-clubs.

partners) who hire him to kill another man, but he simply wants to be like them. He wants to invade their properties, whether through seduction (he wants to seduce the rich girl and take her to the outskirts of São Paulo in search of cheap emotions) or through violence, through blackmail or by threatening to kill the businessmen that hired him. He could not care less what it costs; he only wants to be 'part of it' and, to that end, he pries open the social and cultural doors.

Other contemporary Brazilian films had already indicated this ethical failure and the dissolution of social pacts which, in the 1990s, show up in the mouths of characters as Vítor and Dalva in *Um Céu de Estrelas* [*A Starry Sky*] by Tata Amaral. It takes place in the poor quarters of São Paulo, or in the anarchic-emotional behaviour of the lads in *Como Nascem os Anjos*, by Murilo Salles. The author chooses a territory for the confrontation between the *favela* and the city; a mansion in Barra da Tijuca.[6] The cinema enters these territories like a surgeon penetrates the body of a dying person, with medical curiosity or even passion, but without any hope of a real intervention or 'resurrection'.

City of God and Brutal Death

Fernando Meirelles's *City of God* (2002), an adaptation of Paulo Lins's novel of the same name, is a synthesis of this new brutality. It has, amongst other refernces, gangster films, the Mafia sagas, spectacular epics, and MTV aesthetics. It is undoubtedly a landmark film, a very important historic model of drug trafficking in Brazil. But its narrative has other implications.

If the book pictured, almost in the shape of a collage, brutal and differentiated reports of the appearance and development of drug trafficking in the *favela* Cidade de Deus, the film homogenises the speeches and creates a narrative in the first person. It tells a story from the point of view of a character that is already a classic in film-making: the 'survivor', the lad nicknamed Rocket [Buscapé], whose brother is a thief who is killed in a shooting, and who decides to follow a different path, something that is not so natural as one might suppose. In his attempt to find his place in life, the lad intends to become a photographer. That is the tender thread of a series of other biographies, quite different from his own, the stories of the drug dealers Li'l Zé, Benny, Knockout Ned, and Carrot.

For all of them, adulthood, social 'respect', is going to be achieved through the exercise of violence and crime. One sentence serves as a key to the initiation ritual into barbarism: 'I'm not a boy, no, sir. I smoke, I snort. I've already killed, I've robbed. I'm a man'. The whole film has a tremendously agile language, with virtuous ellipses: time passes as the camera rotates 360°; an alteration of language and colours in the passage from the 1960s to the 1970s.

The scenes of violence are spectacular, with a number of assassinations and marked violence. Personal revenges, strategic massacres of one gang by another, meaningless violence, institutional violence: all are encouraged to feed this vicious circle. The *favela* is

---

[6] Translator's note: Barra da Tijuca: a rich neighbourhood in Rio de Janeiro.

shown as completely isolated from the rest of the city, as an autonomous territory. At no point in the film does one suppose that the trafficking is maintained and develops (guns, money, and police protection) because it has a base outside the *favela*. This *outside* does not exist in the film. Among the most violent scenes are those that show a group of young lads who are forced to kill each other to prove allegiance to the dominant gang and to prove themselves man-like. Rituals of initiation into violence and hatred are depicted in a realistic way. At certain moments, the choreography of the action and of corpses falling in succession reminds us of the gangster films of the 1930s and their rules. The film also shows the attraction and the fascination that the lads in the *favelas* have for guns, for the exercise of power, and for the pleasure of being 'somebody', of being feared and respected. If they are not respected as citizens, then they will be respected as figures in the media, as criminals.

'A gun in the hand, and an idea in the head,' jokes one character. *City of God* is a symptom-film of the reiteration of a sinister social prognosis: the expendable show of the poor killing each other. It is obvious that the 'descriptive' discourses about poverty (in the cinema, TV, video) can work both as a reinforcement of the stereotypes, and as the opportunity for a broader and more complex debate in which poverty is not seen only as a social 'risk' or 'threat' in itself. This might be the political, extra-cinematographic bias that the film could bring about. The narrative, on the other hand, frequently gives us the impression of *déjà vu* from Hollywood action films, the so-called 'tourism in hell' in which the *favelas* appear not as 'museums of poverty', but as new and terrible concentration camps. Does the cinema of the massacre of the poor prepare us for the real massacre that already happens and others to come, such as the American action films foresaw and produced the feelings of international terror and control and the claims for 'infinite justice'? We hope it does not. We are able to produce and circulate our own clichés in which healthy and shining blacks with a gun in their hands cannot think of anything better to do than engage in mutual extermination.

City of God produced a very rich debate in Brazil, thanks to the dissonant voices that were raised in the *favelas*, such as social activists, movements of all types, scholars and common people from the Cidade de Deus neighbourhood. The area's inhabitants, for the first time in Brazilian history, spoke publicly about their misery and their dissatisfaction with the image of them projected in the film and exported as an image of Brazilian violence and people's lives in the *favelas*.

A disturbing question, for which I have no answer, remains: does the massacre of the poor prepare us for the real massacres that are already happening (between the police and society, between the police and drug dealers, between drug dealers and the *favela* dwellers) and those still to come?

Films about Brazilian *favelas* have existed since the 1910s, and some do not carry any form of 'idealisation', but picture them as a 'disease', 'social leprosy', according to the view of the hygienists of the beginning of the 20th century. The lyricism and romanticism around poverty have also always existed, but even this type of cinema has extraordinary films, such as Nelson Pereira dos Santos's *Rio Zona Norte* [*Rio Northern Zone*] and Rio *40 Graus* [*Rio 40 Degrees*]. These are lyrical films, but they are also full of realism, they show criminality, the violence that a black *samba* dancer from a *favela* (*Rio Zona Norte*) suffers, for example. *Rio 40 Graus* depicts, in a critical, realistic, and poetic way the day-to-day lives of peanut sellers.

None of these films shows the *favela* as a 'detached' place. The opposite is actually shown, with the *favelas* integrated into city life. In Marcel Camus's *Black Orpheus* (1959), however, the *favela* is fancied to the extreme. Throughout history, though, we find some interesting and critical films about the *favelas*: *Five Times Favela* (produced by the Centre for Popular Culture [CPC], a centre that is a part of UNE).[7] Despite being at times pedagogical, it tries to understand this environment and its characters and problems. Eduardo Coutinho's recent documentaries show the daily lives in the *favelas*, revealing that people there have cultural, religious, individual, simple and complex experiences, but it does not generalise and does not fall into a pedagogical bias or into idealisation.

Counter-Discourse: Changing the Values of Poverty and Violence

Beyond the images of journalism and cinema, the innovation in the representation of poverty and violence in Brazilian audio-visual production and the discourses about them are found in the field of music and video-clip. When rapper M V Bill sings in a hypnotic beat his war song, *Soldado do Morro* [*The Favela's Soldier*], speaking in the first person, naked torso, a gold necklace around his neck, a gun hanging from his shoulder, and a pair of a famous 'brand-name' tennis shoes on his feet, he epitomises in an all-involving posture the juvenile rebelliousness in its pure state, the fads, the manliness, the rapper's hip-hop 'attitude' sold in the market, and a most legitimate political discourse. These are 'protest' music and images created by youngsters from the *favelas* and poorer neighbourhoods that function today as a counter-discourse. It is a manifestation of juvenile aggressiveness not only translated into the music's lyrics, into the fashion – caps deeply pulled down on their heads, 'brothers' and '*Carandiru*-like' tattoos – but embodied in a community and collective discourse, full of legitimate social wrath that sings and demands changes.

From fashion to activism, from 'attitude' in relation to music to a political discourse we see the emergence of new subjects of discourse that come from real territories, *favelas*, poorer neighbourhoods, ghettos, and rise to the level of the media, carrying within the germ of a rejuvenated political discourse, foreign to the traditional institutions: the State, the party, the labour union, the students' movements, *etcetera*, but close to the young urban culture: music, shows, TV, internet, fashion.

M V Bill is only one of the icons of this new discourse, of an aggressive presence in the media that may make use of the most

---

[7] Translator's note: UNE, National Students' Union, as the name suggests, is a national organisation of students that has always had an active role in Brazilian social and political life.

traditional forms of political participation, but who is not limited to them. In his case, he blends music with the construction of a collection of audio-visual production, called CUFA – *Central Única das Favelas* [*Favelas' Central Union*], whose name is a parody reminding us of an old labour union federation. Also a 'party' was organised, the PPPomar (Popular Party of the Power for the Majority), that has a manifesto, a programme, and projects with an emphasis on racial issues and on the relationship between race and poverty, using as a form of discourse and participation the rap, the shows, the performances, the video-clips, presentations on Brazilian MTV, and now in the cinema (the documentary *Di Menor* [*Under Age*], about the participation of children in drug trafficking). The proposal is to make hip-hop a platform for cultural production, without 'mediators'.

M V Bill plays with the traditional discourses and calls himself M V, the messenger of truth,[8] and thus he can play a thinking drug dealer, as in the controversial *Soldado do Morro* [*The Favela's Soldier*], a political leader in the debates about university quotas for blacks, a performer with a gun hanging from his belt during the Free Jazz Festival, reminding the public that he comes from the Cidade de Deus neighbourhood, but, later, wrapping the gun in a white handkerchief, he shouted the slogan 'I belong to peace!'

We are before a 'displaced' political discourse, that makes use of violence in order to fight it and that brings into focus these new cultural mediators: rappers, funk-singers, b-boys, as well as other discriminated-against groups and voices: *favela* dwellers, unemployed, underemployed, drug addicts, a 'diffuse' bunch of outcasts that appear in the media in an ambiguous form, but that can occupy the place of an urgent political discourse.

The decisive change is the political dimension of these urban cultural expressions and lifestyles forged in the passage from a literate culture to an audio-visual culture and to the media. Maybe an intelligent governmental policy would include cultural experiments that pinpoint the large cities: music, theatre, videos produced in partnership with the *favelas*, and a refurbishment of the poorer neighbourhoods, peripheral cultures that flee the merely philanthropic efforts and state a political and aesthetic 'quality' (certain rap and hip-hop pieces by the *Companhia de Teatro Nós do Morro* [*Us from the Hill*], *The Ethnic Dance Company*, the *Coopa Roca at Rocinha*, *Radio Favela*, among others do so).

These new subjects of musical and literary discourse (writer Paulo Lins and other scholars and artists with origins in the poorer neighbourhoods) discharge the traditional cultural mediators and, more than that, they battle for the same funding and financing for social projects; they give up being 'object' of discourse and become the subject. This is another ironic innovation that does away with any remaining paternalism. The new outcasts, the privileged subjects and victims of urban violence, fight in order to obtain the 'copyright' over their own poverty and image, knowing that the 'mediation' and the mediators between these different levels and discourses cannot be forsaken. Thus

---

[8] Translator's note: M V in Portuguese stand for *Mensageiro da Verdade* [Messenger of Truth].

they continue to run for indication among themselves, or come together in productive partnerships.

There are many forms of the aesthetics of violence and poverty, with different ethics and consequences: some are affirmative, others are reactive, and being stalwart, they can become the symptoms and the expressions of forms of living, valuing, and thinking.

Translation by Edson Martins Lopes

11. The Looks in *City of God*
Ely Azeredo

City of God introduces a new perspective into Brazilian film-making –
seductive, disconcerting, and sometimes shocking – but in a way that
does not hinder the spectator's receptivity. We can forgo the powers of
premonition to affirm that Fernando Meirelles's enterprise will travel the
world with reverberations equivalent to or exceeding the film's praise at
its first public appearance in Cannes. In language and technical
execution, *City of God* absorbs the shift to work-in-progress found in the
movie industry – especially in the work of certain American film-makers
distanced from the institutional restraints of Hollywood.

The detractors of the film created by Meirelles and his valiant
crew excommunicate its profane body, its musical and sensuous curves,
its high voltage as an audio-visual spectacle, as if movie theatres were
temples and the producers, peddlers. Come on, we live in a time of
politics-spectacle, media-spectacle, even religion-spectacle. Why would a
film-maker be obliged to broach any chosen theme according to the
canons of *cinéma-vérité* (or direct cinema), of anthropological exposé or
committed documentary film-making? Spectators can do without didactic
scenes involving the use of drugs, social inequality and the quality of
'salvaging' operations of *favela* communities. These themes are discussed
and illustrated through other means of communication.

Cinematographic spectacles gained importance as a language
precisely with Griffith, during the second half of the 20th century, in a
revolution (aside from ideologies) to give dramatic visualisation to
violence. In the wake of Griffith's invention, Eisenstein copydesked
historical facts and ignored canons of documental veracity to create the
masterpiece of *fake* documentary, the marvellous *The Battleship
Potemkin*. Well-informed cinema students know: Eisenstein, Rossellini
and Orson Welles were not deemed less ethical because of their use of
lies to attain the truth.

Is it absurd to broach the tragedy of drug-dealing youth with
elements of cosmopolitan pop culture? A genius like Stanley Kubrick
would say no. Thirty years ago he foresaw the chaos of urban
delinquency to the sound of *Singing in the Rain* and Beethoven, creating
a choreographic and musical language for *A Clockwork Orange*. Few films
are more a spectacle than Coppola's *The Godfather* – especially *Part 2* – a
major film from which nobody extracted moralism or ideology, although
narrated by a mafia member from the perspective of organised crime.

Art work, which causes rupture, shuffles the primers. I have been
a film critic for fifty years. After its première, I was unable to evaluate, in
my emotional state, the enormous importance of *Rio 40 Graus* [*Rio 40
Degrees*] by Nelson Pereira dos Santos, which is historically indisputable,
despite the clichés of its social protest. Nelson was tracing, to the horror
of dramatists, his film-making's future trajectory. If Brazil today has
bunkers of film-making industry, it is due to this epic – in a large part –
to the 'inappropriate aesthetics' of *Rio 40 Graus*.

City of God is the first Brazilian fictional film with the look from the other side of the 'divided city'. Radicalising the approach used by Paulo Lins (in his novel hindered by a laborious lyricism and an excess of plots which he saw parade under his window, in the city located on Rio de Janeiro's western fringe), Meirelles says that 'what the movie tries to show is what the young chaps see from the inside', meaning what youngsters involved in drug-dealing before the more 'organised' phase experienced (the story ends at the beginning of the 1980s). It is a non-journalistic, non-documentary way of looking and, therefore, not obliged to 'show the two sides'. The film's originality resides in how it conducts us through the terrible and inimitable experience of living in the ghetto as if we were incarnated in those war-torn children and teenagers. Mutilated, because they have had their childhood amputated; not unlike the two young protagonists of *Jeux Interdits* (*Prohibited Toy*) on the outskirts of another war, in the unforgettable film by René Clément.

José Louzeiro, author of the novel *Infância dos Mortos* [*Childhood of the Dead*] and co-author of the respective screenplay, directed by Hector Babenco, said that his was a 'film universal in its pain'. I believe I can say the same about *City of God*. The tragedy of this new film ricochets well beyond the traumatised asphalt between domestic window gratings. Well beyond the horror of drug dealing. Well beyond the agony of adults in a crossfire. What I wrote about *Pixote* in still goes: their creators point out how, for hundreds of thousands of youngsters in our country, the mere exercise of childhood – as a harvest ground for playfulness and a territory for dreams and self-invention – has become literally impossible.

Films that cause rupture breed incomprehension. During the dawn of *Cinema Novo,* Ruy Guerra abandoned the point of view of decent people and shot *Os Cafajestes* [*The Unscrupulous Ones*] from the perspective of the lowlifes involved in drugs. The Cardinal complained to the Governor (Carlos Lacerda, supporter of cinema, although a bad critic) and, in broad daylight, the police interrupted the sessions in Cinelândia and took off with the tins of film. Guerra was an innovator, under the influence of French *Nouvelle Vague,* but audiences were only enthusiastic about the raw scenes, such as the frontal nude of Norma Bengell.

In the feature film that founded *Cinema Novo, Barravento* [*The Turning Wind*], by Glauber Rocha (1961), outlaw Firmino (Antonio Pitanga), a contester of popular religion, is the film-maker's spokesman. Throughout the 1960s, social nonconformity illuminated the violence of the *cangaceiros*,[1] hired-guns and urban bandits. Hidden or explicit messages were demanded as warranties of integrity when broaching social inequality.

In 2002, in view of *City of God*, there are still critics who are scandalised by seeing inhabitants from the *favelas* behaving cruelly. Will Luis Buñuel's ethic's certification have to be registered anew? For Buñuel (his film *Los Olvidados* [*The Young and the Damned*] a brutal portrait of the excluded youngsters in Mexico City), as well as Bergman, evil is not

---

[1] Editor's note: Cangaço/Cangaceiros were 'honourable' armed bandits who roamed the Northeastern region of Brazil from 1870-1940, taking over landed estates and exercising justice.

the by-product of perverse social conditions.

Unfortunate people are also capable of extreme cruelty, like Zé Pequeno [Li'l Zé], one of the protagonists in *City of God*. The troops belonging to this 'Drug Lord' are way beyond reach of any citizenly deeds; two words which to them sound like some ditty at a convention rally. It is worth remembering though, that this cinematographic story is bland compared to the episodes of the war against trafficking permanently shown on TV.

As long as television fragments our perception of the communities harassed by this unending war, cinema concentrates, condenses and offers the sensitive spectator a mature grasp as to what it is all about. The new look of *City of God* arises from the film-makers' openness to multiple influences (it is, after all, a collective piece of work, involving the priceless participation of co-director Katia Lund, director of photography César Charlone, editor Daniel Rezende and others, including the cast). Little does it matter if the camera, here or there, reveals the inspiration of some demoniacal gringo like Scorsese in *Goodfellas*. What matters, in reality, is the heart beating behind the camera. What really matters, and a lot, is the absence of ideological filters.

Arnaldo Jabor wrote, 'we do not see this movie; it looks at us'. A play on words, indeed, but one in search of translating the irritating (and innovating) 'change in axis' in the relations of audio-visual products with the *favelas.* Sitting in their seats, spectators on the right side of the law, tuned with the law and income tax, tremble. There are no shots from 'this side'! The point of view, reaching back to the pages of the novel, was transferred to that which is improperly called a 'housing project', increasingly being pushed into a ghetto state of existence. Now, as a film, it radicalises; it pulls the spectator into the labyrinth that was once the symmetrical proposal for housing in the 1960s.

Meirelles and screenwriter Bráulio Mantovani reply to this labyrinthine 'housing project' with a labyrinthine narrative (an organic and living structure), which uniquely magnetises the spectator's participation. The extraordinary opening scene stops on the threshold of its climax (opening a gap in time for the narrator, Buscapé [Rocket], to lead the spectator back to the 1960s and 1970s) to return to the screen at the nucleus of its nervous centre at the end of the screening. Within this circular narrative, other circles of stories open and close, until the moment when the angel of death opens its wings over the throne of the drug traffic.

This century of cinema has made us used to screenplays with a beginning-middle-end, which evolve through the classic phases of presentation, confrontation and resolution. The screenplay signed by Mantovani, a chain of stories, is re-sculptured as the film progresses with countless landings where the crew imaginatively shuffles their order: one story flows into another. The three presumed 'acts' of each plot are shattered and re-sculptured through editing. And orchestrated in such a way that we cannot separate the pain from the happiness of those living (for how long?) and those dead. The film was 'accused' of being influenced by Tarantino, in its language, which is evident, but it also surpasses in the shift from Tarantino-like fiction to the truth-fiction of

Lins, Mantovani and Meirelles. Time, emotion and critical posture are another.

City of God (with a few exceptions, like the sequence which reveals the bodies in the motel, which looks like some footage abandoned by Scorsese in *Taxi Driver*) exits the tracks of influences, mainly in the creation of its own dramatic timing. 'I believe that what usually leads people to go to the movies is time: lost time, bygone or that not found yet,' wrote Tarkovski, the Russian film-maker. 'Spectators are in search of a living experience, and cinema, like no other art, amplifies, enriches and condenses the experience of one person – and not only enriches, but makes it longer, significantly longer.' I believe that the search and the discovery of this 'living experience' explains (beyond any excitement brought about by technique), the success of *City of God*.

Translation by Charles Anchor

12. Humanisers of the Inevitable: Brazilian Film against Barbarism[2]
Ismail Xavier

Karim Ainouz's *Madame Satã* [*Madame Satan*] (2002) illustrates the transition that makes this film an example of the shift in the tone of Brazilian cinema, whose agenda pre-2000 had leaned towards the accentuation of the destructive behaviour of characters reduced to impotency, or as agents of a displaced violence. From *Orfeu* [*Orpheus*] (Cacá Diegues, 1999) to *Cidade de Deus* [*City of God*] (Meirelles-Lund, 2002) cinema has depicted the opposition between culture (art) and barbarism (violence, murder and involvement in drug-trafficking) as the boundary between the alternatives available to the youth of the *favelas*. In renewing the raft of resentment and exposing the social factors that determine the conformity to trafficking, *City of God* highlights an example of liberation in the face of this dichotomy. Paroxysms of social corrosion cannot hinder the fact that our attention has also been increasingly drawn to the experiences of positively influential characters, rare authors of emancipating actions and gestures that allow them to survive and liberate themselves from the mechanism, whether it be the world of urban delinquency or the traditional family, an inflection that can be seen in Walter Salles's *Behind the Sun* (2002), among others.

In *Bicho de Sete Cabeças* [*Brainstorm*] (2001), the family as an institution and the medical order compose the binomial of dehumanisation. The recurring theme of the prison system in recent years renders the affirmation of the subject problematic, since the stories of the transgressions which cause these characters to fall into the network of this perverse system are not always so pleasant. Such is the problem Babenco faces in his attempt to remove the stigma of 'incorrigible evil' from the prisoners, seeking to combine the story of the inferno with a reference to the history of the prisoners. With its emphasis on the oppressive power and determination behind the state, *Carandiru* adds to the list of recent films that reveal the most perverse mechanisms of violence: transgressors will seek alternatives to the institution whose deterioration is foregrounded by their humanising gestures.

Childbirth, whether metaphorical or otherwise, further features in the 'Recovery of Brazilian Cinema' as affirmation of life while the woman as prisoner and mother fights oppression and barbarism in foundational narratives.

Art *and* Barbarism: Affirmation of the Individual in the Face of Racial and Sexual oppression in *Madame Satan*

At its close, Karim Ainouz's *Madame Satã* leaves us with a question: why should a person so affirmative in his reactions, a person always dignified

---

[2] I borrow this expression from an article by Roberto Mangabeira Unger published in *Folha de São Paulo*. In it, he analyses the difficulties of a leftist 'social policy' in a state without effective powers to face the inputs and perverse effects of the contemporary global economic order.

97

in his composure, who never takes shame home, bear the humiliation inflicted upon him in a bar by a person unknown to him without retaliating, only to ruminate later on the offence while licking his wounds, and then return to the street to follow the aggressor and shoot him in the back?

Such a shot is decisive. It transports him to prison and seals the finale for a flashback that traces his life story. We return to where we started, the close up of Lázaro Ramos's face, to hear in voice-over a new diatribe from the court against the 'bad bloke', as a possible denouement for a life that had been on a downward spiral. However, this is not what happens. The decrepit face is followed by an epilogue in which the protagonist is reborn as Madame Satã in a tremendous finale. What we have witnessed during the course of the film, the construction of a character endowed with enormous self-esteem, pledged to his self-affirmation in the face of racial and sexual oppression, is restored.

In confrontational situations, the emphasis was very clearly on the formula of 'my person', the expression of his character and of his resistance to prejudice. An incisive form that sits well with his face and attitude, and is completely out of step with his shooting someone in the back. Vengeance, at the wrong moment, and in the wrong way. One way or another, the final events of the film, with the exaltation of the values projected onto Madame Satã's' social mask. The confrontation between the protagonist and oppression does not engender self-poisoning. All traces of resentment are absent from the character except for that one momentary lapse, which represents the irruption of a surprising, regressive and anomalous gesture. Perhaps, for this reason, the film does not take long to invert the radical transformation into the affirmative. When I refer to the shot in the night as a regressive act, I do not do so in comparison with the supposed depths of goodness that this act is betraying. The interesting detail in this film is that the demand for an affirmation of the subject (in this case a black homosexual in a discriminatory context) is achieved by the tracing of a course that does not touch on romanticisation.

This trajectory enhances the force of a character who, in spite of being a social agent not exempt from contradictions, is in harmony with the dissident values that he embodies (we are not attempting to underline the condition of a virtuous person who is 'misled' by the corruption in the world). The affirmation of the subject is more complicated here because it does not imply sublimation or rehabilitation within the dichotomy *violence or art* that guides the actions of the diverse self-help groups operating in the pockets of poverty nowadays. The equation in *Madame Satã* is *violence and art*, the construction of himself as a character – a dandy in Lapa,[3] a delinquent.

---

[3] Translator's note: Lapa is a traditionally bohemian neighbourhood in Rio de Janeiro.

Art *against* Barbarism: *City of God* and Others

The central conflict in *City of God* it is 'violence or photography'; previously, in *Orpheus*, it was 'violence or music'.[4] Fernando Meirelles and Katia Lund's film constructs the figure of the narrator, Buscapé [Rocket], who walks on a knife edge without falling into the chain of vengeance – and survives.

Meirelles follows the three-segmented division of the situation in the *favelas* explained in João Moreira Salles and Katia Lund's *Notícias de uma Guerra Particular* [*News from a Personal War*]. There are three poles to the situation: the drug dealers, the police and the population squeezed in the middle. From the opening sequences, Rocket is portrayed as a symbol of those who are caught between two fires. There he is, in the middle of the street, graphically exposed between Li'l Zé's [Zé Pequeno] gang and the police. In the flashback, of which the film is composed, his fear and humour serve to set him apart from his friends (and from his own brother) who hold fast to violence and robbery as a solution to their problems, before the armed gangs find, in the trafficking of cocaine, a way of life and death.

He passes unscathed through this tangled undergrowth, aided by luck and by his own predisposition towards breaking the chain – twice he has the opportunity to kill Li'l Zé, but does not want to fall into the web of violence. The film is structured to make an exception of Rocket, almost a miracle in fact. The dramatic condensations of *City of God* turn its ultra-realism into an allegory, a strong abstraction of the terms of that war embodied in a small group of characters. The film does not picture the variety within the real community, thus generating protests from within it against simplifications that are harmful to its imagery. They wanted a representation of a more nuanced and diverse world, which would correspond to their real experience. However, here the cinema wishes to reaffirm the radical poles of the conflict, eliminating ambiguity, and those who live a routine life in order to oppose the social visibility of the photographer to the fame of the criminal.

This opposition – art versus barbarism – is a pillar of the formulation of the politics of the NGOs [Non-Governmental Organisations], whose premise is the offer of artistic training and cultural practices as a means of education for citizenship. Such practices involve the individual's self-affirmation and the recovery of self-esteem. 'Regular' jobs appear immediately to be beyond their horizon, either because they do not exist or because they are humiliating in the eyes of the young *favela* dwellers who do not see a future as office boys or supermarket cashiers. As in the case of Branquinha in *Como Nascem os Anjos* [*How Angels Are Born*] (Murillo Salles, 1996), they prefer a short life with the money from trafficking – risky, almost suicidal, yet more generous and glamorous. This does not extract them from the circle of resentment present in the poor communities of the large cities of this lay society (or

---

[4] About Cacá Diegues's film and this general issue of resentment in the Brazilian cinema of the 1990s, see Ismail Xavier, 'Brazilian Cinema in the 1990s: the unexpected encounter and the resentful character'. In Nagib, Lúcia (ed.), *The New Brazilian Cinema*. London and New York: I.B. Tauris, 2003, pp. 39-63.

at least where the role of religion has changed), geared towards the valorisation of consumerism.

Although not completely absent, we see there the weakening of the ascetic moralism inherited from the Jewish-Christian tradition. The immediate demand for participation in consumption is far more attractive to the young than movements related to spiritual ascetics and renunciation, shifting in their minds the terms of a supposed elimination of the 'existential resentment' of the excluded. The adoption of a political route, which would require long-term participation in a collective effort to resolve their problems,[5] is an even more remote possibility.

Helvécio Raton's *Uma Onda no Ar* [*Something in the Air*] (2002) had its script and *mise en scène* problems potentialised in its reception by the critics, to the extent that such problems were associated with what one understands as a 'forced affirmation', idealising the protagonist (mainly in what is referred to as the 'superior' side of the protagonist, flawless since his days on the benches of the bourgeois school he attended). Overcoming the personal retaliations of an oppressed – by means of a collective and thus more political practice – is but an example of what seems to demand more from the film-maker than other situations in which today's privileged dichotomy is valid: either violence and drug trafficking or assistance work which prepares one for artistic performance.

In this way, what the film-maker brings as an original piece of information in terms of choice, otherwise based on real experience, ends up being a problem. Remembering Aristotle, what is valid here is the rule according to which the decisions taken by the characters, and judged unlikely by the audience (or by the critic), require more dramatic elaboration in order to convince. On the other hand, everything is smoother when the film moves along the lines of verisimilitude in the recreation of an era and yields dramatic returns from them. This happens when the logic of vengeance is explored in the drama, whether as an ancestral rule, which every generation should obey within the family regime, or as the law which regulates the relationships between the gangs and soldiers in drug trafficking.

Problems with the screenplay disappear and value is given to the forcefulness of the types and the incisive, less reflexive manner of their actions. The speed of a dramatisation with a behavioural basis renders a

---

[5] Religion scholars highlight the advance of beliefs that imply the direct negotiation of immediate material advantages to compensate for the rules that the church imposes on its followers. The relationship between religion and negotiation of the earthly world emphasises immediate gratification within life's immanence, not in its transcendence. What then can one say about the political utopias whose language would be even more complex and whose accomplishment would be pin-pointed by discipline and long-term actions? The expression 'existential resentment' refers to the theme of Nelson Rodrigues's play *Boca de Ouro*, the analysis of which by Hélio Pellegrino emphasises the way in which a tragic vocation is born out of greed and also out of a deeper misunderstanding of the condition and of the meaning of human existence. See the discussion about this topic in 'Boca de Ouro: o mito, a mídia, o drama doméstico e a cidade' in Ismail Xavier's *O Olhar e a Cena* (São Paulo: Cosac & Naify, 2004).

lively telling of the circle of violence which is reinforced at every new turn of the war, interrupted at times by the selflessness of a young boy who sacrifices himself, as in *Abril Despedaçado* [*Behind the Sun*], or by the social work which has an effect on the youngster, revealing a talent which could lead to the 'social inclusion' of the destitute character. These are cases of redemption in which the actions of certain characters function as humanising agents of the inevitable. Such an intervention, whether it comes from a force from within (affection) or from without (for example, via the work of an NGO), saves the protagonist from the circle of hell without touching upon the foundation of the natural order of these worlds.

The Progressive-Regressive Movement: *City of God* as a Synthesis of Urban Conflicts

The scandalous side of the configuration of power in Brazilian urban life has earned repeated representation in national cinema, which has focused on various forms of sociability and authority, typical of territories where family or gang law is valued, and almost always observed as systems sustained by tradition (when feudal) or by money or arms. There is, in these areas, more than sufficient material for the construction of drama, being, as they are, settings for agonising experiences *par excellence*: confrontations with the risk of death, in which initiative and personal charisma are imperative, and stories of courage and cowardice. The film industry has always explored this material because it is situated before (or beyond) the security of bureaucracy, work routines and the life of the ordinary citizen.

Violence as a system imparts intensity to conflicts and restores the strength (but not the meaning) of the gestures associated with classic tragedy to modern drama. The thrust is to project a certain glamour upon urban conflicts, which, finally, define a context of regression in which death is the by-product of the circulation of special commodities that require 'free territories' and cheap labour (*City of God* is the synthesis of this).

We are, therefore, a long way from the full tragic dimension of the hero who sacrifices himself for the community's sake, seeing that the values on the agenda are those of the profitability of illegal commerce. In the same way one cannot demand a true current representation of violence in the epic dimensions of a mythology such as that of Westerns, for example. This industrial genre departed from the premise that its particular representation of barbarism was the revision of a process of formation, which had its heroes and its sacrifices in the name of the law and future citizenship.

The movement now is regressive. The city subdivided into zones of power construes a new version of what were the rural spaces previous to 1930, dominated by the politics of *coronelismo*[6] – a well-known term that arrived together with *latifundium* (system of large land estates), a

---

[6] Translator's note: *Coronelismo*, Brazilian political-social practice in which the great landowners were given the title of 'coronel', a symbol of power and status in society and in politics, roughly from 1889 to 1930.

geography of hunger, bigots and bandits. The crime bosses in the current big cities bring this same dimension of clientism, meaning protector, owner of the 'patch', judge of good or evil, in the territories they control. *With one difference*: *the colonel was the armed branch of the 'national order' in its archaic fashion, the trafficker is the victory of the market over the Nation State reduced to impotence.*

Survivors and Saviours: Walter Salles's Inflection in *Behind the Sun*

Within institutions: iniquity. Outside them: violence. As a rule, the continuous chain of vengeance, without values or projects, stretches beyond the roulette of finances and weapons. Yet there are characters that do not succumb to the labyrinth and find a way out which elevates them to exemplary figures in the affirmation of the individual. In this opposition between the affirmative and the reactive gesture, *Behind the Sun* (2002) brings a new inflection to the trajectory of Walter Salles Jr.

In his first films, drifting and violence dominate the agenda until the very end, as in *A Grande Arte* [*The Great Art*] and *Terra Estrangeira* [*Foreign Land*]. In *Central Station* [*Central do Brasil*] a melodramatic design construes a course of redemption for the old lady (Dora) and salvation for Josué, the young boy who re-encounters his family and re-centres his life, when everything indicated disaster for the orphan who had to sleep in the train station. If *O Primeiro Dia* [*Midnight*] restores despair and sabotages hopes for the new millennium, *Behind the Sun* weaves a more complex plot, a variant on the theme of salvation already witnessed in *Central Station*. This time the inferno is not the city, but the rural world that had been depicted as an oasis of humanity in the other film.

Here it is not the child who is saved at the hands of the older figure; it is the youngster marked for death who is saved by the work and grace of a child, his younger brother who puts himself in his place to take the bullet from the rival family that is in search of vengeance. Tonho escapes what the traditional family determines: kill and be killed in the chain of violence (himself and the next in succession), in a traditional and heavily ruled feud. On the one hand, therefore, we have the rural patriarchy and its order, its austere customs, its discipline – the force of tradition. On the other, the altruism of the innocent, the unselfishness of a boy for whom the life of his brother was more important than the family dictates – the force of brotherly sentiment breaks the line of the father and undoes the chain. His sacrifice, by choice, affirms the liberty of the subject in the face of the order of repetition which denies individual choice – 'as it was, it will be'.

This order is transformed into a picture in the resigned rotation of the oxen tied to the cane wheel, in the silent face of the mother, in the way the father observes the faded blood stains on his dead son's shirt, the sign that the moment of vengeance has arrived. It is also present in the natural space which, although sun-drenched and with great open spaces, composes the stable scene that is always crossed via the same paths, without glancing elsewhere, without curiosity. In counterpoint, liberation is transformed into a picture in Pacu's uneasiness, in his curiosity about the book he gets from the girl from the circus, in his affinity with the world of stories and imagination. A boy full of life, whose law is communication and not silence, who chooses death in the name of love, who saw the oldest son die according to the same rules which could now take his remaining brother.

It is not by chance that he is the narrator at the beginning and at the end of the film, extremes where the decisive moment is repeated: that of the imminence of his death, during the night, when he could be mistaken for his brother and take the bullet in his place. It is his voice, therefore, that recognises an interlocutor outside the circle and retrieves the subject from his memory. It is his voice that opens and closes the narrative – already with the certainty his imaginary listener completely understands what is about to happen. Mediator between the world of the family and us, Pacu is also the mediator between Tonho and the circus, between Tonho and his sexual experience with the circus girl, between Tonho and the world that opens for his pilgrimage, free from paternal condemnation.[7]

In the patriarchal matrix of *Behind the Sun*, there is the judgement of the father and the silence of the mother (only broken in the finale after Pacu's sacrifice) – we are in the *sertão* in 1910. On the outskirts of São Paulo some decades later, the protagonist of *Bicho de Sete Cabeças* [*Brainstorm*] (Laís Bodansky, 2002) is the victim of a family plot which is also characterised by the 'dictum of the father and the silence of the mother' which engenders a dearth of suffering, under the power of tradition. Those events unfold into a strange liberation.

A restless youngster from a provincial family survives a long period of repression and dehumanisation in the insane asylum in which his father deposits him. And, as if to compose a parallel to Foucault's view – that wherever there is work, there is no madness (or inordinate violence) – the process of overcoming the 'inferno' is driven by the survivor's unique will, which resists and reunites against a colossal force, to liberate himself from the framework of the institutions (familial and state medical).

Once again, the father is the figure of resentment (reminiscent of Lima Duarte's character in *A Ostra e o Vento* [*The Oyster and the Wind*], who represses the daughter's vitality), a small man at the end of his days who seeks to project his grievances onto his son, and to avenge himself for not being able to control him, to belittle him. 'I got this far, and you? Where are you going?' It is the symptomatic examination which the son would denounce in such a crushing way later on, in the incensed

---

[7] In the epilogue, the film brings the sea as the *telos* – final term, goal – of Tonho's pilgrimage, in an evocation of Glauber Rocha's *Deus e o Diabo na Terra do Sol* [*Black God White Devil*], in Truffaut's *The Brats*. This final gesture as a metaphor for space brings, as in Rocha's film, the sense of walking towards a promise that contrasts with a life so far made up of circles inserted in a perverse order, but the relationship between the *sertão* [waste hinterland], circle and straight line, past and future, is not made up here by a number of reasons apt to suggest the specific field of the metaphor and the content of the relationship evoked by the quotation. This ends up in a formula, not exactly the image of a consideration of history.

relationship-breaking letter that he hands him while already in custody and desperate, under the control of the doctors to whom the father has delegated the power of repression in the name of science, in order to keep him away from marijuana.

We have the woman as a representation of repressed sensitivity and obedience to the father (*Mater Dolorosa*). We have the sister with the petit-bourgeois pretensions, somewhat fickle and blind to her brother's problems (rivalry? envy? alliance with the father?). We also have the son in conjunction with Tonho, in terms of timidity and hesitation, who seeks a commitment to order, and with Pacu, because he has rebellion in him, the force of affirmation of the individual against a coarse institutional power. His stubborn resistance reaches its maximum expression in his resorting to suicide in the solitary cell in the insane asylum, the breaking point of his dramatic 'rebirth' at the end of the film.

The paternal circle demands growth, but acts to make sure that he does not go far. The hospital obliterates. However, the boy survives to tell his story, to denounce the perverse side of the paternal gestures, and the hokum of the institution that imprisons him. His labyrinth was much more systematic in its pitfalls than that faced (in the Kafka-esque order) by the protagonist of Ruy Guerra's *Estorvo* [*Turbulence*] (2000); and were *Bicho de Sete Cabeças* [*Brainstorm*] a fiction without ballast in a true story, it would be difficult to legitimise such a miraculous moment, the moment of returning to life, which serves in the film as a metaphor for future freedom. There the narrative is interrupted, at the climax of oppression, and leaps forward to the closing credits, which evoke the thought of where the written testimony started, a thought that the film translates into images and sounds.

Hell Station and the Invention of Everyday Life: The Carandiru Prison

Affirming the subject while depicting the experience of the institution from the point of view of the prisoners is the problem that Babenco faced in *Carandiru*.[8] Alongside the gallery of characters and what opens as a panel of experiences – routine or unusual, folkloric even – inside the prison (point of anchorage of the film which explains its successful composition of friendly characters with their particular idiosyncrasies), Babenco felt the need to insert some flashbacks, which explain why one or another of the spotted characters is in prison.

One may say that he takes a step too far in his tendency towards Rousseau's allusion, already present in *Lúcio Flávio, O Passageiro da Agonia* [*Lúcio Flávio, Passenger of Agony*] and *Pixote*[9] [*Pixote, the Law of the Weakest*], but which more recent cinema had done away with in its representation of the criminal experience, preferring ambiguities and a form of more radical ethical impasses. In this specific case, the weight of the *Carandiru* massacre – true state terrorism – created an infernal aura

---

[8] Translator's note: *Carandiru*, a state prison in the city of São Paulo, which has been demolished. It is also the title of a book by Dráuzio Varella, and of the namesake film by Argentinian-Brazilian director, Hector Babenco.

[9] Translator's note: *Lúcio Flávio* and *Pixote* are also part of Babenco's filmography.

of institutional catastrophe around the prison. This redeems the image of the inmate and guides a representation whose tone is humanisation, which, in the film, heads in the direction of melodrama, in opposition to the more dry tone of Dráuzio Varella's rendering. He does not dramatise, he is laconic and less sentimental than Babenco in his anthropology of the prison, marked by the construction of a humanising point of view, against stigmatisation.

The state casts the detainees into a situation of frank vulnerability in relation to their enemies, in what constitutes a perverse part of the punishment (it is common for a prisoner to state 'I don't know if I will get out of here alive'). In Babenco's film, however, the climate of community appears less unbearable than is presaged in the opening sequence – the disposition of permanent threat is rarely manifested. The film-maker is more interested in what is to be found, emotional or confessional, in the relationship between the prisoners and the doctor, in what every personal story reveals of a universe ignored by prejudice. Humanisation, therefore, is the word of order, the gestures of affirmation of the individuals who stress the deterioration of the institution's role, now reduced to a repressive warehouse. What matters is what it does to each individual and how each individual reacts to it, placing the problem of the organisation in the shade, the more complex side of the motivation behind the conflicts, generally what could lead to a more realistic discussion of the problem.

These infernal 'warehouses' generate a justified phobia among the transgressors to the point that they would prefer any alternative other than prison (a central theme in José Padilha's documentary Ônibus 174 [Bus 174]). Beyond the material misery and resentment, there lies the terror of falling into the perverse nets of the correctional system, a perspective that breeds desperation, the 'all or nothing' that characterises Sandro's behaviour. Bus 174 constructs this cycle of the denunciation of violence in the disciplinary institutions that have marked Brazilian cinema. Notably, the documentaries promote the meeting of the film-maker with the 'other', whether the theme is religion, violence or drug-trafficking wars in the favelas.

If we look at the question of life within the prison, Paulo Sacramento offers a film that is a synthesis – O Prisioneiro da Grade de Ferro [Prisoner of the Iron Bars] (2003) – in which the call for the subject's affirmation attains new levels: it involves the inmates in the actual process of filming and composing the sequence of images and points of view – that results in workshops on the operation of video equipment. The inmates faced the challenge with enthusiasm, integrating the process into their day-to-day activities, involving different, and already existing personal creative forms, even hobbies, which construe a work discipline and personal affirmation.

In this way, cinema does not simply register the cloistered life with its threats and dramas, but also sums up the things that go towards inventing the day-to-day, towards establishing a routine of varying practices. Among them: sports, music (the omnipresence of Rap as a means of inquiry into the world, by itself a complex field for insights), arts and crafts, services, commerce, communication with the outside world (letters and other objects to be sent out) – all pastimes which help to maintain a sense of humanisation, a commitment to carry out tasks which sustain self-esteem – an extremely difficult thing to do under conditions of confinement.

One symptomatic fact is the way in which, in the film, it is possible to construct a social fabric that seems to dispense with the institution. A fabric that is woven in the rifts of the direct action imposed upon the inmate. There are, in truth, interviews in some of the passages that denounce bad treatment, risks, absence of hospital treatment and medical care, manoeuvring to avoid eventual violence and retaliations, terrible food and humiliation. Then there is the register of notoriously illegal practices (such as selling drugs) that generate tensions, even though they bring relief to others, according to the prisoners. This nevertheless creates a plot which never comes to the forefront, since the film does not turn its attention to investigating the organisation (such as the *Terceiro Comando*[10] [*Third Command*]) which structures the disputes of power and claims. The incursion into day-to-day life is given precedence, and the prisoners are given the word and the perspective to create a self-portrait, in contrast to the impersonal numbers and codes imposed by the institution.

The word of order is: get close, sound out an internal point of view, get to know the experience better by means of conversations with, and images of those with names, to create a character before our eyes.[11]

The Recently Born: Childbirth as Affirmation of Life in the 'Recovery of Brazilian Cinema'

In the films released in 2002–2003 that we have discussed, the protagonists overcome, or find incisive forms of affirmation in, radical situations in which importance is given to drama and severity. For these survivors, to escape is to be reborn, which can be projected into a more ambitious metaphor on the social plane (when certain traditions or the institutional system are on the agenda). However, fiction has found other terms, and works the same metaphor of 'overcoming' (liberation) as birth, rebirth, in different contexts and tonalities of experience, as in the tragicomedy *Durval Discos* [*Durval Discs*] (2003). In this film, Anna Muylaert encounters a dialogue with the family strangeness already worked upon in Ana Carolina's films, affirming the metaphor in the bosom of a small family drama, in which a radical youngster, in his clinging to the past, ends up creating a new image of the survivor, in milder conditions.

This is instantaneously announced by means of a biblical parable. The passage of Jonah in the belly of the whale is evoked by the music

---

[10] Translator's note: *Terceiro Comando*: One of the main criminal organisations of the *favelas*, outskirts, and prisons.

[11] Coutinho's cinema constitutes the extreme point of this search for affirmation of the subject under diverse conditions. For further observation of what is produced as an idea of a person or character, see Ismail Xavier's '*Documentário e afirmação do sujeito:* Eduardo Coutinho counteracts resentment', in *Estudos de cinema* [Cinema Studies], SOCINE ANO IV, org. Afrânio Mendes Catani, Fernão Ramos, Mrairosaria Fabris et alli (São Paulo: Editora Panorama/FAPESP, 2003).

that punctuates the extraordinary opening sequential plane, in the Pinheiros district. A plane which defines the space in which the protagonist rejects the passing of time with his music shop which only sells old, long-playing vinyl records, and does not accept the era of the CD. The turning point, nevertheless, is the tale of the protagonist's life of confinement, and his life with his mother, which reinforces the idiosyncratic profile and the isolation of this domestic life. There are rituals, entertainment – the house serves for everything. We are dealing with another film with one single setting (with just one or two outside scenes), which ends up becoming tangled in social violence. The girl employed as maid, right at the start of her unfair contract (which only someone with other purposes in mind would possibly accept), leaves a young girl, a victim of a kidnapping, in the care of the boy and his mother.

The mother, like a whale, retains everything that falls into her entrails and initiates a psychodrama that turns into a theatre of the absurd in relation to the possession of the girl, whom the mother refuses to hand over, even when the situation of kidnap becomes clear. Even though he hesitates and delays his reaction, the son finally realises that he should put an end to this whale delusion. He calls the police and his gesture transforms the moment of the girl's (Kiki) rescue into the moment of the protagonist's release.

In not carrying out the wishes of the mother and delivering the girl, he leaves the womb; he survives, in the same way in which the victim of abduction does. Finally, he too is a victim, inside his own house, in a regressive symbiosis with a due date. As in the uterus, staying beyond the allotted time would be fatal. Durval finally manages to free himself, late in the day, from this maternal kidnapping, in counterpoint to the outside world, which happens perhaps in a kind of secret synchronicity with the changes in the neighbourhood that are expressed in the demolition of what was Durval's refuge, retreat and uterine prison.

Childbirth, a central metaphor, shifts into a literal presence in such films as *Latitude Zero* (Toni Venturini, 2002) and *Desmundo* (Alain Fresnot, 2002). In these, birth is a concrete fact in the diegesis, the denouement serving as a support for a figuration that, in each one of these films acquires a completely different sense. In these cases, we see a return to the type of treatment of space and dramatic situations in which the characters' individual (and family) experience is remitted to a wider social and historical plane. Be it because the couple in *Latitude* are isolated in a desert-like location, an 'aftermath' composed of the exhausted ruins of a former mineral exploration and source of wealth, or be it because *Desmundo* steps back to the 16th century to effectively compose a 'foundational narrative'.

They are films that tread on a terrain that has proved to be quicksand in the *Cinema de Retomada* [Cinema of the Recovery] – in relation to history – as I commented apropos, *Behind the Sun* by Walter Salles Jr. From the outset, *Latitude Zero* creates a laboratory with minimal resources, capable of reflecting on the most elementary relationships. A place at the end of the world, a restaurant-inn rendered useless by the collapse of the goldmines and economic activity. The highway remains, but no-one ever stops. Alone, the protagonist takes care, very badly, of the place and of her pregnancy. Hungering for sex, however, she is aggressive (at first) towards the first person who knocks on the door and is received as if ready for battle.

Her law is confrontation, she relates to other human beings as if she were in a jungle, a barbaric land, because she is full of resentment and mistrust. In her solitude, she has reached her human limits; she is a hermit without inclination towards the ascetic life. Everything is conflict, privation and aggression. The person who appears is a policeman in flight, sent to this 'end of the world' by his commander, an absent figure who is repeatedly mentioned, because he had some kind of relationship with the girl in the past. This person came to stay until things cooled down – he had murdered someone (this is a fact that she keeps to herself the whole time). Between attraction and hostility (always ready to emerge), she accepts this 'partner' in their occupation of the void and the relationship evolves. However, any attempts at colonising, to build a home and start a business there, prove to be mere illusion.

Disloyalties, his temporary disappearance, which leaves her alone at the moment of childbirth, lack of consideration for her recently born child (he has issues in this area, as he left behind a child and now is distilling his resentment), all brings the woman to confirm her mistrust and anger. In a desperate fit of drunken rage, she defends herself (or rather does what she deems necessary for the defence of the baby) and shoots him dead.

The catastrophe carried out, she burns the inn and abandons the place. She makes up an icon of the mother with child on her lap, survives and leaves the refuge in the name of her new function; she has the will to do this as she demonstrated in the solitude of the childbirth. Of the basic nucleus – a man, a woman and a child – neither was a family created nor a place civilised. She is resentful towards men, he is resentful towards life. The assignment failed. She hitches a lift in a lorry and distances herself from the building in flames, to erase the crime, the past and maybe to give a chance to the child in some other place – for here nothing remains.

The Woman as Prisoner and Mother against Barbarism

There exists a 'non-foundational narrative' in *Latitude Zero* in the sense of the inversion of the usual paradigm in which the myths of national foundation are focalised, in literature and the cinema. Starting with family dramas, the characters, by their strategic position, acquire a symbolic dimension as focal points of a formation, according to rules which, in the majority of cases, celebrate the birth of a nation as a melodrama – nothing but an extension of family and blood ties (let us be reminded of Griffith).

In *Latitude Zero*, from the outset, nothing is created. Above all because the masculine figure is not adapted to such an undertaking, beyond all of the non-viabilities of the geographical location, tending to desert. Alain Fresnot's film *Desmundo* (2002), on the contrary, ends with a childbirth that serves as another reference in the face of the varying settings of the foundational narratives, which deal with the settlement in the new land in the 16th century, of those who commanded the rustic colonial undertaking, enslaved the Indians, had sex with their wives, and assumed a lifestyle which shocked the church. We are nevertheless dealing with the drama of birth, but the bill makes it clear that the objective is to explore contradictions and ironies outside the usual frame of idealisations, which this type of tale usually contains.

We start from the framework of sexual promiscuity in the life of the colony in the 16th century, a space of liberation and domination that so disturbed the priests who adhered more to moral precepts (a theme of historians such as Paulo Prado and Gilberto Freyre). The story begins when virgin orphans arrive in the New World, sent there with the blessing of the church, with the mission of transforming adventurers into patriarchs, founders of a new Christian society whose hidden story was built on ocean crossings such as these.

The film features Oribela, the girl who does not accept the conditions imposed upon her, a rebellion that makes her an outcast in this world of obedience. Proudly, she states: 'I am not a stubble', 'I am not an animal'. It falls to Francisco de Alburquerque to subdue her. Of few words, she reveals her dreams by means of gestures, as when she pats the woman's stomach in the hope of a sign, while she, also in silence, conceives plans to flee. These plans, once put into practice, lend a coming and going movement to *Desmundo* – between the *sertão* and the ocean. An alternating scenario that is articulated with others, on workdays and during the long tense nights; a congeniality conducted with mute gestures of command, appeals for understanding and patience. An arrangement, which is sometimes oppressive, sometimes tender (since Francisco loves his wife, apart from the harsh treatment in the game of power).

Oribela always brings the ocean with her, the hope of return. Once, her dream is projected onto the figure of Ximeno Dias, the New Christian who gives her shelter and affection, and her first happy sexual experience, which draws a rare smile on her grave countenance (the suggestion of a fertility which will echo later). It is between that hope of liberation and Francisco's stabilising power that *Desmundo's* biggest conflict springs. Confinement and expansion: *sertão* (fixation) and ocean (liberty) newly opposing in Brazilian cinema to define the destiny of the feminine figure, as Francisco's movement is 'in gear for the west', like a *Protopaulista*[12] from the north coast of what is nowadays the State of São Paulo, a coarse man who wishes to free himself of priests and even the crown. Twice attempting to escape, twice recaptured, Oribela has to accept Ximeno's death and Francisco's victory.

Desmundo is a suggestive title for this tale of the history of birth in the tropics, a childbirth which condenses the idea of the stabilisation of a social contract initiated forcibly, as lived by the prisoner who along his trajectory sees his presence in the New World change his senses, without redeeming facilities. The style of representation is serious, composed of a

---

[12] Translator's note: Protopaulista: Paulista is someone born in the State of São Paulo. *Proto*, from Greek, previous, anterior. It refers to a settler in the area that was later to become São Paulo.

dry appropriation of a code recovered from classic cinema, competently conducted with excellent art direction, which avoids the conventional and is not directed towards the spectacularisation of history. The perspective of the film is neither epic nor nationalistic, since the point of view is of the captive woman who absorbs the blows and ends up inserting herself into the order of things, carrying out the role that is expected of her.

The contradictory situation and the dramatic/serious treatment serve as a repositioning of a realism difficult to find nowadays in the historic film, more given to comedy and the satiric vision of the colonial period, sometimes restoring the good humour of Oswald de Andrade's *Anthropophagy* which dominated the cinema between the years 1968 to 1975. Contrary to this, Alain's film, from the beginning to the end is dominated by the tonality of pain, the rhythm of anguish, the sombre gaze that must evaluate what encircles and constrains, as Oribela does. Re-treading a soil already weary of mythical paths, *Desmundo* moves against the grain of the mirage of joyous sex in the tropics, or of the complacent readings of Gilberto Freyre. It exposes the violence of the consolidated colonial family. The farm in its budding phase, a sombre, rustic world, a place of the better administrated search for wealth (after the first moments of the colonies).

The couple who come together in the finale do not unite either because they love each other or because in the destiny of the romantic couple, a union is accomplished which is projected into the community, and on the happy couple lies the promise of what will be the future. We are dealing with the formation of the family and reproduction. It was for this reason she came from Europe. She was brought against her will, she stays against her will to live a difficult experience, well expressed in the childbirth scene (squatting as the Indians do) when her face carries the scream of pain while she receives noteworthy help from the Indians, and local wisdom hints about the essential things of life.

They receive the baby with smiles and friendliness in a ritual that aims to ease the mother's pains. In this symbolic moment, Oribela and the Indians compose the image of the experience of the affirmation of life in extreme conditions, there where continuity is made and the future is announced, even in the wake of a constraint, an acknowledged *fait accompli*. With resentment she finally recognises that her destiny is to live within this mixture of prison and shelter, which the final image of *Desmundo* condenses so well into the hammock, in which she and her baby are harboured. A displacement which we are unsure as to its being a routine episode by the sea or a moment of another step in the direction of the *Planalto Paulista*,[13] to sediment a colonisation project.

Oribela's face in the foreground traces the image of the woman as prisoner and mother, out there carrying out the civilising mission, which the foundational narratives attribute to her, almost always with milder plots, and celebrations, which extinguish the actual nature of what was oppression in the course of history. And Brazilian cinema gives another expression, now on a more all-embracing historical plane, to what has

---

[13] Translator's note: Planalto Paulista: The higher lands of the plateau, where the city of São Paulo was to be built later.

been a stimulus for most recent urban films and which observes the current combination of events. It features the poles of resistance to barbarism, in an impulse to reflect its own image of cinema and art as a means of salvation in the face of a social order with an agenda of inequality, concentration of power, and violence.

Oribela is the projection of all of this in a film, which makes the archaeology of the patriarchal Brazilian family and turns over its subsoil of violence. She, in her way, is a humaniser of the inevitable, that is, of globalisation in the 16th century.

Translation by Maurice Blackford

PART II
RESPONSES TO FERNANDO MEIRELLES'S
CITY OF GOD

13. Screening *City of God* [1]
Luiz Inácio Lula da Silva

This week in São Paulo I watched the preview of a good film: *City of God*, directed by Fernando Meirelles and inspired by the novel of the same name by Paulo Lins. It is a dive straight into the guts of the excluded youth of a Rio *favela* – in fact, a poor people's housing area, of simple architecture, constructed by Governor Carlos Lacerda between 1962 and 1965 and today home to 120,000 people. Across three generations, the narrative documents the evolution of growing levels of violence.

What is seen on the screen are simple lives that have been ground down to a level without horizons – other than that which can be seen through the sights of a gun. The target is the very image of each character caught in the bloody and daily fight for the drug dens.

The best thing about the film, which is edited with mesmerising rhythm, is that it does not descend into a mere theoretical social discourse. The emptiness – and the blood that fills it – speaks for itself. In the *favela*, where the state is absent, except for the occasional robberies of an ill-prepared and equally brutal police, the social and psychological dynamic begins to be controlled by the worst element in the universe of the excluded periphery: mad and unrestrained violence, within which the logic of death comes to dominate.

However, *City of God* is not a pessimistic film. In the place of defeatism, between the debris and the lacerated bodies, what emerges is the twinkle in the eyes of Buscapé [Rocket], a young boy saved by a camera, with which he documents the hell that is the *City of God*. And, incredible as it may sound, he manages to catch a glimpse beyond this hell – which may be the only hope of escape for millions of other 'Buscapés' – through art, culture and ultimately public policies that transform such situations.

Violence begins before the police enter the story. It is not worth simply trying to combat it only with more weapons and more police. When the police arrive, they will see that the criminal is ready. This is why our Public Security Program for Brazil also includes culture as a method for combating delinquency.

There are proposals at the federal, state and municipal levels of government. There is also a clear distinction between what can be done immediately, without waiting for legislative changes, and what will require constitutional changes. And there are, still, clear measures to promote the efficiency of the police and the indispensable participation of the communities' citizens in dealing with the problems of public security.

This means that the project can meet the task of confronting the current criminality and violence, that is, those who are already leading a life of crime, and also propose effective measures to prevent others from being attracted to or won over by criminals. In this case, we need to

---

[1] Editor's note: This text was produced when Luiz Inácio Lula da Silva was the candidate of the Partido dos Trabalhadores [PT – Worker's Party] for the Presidency of Brazil. In a landmark election, the polls soon confirmed him as the first working class president in the history of the country.

mobilise the whole of society, particularly the youth who are already citizens, to compete with organised criminals and drug dealers for the millions of youths living in the suburbs and the *favelas* of our cities who want to lead a dignified life, but who are constantly harassed by criminals.

The absence of the State – in terms of schools, leisure, and employment – can transform housing estates like Cidade de Deus into a site of banishment, places where poor people are concentrated in order that they do not to disturb the peace of the other section of the country that is socially included.

Our government programme does not overlook direct investment in police training, equipment and structural improvement. But this is not enough. Either the State invests heavily in policies designed to integrate the youth or we might as well give up. The State has to be the architect of hope for children and young people.

How might we accomplish this goal? By deciding, acting and negotiating. Brazil's problem is not only economic. It seems economic. But it is political. 'Cities of God' exist in many regions of our country. This is not a merely economic problem, but the fruit of political choices. Available money leaks out because the government's priority is not and has not been social policy.

The writer Paulo Lins, also present at the preview, spent his youth in Cidade de Deus and took ten years to finish his book. He told me that in this period the violence worsened, the gunfire escalated, and the age of initiation into crime grew younger. Just last year three hundred new *favelas* emerged in the city of Rio de Janeiro. Lins's new literary project intends to chronicle this absurd growth in violence that has already invaded Rio's Zona Sul.[2] It is not for nothing that Governor Benedita da Silva, who took on the state in such precarious conditions, is paying so much attention to public security.

More barbarism or solid investments in public policies? What other option does Brazil have?

Luiz Inácio Lula da Silva
President of Honour of the Partido dos Trabalhadores – PT [Worker's Party] and Councillor of the Citizenship Institute

Translation by Juliet Line

---

[2] Editor's note: in the marked social divide of Rio de Janeiro, Zona Sul [Southern Zone] is associated with the upper middle and upper classes, the impressive architecture along the coast and the city's beach culture. It contrasts with Zona Norte [Northern Zone] which tends to be working-class and has *favelas* uphill.

14. City of God and of the Devil
Luiz Eduardo Soares

City of God, directed by Fernando Meirelles and co-directed by Katia Lund, based on the novel-testimony of the same name by Paulo Lins, is an extraordinary film. The book is a remarkable tapestry within which short and obscure biographies are woven, constructing the history of violence in Rio de Janeiro from the 1960s onwards. The ocean of tragedies in which we find ourselves shipwrecked today was once the localised drama of a few boys trampled by the brutality and shamelessness of the police. The latter, in turn, were protected by the ferocity of the military dictatorship in the context of the state's neglect of the suburbs and *favelas*.

After the period in which (almost) innocent thefts and robberies prevailed, drug- and arms-trafficking and the cavalry that today we know so well, imposed themselves. The film, faithful to the book, relates the human and social complexity of this progression with sensitivity and realism. The behaviour of the protagonists in the 'romantic' phase of urban violence was a rebellious deviant of the cultural codes that prevailed in the community. Basic principles were not questioned, either in feeling or in practice. The authority of the elder ruled. The family remained the decisive point of reference. Vanity was satisfied by an extra handful of *cruzeiros*[1] and the coveted girlfriend. Yet the feeling of pride derived from transgression was subordinate to the shame caused by society's criticism of the deviant act revealed. No one thought about killing or assaulting. No one dared abuse anything besides property, and even then only in miniscule degrees by our current standards. The fear of the father, of the community's judgement and of the police exceeded the will to break the rules of the game. Today criminals follow their own rules inspired by the pacts that govern marginal organisations.

In spite of the stigmas, the community still managed to retain the natural respect that exists in any human group that fulfils its duties, and gives shelter to its members. For the boys who robbed, belonging to the community was enough of a disguise; indeed, all that was needed, in order to trick the police, was to mingle with the players in the middle of a football game on the vacant lot. The owner of the corner shop turned people in and was feared; he was not labelled a 'grass' to be humiliated and sacrificed. The drug of choice was still marijuana, the contemplative and innocuous stimulus of street roguery – it was not cocaine, that insatiable fuel of anxiety. Smoking was the opposite of the snowballing omnipotence that today blows up boundaries. Children were reprimanded with a tap on the head and by the playfulness of adolescence – not with gunshots to hands and feet. Violent death was rare, shocking and surprising. And crimes of passion were the result of the Northeastern migrant's pride that would not stand for adultery. The desire to transgress was the biggest sin; woman was the main victim.

The first professional dealers set up drug retail businesses that,

---

[1] Editor's note: Brazilian currency at the time.

117

distinct from the previous predatory practices, were more sedentary than nomadic, inasmuch as a fixed headquarters is required to permit economic success. Besides, it needs to root itself in a territory that is protected and able to guarantee consumers' safety. In other words, retail dealing, of the type established in Rio de Janeiro, does not sell its product furtively on dark street corners, whispering in the ear of potential clients. Drugs are sold in the *bocas* [dens]. These are defended against possible competitors by the use of weapons, the organisation required to use them, and the ability to impose upon the local society a system of power with sufficient authority to control and limit the use of force and thus the occurrence of crimes. These are the bases upon which local armed tyrannies are erected, arbitrary and trigger-happy, whose cruelty is rivalled only by corrupt sectors of the police.

Instead of leaving the community to rob (the film describes the attack on a motel, the pinnacle of the audacity that characterised 'the Golden Years') the new protagonist, the professional dealer, awaits the visits of the 'junkies', represented by Thiago [Tiago], the addict who ends up being drawn into the drug trade. Before the motel robbery, the boys, more scared than their victims, make an oath: they will not kill. They want fun and money. They enjoy risk and are fascinated by their own cunning. They are not murderers. Their prowess lies in dodging the law and its guards, penetrating a space forbidden to them for economic reasons and inverting the scene that encapsulates our social hierarchy. If events do not go according to the script it is because the future had already insinuated, developing in the broken-hearted child who is the new character in embryo. The future was already among them, cultivated by Dadinho's [Li'l Dice] resentment in anticipation of the rupture that Zé Pequeno [Li'l Zé] will introduce into the narrative. The Hamlet-esque meeting with the *Quimbanda*[2] priest symbolically inaugurates the new era with the baptism that actualises the previously intuited and gestated project: Dadinho receives the name Zé Pequeno and becomes the focus of the world that emerges. Malediction suddenly shakes the ironic tone of the name of the neighbourhood condemned to its own misery. The city, now, is of the Devil. The cinematographic language punctuates the new imaginary horizon: the Devil among us brings with him the discursive vortex that pulls together the plot's several threads. Previously, the plot had been propelled by the centripetal impulse of the growing dramatic possibilities and by the broadening of the characters' paths. With the rupture, the centrifugal and increasingly claustrophobic dramatic force gravitates around the diabolic axis. Zé Pequeno is the magnetic nucleus of the plot who withdraws into the den that he conquers. He shifts Cenoura's [Carrot] role to that of counterpoint, antipode to Zé within the sphere of evil. Acting as a prop to Zé's role of protagonist and structurally an equivalent to Bené [Benny], the 'nice-guy-dealer', full of good will. Bené is the 'coolest', most respected and liked bandit in the community; he literally puts his neck on the line to avoid conflicts, protect life and

---

[2] Editor's note: Afro-Brazilian cult, also known as *Macumba,* characterised by black magic and the conjuring up of mainly lower spirits, known as the 'obsessors'. It opposes *Umbanda.*

defend innocents. His destiny delivers him redemption before death (as he is killed by mistake). In other words, his trajectory leads him to discover the virtues of love and a pacifist way of life, the celebration of which fills the stage with the tragedy hastened by a twist of fate – a *carioca*[3] version of the classic matrix. This end defines the feeling of claustrophobia also in the sphere of morality: the good-bad dialectics no longer applies. Nothing resists this homogenising logic: Bené dies and Mané Galinha [Knockout Ned], who plays the role of the vengeful hero, ends up being absorbed. In seeking revenge, he allows himself to be co-opted and reproduces the dynamic of which he had been a victim. He ends up getting caught up by his own trajectory reflected in the mirror: he gave up his job in order to gain revenge for the cruelty to which he fell victim, but has now broken his promise never to kill innocents, thereby condemning the son of his victim to reproduce his own trajectory. Reflecting destinies cross paths in death.

Victim and torturer continually meet and swap positions, until the very distinction loses meaning, because it is the agency itself that dissolves in the inexorable reproduction of the dynamic set in motion. The only subject of this story is the self-devouring and homogenising greed that unfolds it as one, identical to itself, without porosity, contradiction and dialectics: there is no lucky escape, no change of quality or transforming synthesis. The triumph of the police will eventually be the victory of one more infamy that will contaminate Buscapé [Rocket] (the narrator-photographer and cinematic replica of the narrator-writer of the book by Paulo Lins). In the film, the narrator will have to be the wily chaser of images, an Antonioni of the tropics whose professional success will cost him the role of silent accomplice, demanding the omission of the most revealing photographs. Buscapé-narrator makes the painful journey of losses: from the girl he desires to fame, whose price will be the risk of death. Opening and closing the film, in a truly memorable scene, the dove of peace submits itself to the collage of aesthetic invention. In this cacophony of symbols and sensitivities, serving the cultural sublimation that substitutes Oswaldian *Anthropophagy*[4] for post-modern ironic dislocation, this dove transforms itself into the chicken that escapes decapitation, slipping deftly between the hands, knives and bullets whizzing uncontrollably through the *favela*, eagerly dodging the police van's tyres only to find itself captured by the narrator, at the moment when he divides the road, and is himself divided internally, between the police and the gangsters, all criminals and all partners in this infernal business. We do not know the eventual fate of the chicken, and whether it is turned into a feast. Mané Galinha did not have another chance. We know that the narrator sacrificed the Truth for a life without risk – giving us, paradoxically, this unforgettable film that unmasks what he disguises. Peace and freedom return to the banquet for the sacrifice. The police sell

---

[3] Editor's note: pertaining to Rio de Janeiro.
[4] The anthropophagic metaphor is the core one of the *Anthropophagous Manifesto* by Oswald de Andrade and of Brazilian Modernism (1920s) which set out to 'digest' all the positive foreign influences and combine them with Brazilian input. The idea was to create a new language and a new cultural identity.

arms and freedom to the criminals. But now it is the children who assume power, only to dice with death – perverse and extremely fragile little gods. Fate proceeds without a way out, down the street, down the throat, between hands, knives and bullets, whizzing desperately through the *favela...* after what?

What magic the directors worked to turn little boys into great actors, I do not know. All I know is that a masterpiece like *City of God* teaches us one lesson: in looking closely through the keyhole, with the persistent voyeurism of the photographer-narrator, with the acute sensitivity of the directors and the author of the book, it becomes possible for us to understand that behind the story there is a History of violence and a cruel Brazilian capitalism; behind the story there lie plenty of smaller stories. Each of these stories is the size of one of us, lived by characters very similar to us, or possessing some of our subjective dimensions, performing some of our possible lives. The confused and entangled result of the individual plots carries the same dose of humanity of which we too are capable. For better or worse. Neither more, nor less.

Translation by Juliet Line and Nádia Alves

15. Cidade de Deus: History's Silent Protagonist[1]
M V Bill

Art, Screen, Poetry: Meditations on *City of God* (December 2004)

I have never meant to be the messenger of truth, even if my name suggests otherwise.[2] Actually, the only truth that I want to stand for is my own truth. Many people share my multiple truths, and this 'family' has increased a great deal in the last few years.

I was born and raised in Cidade de Deus, a community that I learned to respect, about which I have a dream: I dream of helping the people of the *favela* find a goal. These are people who lack self-esteem, who lack health, and who lack peace. They are people who have been cut off from all emancipation mechanisms; they are people who have never been regarded as people.

Even regarding this dream, I do not picture myself, as I write these lines, as a rightful representative of Cidade de Deus, since I have not been elected to speak on its behalf. Thus, there may be some people who disagree with me, a natural fact in a fake democracy.

When I made my concerns public, during the film's debut, I did it for a single reason: to give a voice to the people of the *favela*, who up to that moment had never been heard on the issue.[3] I have never meant to disrespect, and even now do not mean to, the film's or the story's owners. But I have always felt that those strangers to us all had to find a channel of communication between the capital that they represent and the poverty and violence that they reproduced through this film. We cannot forget that those in the film exist as real people, and that this *favela* exists, that the families and the people who suffer these evils exist.

By this, I do not mean to say that the producers and directors of *City of God* have to share the film's proceeds with the *favela*, or that everyone is supposed to think the way people in the *favelas* do. Not at all. But for a film that intends to provoke, in Brazil and in the world, a meditation on poverty, and, as a direct consequence, the violence that it produces, the first concern for the film's producers and directors should be to bring alternatives and hope to the people in the *favela*. At the very least, the film-makers should organise humanitarian discussions about ways of providing better living conditions for those whose lives they disclosed to the world. Brazilian *favelas*, and maybe *favelas* throughout

---

[1] Editor's note: On the last day of 2004, M V Bill, in response to my invitation, dedicated some of his precious time and, in a much appreciated gesture, especially on such a date, revisited his meditations on what he considers the important issues interconnecting the population of the *favela* Cidade de Deus and the film *City of God*. Two years before, at the height of the debate around the film in Brazil, M V Bill had used the website *Viva Favela* (www.vivafavela.com.br) and other media to draw attention to these issues (messages included here).

[2] Editor's note: The initials M V in his name stand for 'Mensageiro da Verdade', in English 'Messenger of Truth'.

[3] Editor's note: M V Bill, in the message of January 22nd 2003 (see below), raises public concerns that the film has brought a bigger stigma rather than any social, moral, or human benefit to the *favela*.

the world, are large cradles of ignorance and depression, because there one finds the 'human cast-offs', the most desperate families on the planet. This is where one sees the largest display of misery. This fact makes 'men from the asphalt'[4] think that they may satisfy us by allowing us to appear in their films; for some even to get a tip or a wage may be enough. This may satisfy some who are hopeless, or even some who have a flair for acting and may be willing to take part in the film. I myself would have participated if there had been a well-defined and humane policy of return for the community; I would even have left if I had been participating and the promises were not fulfilled. What I mean is that my criticism is not because I like to criticise for the sake of criticising, but it is to claim a right.

I expressed my views because up to that moment, I was one of the few people who would be heard outside the frontiers of Cidade de Deus. At that time, the only people who had taken a position on the film were the critics. But for us in the Cidade de Deus this was not enough. The film would tour the cinema circles, and then it would no longer be like any other film – but the history of Cidade de Deus would be even more doomed to failure, to neglect.

I could write about many points of view that I think are correct or at least consistent, but I am going to finish with saying that I surrendered to Brazilian hip-hop, which is moved by a social and political practice. I studied at CUFA, which is Brazil's largest hip-hop organisation. There are no half-measures there; you either believe it or give your life for it, or you kill yourself.   '

I have nothing against films or against this film in particular, but I think respect towards the community was missing. I may prefer to believe that it was because those involved with the film were too busy to think. The fact is, I agree, that no film can solve the problems in the lives of the people depicted in it, but all films must offer some hope to the sick when they make money or receive a lot of prestige (which is a type of capital); it is the same when films tell stories about mental institutions. It is a simple human rule: render unto Cæsar the things which are Cæsar's, give the *favela* what is the *favela*'s. And the only thing that the *favela* has asked for is love and respect.

I am sure that today people would think twice and pay more attention, because the only thing that the *favela* has is poverty and suffering. The film-makers cannot take this human degradation and transform it into art with the resources of the State (in the form of tax incentives), and ignore that this selfsame *favela* is not assisted by this same State.

That's it. We want to love the film, but we could not accept that Cidade de Deus would be forgotten exactly at the point it was the protagonist of history.

---

[4] Editor's note: A distinction is established here between 'men from the asphalt', meaning those who live in the urbanised areas and benefit from access to all services and those who live otherwise in the unpaved *favelas* uphill.

The Bomb Is Gonna Blow Up (January 22nd 2003)

This text is gonna be blunt and tough!!!

I gave Paulo Lins, Katia Lund, VideoFilmes, 02, Globo Filmes and all their allies a chance to revert and re-think their social attitude in relation to the community of Cidade de Deus. Everybody knows what I'm talking about. I have never made open criticisms about the film. I just said, and I repeat, that *City of God*, the film, would win an Oscar, and that our *favela* would win an Oscar for violence.

However, nobody has done anything about it; they continue to ignore people's capacity to think. A war seems inevitable! I have just pressed the button. Now, let's just wait for the countdown... I shall begin with a press conference on February 6th, at the *favela* itself. Those interested in participating may enrol by telephone [...] I warn you that I am going to call everybody to the battlefront. The whole world is going to know that this film has brought no good to the *favela*, no social, moral, or human benefit. The world will know that they exploited the image of the children who live here at Cidade de Deus. What is obvious is that they are going to carry a bigger stigma throughout their lives; it has only become greater because of the film. They turned our people into stereotypes, and they have given them nothing in exchange. Even worse, they stereotyped them as fiction and sold it as if it were true.

I remained silent about it, no doubt. Out of respect for Katia Lund and for Paulo Lins, due to our friendship. But I believe that my behaviour was unworthy, and I was not faithful to my principles, to my origin, to my community, and even more, I betrayed my own conscience.

All of them know we do not want any money. We only want respect. They, the owners of *City of God*,' the film, have the media's support. But in our case, unfortunately, the support of hatred is the only thing left to us. I did not want to show off, so much so that here, in this same space, I never said anything. But then, who would? I take this role upon myself. Somebody has to tell them this. And I am just doing that!

The newspaper *A Folha de São Paulo* itself has just published an article on the community, but I refused to say anything to them, once again out of respect for my friends and in order not to stir the community. I did not speak – not because I was not aware of my responsibility. But now I am tired. It is about time we put the blame where it belongs without being concerned about the consequences. What is right is right, what is wrong is wrong.

On February 6th the chaos will begin!

Certain authorities, after learning about my position, started to understand our feelings of neglect and started mobilising, but I still feel it is not enough. The Mayor may do much for Cidade de Deus; he may carry out 200 projects, the National Secretary for Security may carry on another 200. I hope they do since it has been promised.

But the humiliation that we are enduring may serve as an example for other communities of misery. If someday, somebody should transform their lives into a circus, tell them to demand a reward to match, even if it is simply the role of a clown. This way, at least some cheer will be guaranteed.

If a third of what Celso Athayde said about Hermano Viana is true (in which case, I will have to reconsider my opinions about scholars, since I have had some reservations about them), Cidade de Deus will be forever indebted to Hermano. Cidade de Deus is going to learn that this bloke, Hermano, when he expressed his opinion in our favour, had the guts to come to the *favela* last Saturday, to debate with the locals, at night, under the pouring rain (he must be crazy!). More than this, he had the courage even to confront the 'friends' (he's a crank). After that, he discovered that the community wanted no more than affection.

February 6th is coming. But first I must talk with the people of the *favela* to see what they think.

Again, I thank the Mayor for his support and the same must be said of the Secretary and of Hermano. But 'the film' must also take a position. They have to sit at this table, and re-think the meaning of the word 'love'. Then I will be able to see Cidade de Deus happily waiting for the Oscar to be awarded to the film, with a reason to celebrate. Because, up to now, the police have been the only ones to benefit from our misery pictured in 35 mm!

02 and VideoFilmes: 'God exists and only He can help with the Oscar, but maybe it would be convenient to count on the prayers of His City'.

See you.

It Is Possible to Build a New Mentality (January 24th 2003)

Many years ago, many people promised they would do for Cidade de Deus what the community needed. But nothing happened! Then, the film came along; it has its merits (I have already talked about them). It also has errors (I have also talked about them). It does not matter, because nobody has done anything to change our reality. No one! Not even me! What is the right attitude? Does anybody know? I do not think so, right? If I knew, I would already have said so!

I am not, and I do not intend to be, the unanimous voice in my own home, let alone in the Cidade de Deus. I knew very well the risk I was running when I decided to write in a more aggressive way. I knew that many would understand, but not others. But I also knew it was the only way out.

City of God, the film, was a success, but the Cidade de Deus remained the same – without the electricity it deserved. I am not blaming anyone for it. I also know that Brazil has so many problems, so many *favelas*, that the government could not set Cidade de Deus as its priority. But this was our turn, our moment. Our ship was on its course, but our dream was being sent adrift.

I agree that the film was important for Brazil; I recognise that. But having the film as a starting point was also our only chance to change our history and the history of Cidade de Deus.

The film went out into the world, sold tickets, stirred the public, and was the reason for celebration. Great! The film toured the world and fulfilled its role. But, here, nothing changed. Blaming it all on the politicians was easier. We had done this all our lives. The issue was how to turn the discussion that had been generated into a form of investment. It was our turn, my friend. It is a matter of now or never. If the film wanted to provoke a debate, it managed to do so. If it wanted to make the problem surface, it has done so! If the film wanted to show this to the world, it did!

But for those who live outside our community, the discussion was mainly on technicalities. We never mobilised in order to reverse the picture!

Discussion was restricted to whether Li'l Zé was black or not, if he was darker or lighter! If the film was shot at Cidade de Deus or not. If the story told was true or mere fiction! But in a few days, the film will be gone from the theatres and that will be the end of the story. So our only real chance for change will end. The *favela* has just accepted a lift on history's train, but the rails also belong to the community!

I knew I would run the risk of being accused of showing off, but I also knew that Mr John Doe, the bartender, or Ms. No One, who sold home-made sweets on the streets, would never appear.

Today the film may say that it is fulfilling its role; those involved may say in their CVs that the movie helped change the reality it showed. You may say that it meddled with our sense of honour, so the people who live there have responded to the bugle call, and thus have had their claims attended to. This is not a dream; it is a fact.

But now it is time to celebrate, it is time to give thanks, it is time to party! We have already won some unimaginable partnerships. Several ministries and secretariats are already mobilising, making commitments to the *favela*, making it the landmark of change. And other ministries are joining in.

The Press Conference

What is going to take place on February 6th at Cidade de Deus is nothing more than a ceremony for the signing of a letter of commitment, a national crusade, so that all participants may publicly formalise their participation!

We are sure that the firms that sponsored the film will also participate in this crusade and will show the other faces of our community, the positive things that we also have.

This is the last time I will speak about this issue. If you want opinions about the film, ask cinema critics and the film's creators. If you want to know what kind of benefits the film ended up generating, look at the list of partners we now have:

Brazilian and International Press
Rio's City Hall
Federal Government
State Government
City of God (Production; we're waiting for you too, Katia, Paulo, Fernando and others).
Ministry of Culture
Secretariat for Housing
Secretariat of Labour
Special Secretariat for Events
Ministry of Social Action

Community
Hip-Hop Movement
Cultural Group Afro-Reggae
Viva Rio Movement

If you want information about the needs in our community, call up the community leaderships at Cidade de Deus. They do not have space in the media, but they have a big heart waiting for you.

If it is possible to move so many people through a mere e-mail, I then believe it is possible to build a new mentality, starting from this historic moment – I do not know if it is possible for Brazil, but it certainly is for Cidade de Deus.

Translation by Edson Martins Lopes

16. *Cities of God* and Social Mobilisation
Paulo Lins

It was not an e-mail from M V Bill that mobilised a number of people around the problems of Cidade de Deus,[1] the *favela* in the neighbourhood of Jacarepaguá, Rio de Janeiro, but the 10 years that it took me to write the novel *Cidade de Deus* [*City of God*] and five more that it took director Fernando Meirelles and team to make it into a film. This film has won a prize more valuable than a likely Academy Award by becoming a box-office hit with more than three million domestic viewers, and by provoking intense debates, nationally and internationally, around themes such as poverty, racism, and violence. As can be seen, the research, book and film are all fated to continue to stir social mobilisation.

The statement that nobody does anything for the *favela* Cidade de Deus is a misconception. I lived there from 1966 to 1994, and at a young age I engaged myself in social, cultural and scientific projects (black people movements, community councils, academic tutoring, film club, carnival groups, music festivals, the creation of a public library in my own home and an assistantship to the anthropological survey carried out at the *favela* Cidade de Deus by Doctor Alba Zaluar, a scholar much respected in Brazil and abroad). However, I do not want to boast because many people, both those living in the *favela* and outsiders, have already developed or have been developing social and cultural projects. Actually, many people have promoted and still promote many positive actions in Cidade de Deus. I do not want to mention names so as not to forget anyone.

The anthropological research, in which I took part, and which I consider, among all my works, the most important one, depended on Alba Zaluar's efforts to get me a grant to allow me to go back to college life and develop a novel about criminality in the *favela* Cidade de Deus in the sixties, seventies, and eighties. Zaluar followed the readings, gave lectures, and organised debates about our research topic. To finish the work, I also received the support of literary critic Roberto Schwarz and the Vitae Foundation.

It was not easy to write the novel. Besides the remarkable intellectual effort and the extreme shortage of money, the object of research was intrinsically weighty, but even so I plunged into the vast ethnographic research with the people living in the *favela*, who were directly or indirectly involved with crime and criminality, and with the inmates at the Lemos de Brito Penitentiary and at Frei Caneca Prison. Besides the ethnographic survey, I also researched the newspapers *O Globo*, *Jornal do Brasil*, *O Dia*, *O Povo*, *Jornal dos Esportes*, and examined the archives of the Secretariat for Public Security (of the State of Rio de Janeiro). After several interruptions in the narrative process, finally, in 1997 *Cidade de Deus* was published.

Every literary work is, before anything else, fiction, since it is an

---

[1] Editor's note: Paulo Lins is responding to the messages that M V Bill produced in January 2003 (see previous chapter).

artistic creation. And like *City of God*, there are several other books based on real facts, and, since they are art, they must be allowed poetic licence. Any schoolboy knows that poetic licence is used to give the work rhythm, to elaborate the narrative, to create the plot and the suspense, to establish the difference between an account and art, finally to thrill the reader. Both in the film and in the book, this poetic licence was used in order to achieve such artistic goals.

The film is true to the reality of the large Brazilian cities. In 2002, I visited several *favelas* in Brazil, and the people living there told me they identified themselves with *City of God*'s narrative, saying that it looked like their own story. It was the same from north to south in Brazil, including *Capão Redondo*,[2] the very home of Férrez[3] and Mano Brown,[4] who told me the same thing. Anywhere in Brazil, the outskirts of the cities are *favela*-like gatherings. I was talking to Brown yesterday and he praised the film and told me that the book was pure poetry and real life, which made me very proud, of course, since I consider the band *Racionais MCs* one of the most serious and critical hip-hop groups in Brazil, and Mano Brown the greatest name of social art that this country has ever known.

The former governor of the State of Rio de Janeiro and now a minister in President Lula's staff, Benedita da Silva, told me, after seeing the film, that she had seen *City of God* all her life, and that she had already lost two relatives in the urban violence of Brazil. She added that the film *City of God* was her own life.

Obviously, neither the film nor the novel faithfully follow the history of criminality that exists in Cidade de Deus, otherwise they would be a documentary and an historical work. Rather the film and the novel are based on social reality that brings 'our degradation to light' and stirs political action to change the world. The Russian poet Mayakovsky has referred to the artist's duty as that of carving the log that is to become the human head. My commitment is with reality in the work of art, and not immediately with the historical reality that we want to change. One historical mistake here or there does not alter the political load of the work.

My communion with art is political. I have nothing against those who do not have this commitment. In art, everything is possible and that is why it is art. Thus, I do not accept (and with total legitimacy, I believe) that any mortal being, happy or unhappy, can say what can be done or what cannot be done in art, since art stretches through the eras of all

---

[2] Editor's note: Capão Redondo is a most violent district, made up of four neighbourhoods in the periphery of São Paulo. This is one of the many areas that have given rise to marginal art as the foremost creative artistic trend in Brazil over the last two decades.

[3] Editor's note: Férrez is the pen name of Reginaldo Ferreira da Silva (born in São Paulo in 1975), a marginal writer and a resident of the Capão Redondo who became known through his work concerning this neighbourhood.

[4] Editor's note: Mano Brown (Pedro Paulo Soares da Silva, 30) is a radical rap artist who lives between Capão Redondo and Vila do Fundão. He is a member of the group 'Racionais MCs', which acts as a mouthpiece for the black community via its association with 'committed rap' that addresses the problems of marginalisation.

humankind.

To be precise, there is nothing new in the film *City of God*. Every day the news programmes throw at us a picture of the chaos in which we live. Katia Lund and João Moreira Salles's documentary *Notícias de Uma Guerra Particular* [*News from a Personal War*] had already fulfilled the proposed goal of the film *City of God*, and, even though the public for documentaries is very small in Brazil, it caused some impact when it was released because it was a work of art. Thus, it attracted a larger audience.

The characters depicted in the film, based on real people, had already gained public visibility in the Brazilian press by the time the researched facts surfaced. The film itself, for example, shows an interview with Mané Galinha [Knockout Ned] given to Rede Globo [Globo TV Network]. But the press does not have the power to stir emotions and to surprise that a work of art has; that is the reason for the controversy.

My commitment as a writer was to look for the imaginary of those who were socially segregated. And, for the sake of verisimilitude, it was to call attention to the appalling inequities of income distribution in Brazil, to spur the creation of forums about racism, to reprove the abandonment of aged people, to rebuke the government's continuous disregard of children, pervasive violence, police arbitrariness and corruption, and to challenge the lack of public, social, and cultural policies.

After a screening of *City of God*, during the presidential campaign, the candidate Luiz Inácio Lula da Silva declared in a press conference that the problem of violence is not to be solved only through law enforcement by the police, but that it is necessary to give these thousands of forgotten youngsters in the outskirts of Brazilian cities better opportunities to allow them to follow a path different from that offered by crime. President Lula's statement was one of the best I have ever heard in my life – especially knowing that he was elected by an immense majority of voters.

The National Secretary of Security, Luiz Eduardo Soares (an admirer of my work), stated that he would begin the deployment of his Security Plan for Rio de Janeiro at the *favela* Cidade de Deus, which includes, among 11 national projects, a community gym, a sports equipment factory that will offer 300 direct jobs, and a multimedia studio. So, our efforts via anthropological research, the novel and the film have not been in vain, but rather they are breeding positive results, especially for those who live in the community that inspired it all.

Many agree that the President's statement is fitting, and it is for no other reason that the NGOs, the PPPomar,[5] the CUFA,[6] the Viva Rio Movement,[7] and community associations have long existed. We have

---

[5] Editor's note: PPPomar stands for *Partido Popular Poder para a Maioria* [Popular Party Power to the Majority]. Founded in Cidade de Deus by M V Bill, it is also called *Partido Negro/Black Party,* which confronts racism as the basis for the marked social inequalities in the country.

[6] Editor's note: CUFA stands for *Central Única das Favelas* [The *Favelas'* Central Union]; it was organised by the Hip-Hop movement associated with PPPomar.

[7] Editor's note: Viva Rio is another movement seeking to speak on behalf of the *favelas*; it started in 1993 as an expression against violence.

witnessed the commitment for social change move beyond the already large number of literary and film professionals to other artistic endeavours including hip-hop. Many supporters are working with issues relating to politics, education, sports and culture in the so-called needy communities.

Thus, I encouraged the development of a hip-hop project, with the support of Adair Rocha, former sub-secretary of Culture of Rio de Janeiro, and Celso Athayde, creator of the Prêmio Hutus [Hutus Prize], for the DESIPE and the DEGASE[8] (Rio). But unfortunately it was not implemented due to the lack of resources during Benedita da Silva's term of office. Nevertheless, while I was still at the Secretariat of Culture, I created and implemented, with Adair Rocha and Virginia de Oliveira Silva, the *Cidadania Mandando uma Letra* [*Citizenship Sending a Letter*] project, a project to encourage reading and to improve libraries in government-sponsored schools located in needy neighbourhoods, believing that it was going to work as well as *Nós do Morro* [*Us from the Hill*], the Afro-Reggae, The CEASM, the *Nós do Cinema* [*We in Cinema*], *etcetera*. I hope the present State government will continue to support these programmes.

As to the remark that the film stigmatises even more the people living in Cidade de Deus, I believe the opposite to be true. *City of God*, as a work of art, sheds light not on the micro aspect, but on the macro conditions, that is, on the problems and infamies of a national policy that is, so far, faulty. Besides, as said before, it affronts the wicked income distribution of a sick country that was led by all kinds of stupid prejudices, by a slavery that is almost never discussed in Brazilian classrooms, and that up to now has exerted strong influences on our society. If there are doubts about that, they can be dispelled merely by looking at the involvement of children with criminality, a fact that happens all over Brazil, and not only in a special community, as newspapers have reported, but across the decades depicted in the book and the film.

Today, we have something that was unheard of until the 1980s: the famous 'microwave' (drug dealers set fire to a stack of tires and place a rival within them) that a convict at the DEGASE explains in detail in the documentary *Notícias de Uma Guerra Particular* [*News from a Personal War*]. The number of *favelas* has multiplied, poverty has increased, and public policies have languished, thus making violence grow. I myself lost two school age stepchildren, brothers to my son, who were killed in this fierce Brazilian life in Cidade de Deus.

I do not mean to say that only poverty leads people towards a life of crime, but it does help. Yet, there are many factors that cause criminality – the processes are varied – and it is not our goal here to point them out. If schools, however, and all public services are efficient, if economic inequality decreases and if we really achieve zero hunger,[9]

---

[8] Translator's note: prison institutions in Rio.
[9] Translator's note: Reference to a nationwide programme established by the Federal Government under Lula to zero out hunger through different actions, such as food distribution and wage programmes.

surely Brazil will have a new History.

Without a doubt, the research, the book and the film, together with the new policies to face violence in projects fitted out by the municipal, state and federal governments, as well as by the NGOs, will bring international incentives to the socio-cultural works in Brazil. Many Brazilians and foreigners, who did not have the slightest idea of what a *favela* was, are seeing for the first time that our nation is not only carnival, football and beaches. Moreover, the world is learning that for a few to squander wealth the vast majority survive in the most complete poverty.

Those who should be ashamed of the film are those who created and perpetuated poverty, those who discriminate by the colour of one's skin, by social origin, those who govern only to favour themselves, the misers and scrooges. These are the ones now being stigmatised.

Finally, we know that marginalised people are dragged into crime simply because of a complete lack of options – this is especially true for the children of the *favelas*, since the great majority of the mainly black, mulatto, Northeastern migrant youngsters killed in the conflicts between the drug gangs and the police live in needy communities. We also know that those living in poverty are drawn to crime and violence because Brazil has provided few alternatives. The people of Cidade de Deus, now seen in a larger picture, have been thus stigmatised for almost 503 years.

The wealthy Brazilian elite ride in armoured cars and are surrounded by bodyguards, while members of the middle class are afraid to roll down their car windows when they stop at traffic lights. There have been thousands of victims of violence throughout the years. However, I feel that the main objective of the research/book/film is being achieved since several official institutions and non-governmental organisations are devoted to helping *Cidade de Deus* and Brazil. And it is proper to remember that many other works have been carried out with the same objective by hundreds of people. *City of God* (research/book/film) is only one more ally in the search for the changes that this country needs.

It is also proper to warn the most optimistic citizens that the book, or the film, or hip-hop, or the NGOs, or even the government alone will not change this reality overnight. More debate forums, hard work and political will are needed to make this country into a social and economic democracy. However, I believe that today our society is changing, for people are becoming aware that our political model did not work (because of that, Lula was elected), that a better income distribution must be implemented, and that public services, especially educational, cultural, and athletic policies must be taken more seriously.

Let us have faith in the social pact and in the Zero Hunger Programme in Brazil. Cheers for the will to change shown in the soul of the Brazilian people. I am willing to continue working for a more just society.

Translation by Edson Martins Lopes

17. *City of Men*: The Social Fabric on TV
Leandro Rocha Saraiva

More than three million people saw *City of God*: for Brazilian cinema, a great box-office success; for a country of 180 million people, insignificant. Even before the première, there had already been signs of interest in the project of fictionalising ordinary and marginal lives in a much wider way than that small cinematic reserve of the middle and upper classes. During the actors' workshops that Meirelles organised in the film's pre-production phase, he directed a short feature that went on the air for Rede Globo [Globo Network], on the first showing of a programme dedicated to independent productions, *Brava Gente* [*Brave People*]. *Palace II* served as a laboratory for *City of God* and as the pilot for what would become its television offshoot: the series *Cidade dos Homens* [*City of Men*].

Although set in the same world of the *favela* and with several of the same actors from *City of God* (in the film, Douglas Silva, Acerola, is Dadinho [Li'l Dice], and Darlan Cunha, Laranjinha, is Filé com Fritas [Steak and Fries]), the short film has a very different dramatic concept, which is the basis of the TV series. Not the protagonists of organised crime but two ordinary boys, Acerola and Laranjinha are at the centre of the narrative. Like Buscapé [Rocket], they represent the vast majority of the people living in the *favelas* who are uninvolved in drug dealing, but who are forced to learn to live with its destructive influence. Also like the photographer-narrator of *City of God*, this refusal of criminality comes about through practical calculation, without moralising, and does not exclude occasional expedients outside the law.

According to Fernando Meirelles, 'City of God is a drama, with touches of comedy, about drug dealers in Rio, where the community only appears as a backdrop. *City of Men* is a comedy, with a touch of drama, about the community of Rio de Janeiro, where the drug dealers appear only as a backdrop'.

The series explores the social fabric that in the film was, let us say, 'promised' by the presence of Buscapé [Rocket], but that remained merely latent. If Zé Pequeno [Li'l Zé], Bené [Benny], and the criminals of Cidade de Deus formed an almost autonomous group in the film, immersed in their own logic of war, the adventures of Acerola and Laranjinha develop more within a dense communal network made up of friends, parents, grandparents, sisters, and neighbours. The comic characteristic noted by Meirelles points, beyond laughter, to a principle of conciliation, of the mediation of conflicts. In popular language, Acerola and Laranjinha 'dribble' round conflicts and violence, avoiding going 'head on' against whomever.

Juvenile irresponsibility favours a connection with the logic of the *malandro*, but the peculiar design of the series nevertheless allows a variation of approaches to people's lives that goes beyond this traditional figure. Every October, Rede Globo shows a series of five episodes of

Cidade dos Homens, produced by O2.[1] The eternal protagonists Acerola and Laranjinha are, each season, a year older, which allows for progressively more adult themes and thus more serious moments. Each episode is autonomous, a complete story built around a central theme, but which lacks the intense dramatic concentration that characterises *City of God*, allowing for the presence of several sub-themes. The actors are almost all from the group *Nós do Morro* [*Us from the Hill*], from the *favela* of Vidigal. The choice of locations and the field research on which the scripts are based are also done in the *favelas* of Rio.

Let us look at a few examples. In *A Coroa do Imperador* [*The Emperor's Crown*], the first episode of the series, Acerola and Laranjinha have to raise money to pay for a school outing to the old summer palace of the imperial family. Their adventures in pursuit of money – which make up a small portrait of the 'scrounging' of daily life – take place in the midst of a drug dealers' war, which is emotionally intensified by Laranjinha's need to take some medicine to his sick grandmother. On a parallel level, the school theme allows the inclusion of historical commentaries, with the logic of the Napoleonic Wars, which motivated the transference of the Portuguese royal court to Brazil, being compared to the logic of the disputes in the *favelas* between different factions in the drug trade. The episode also features an interruption of the narrative for the insertion of documentary testimonies of the actors, residents of the *favela*, on cases of violence in their families (testimonies given in a tone of narrative spectacle, tuned to the rhythm of the videogame contests that come before them in the narrative).

Buraco Quente [*Hot Hole*], the last episode of the second season is, by contrast, more dramatic. It focuses on the dilemma of Laranjinha's cousin Espeto, who is involved in drug-trafficking, and, who, while being pursued by the police in the woods surrounding the *favela*, loses a backpack with the money from the day's sales. Before the ending, when the two boys save him by finding the backpack, amid intricate plots and betrayals involving dealers and policemen, a series of Espeto's relationships are revealed, involving the dispute between his girlfriend, who wants to get married and tries to get him a city job (as a street sweeper), and a lover fascinated by his status as drug dealer – composing that social fabric that is absent in the film.

In the third season there was a change in the structure of the series, which should be maintained in the fourth and final season (in 2005, when the protagonists come of age, the series will end). Now the linking of the episodes is greater, with the adventures of the duo connected to the general plot of the formation of a family, with the pregnancy of Acerola's girlfriend. This, however, has not changed the principle of broad inclusion of characters and sub-themes; it has only made them more adult, with family worries and a concern for more lasting support becoming more and more central.

The cultural effect of the series *City of Men*, in terms of the

---

[1] A matter worth noting, for in Brazil nearly all programming is produced by the networks themselves. *Cidade dos Homens* represents the most significant partnership of the largest national network with an independent production.

presence in the media of the life of the poor, is historic. For decades, the teledramas have included idealised 'popular nuclei' in their stories – a kind of 'studio poor', who even in the rare cases of the presence of black actors, are represented by stereotypes that 'sanitise' any social difference in the conflicts. Douglas Silva and Darlan Cunha have become national pop stars, decisively contributing to breaking the monopoly of rich white characters on Brazilian television. Even more important than this, *City of Men* has brought to the programming of the largest television network in the country, with spectacular audience ratings (never lower than 50 percent of all sets turned on), stories and environments of the daily life in the Rio *favelas*, avoiding the clichés that equate *favelas* with crime. This is surely an important contribution to make more concrete and complex the nearly always innocuous discussion of 'citizenship' in Brazil.

18. The *We in Cinema* Project: Film-Making by and for Marginalised Youth
The Original Cast of *City of God*

Nós do Cinema is a media arts-based organisation in Rio de Janeiro, Brazil, giving disadvantaged youth a unique opportunity to receive cinema training and access to the job market while giving voice to their realities. *Nós* empowers youths as they explore, discover and recreate their own identity and life history through the most powerful tool of the media.

The Origin of the Project: Selecting and Training the Cast of *City of God*

Nós do Cinema was originally founded as a group of 200 boys and girls from Rio de Janeiro's poorest neighbourhoods. These youngsters were selected in August of 2000 and trained for several months by film and theatre professionals to form the cast of the film *City of God*.[1] The acting workshop ended upon completion of the film. However, with the determination of the students and the guidance of co-director Katia Lund, *Nós do Cinema* has become an on-going organisation that offers a unique solution to the problems facing young people in the *favelas* by providing information, training in media skills and other areas related to film-making, and access to the job market.

The Problem Targeted

Violence in Rio de Janeiro is extreme. An estimated 100,000 people currently work in the drug trade (the same number as in the State government) and every hour a person dies from gunfire. Between five and seven thousand people under the age of 25 are killed each year. Today's soaring crime rates in Brazil are directly related to Brazil's sharp social and economic inequalities, whereby a large portion of the population is excluded from the economy and from participation in mainstream society. The public school system is exceedingly poor, and young people in the *favelas* lack access to information, education, jobs, legal services, consumer goods or society – unless they are working as servants for paltry wages.

These young people have seen their parents and grandparents work for entire lifetimes without making any progress. Now, they seek channels through which to excel or become 'someone', however rare these channels may be. Unemployment in some of the major cities can be as high as 20 percent.

Their lack of usefulness and participation in society, and their consequent 'invisibility', lead to feelings of anger and revolt. With little

---

[1] Editor's note: See Fernando Meirelles's description of the process of finding and training the protagonists of *City of God* in this volume (pp.19-37). See also Ismail Xavier's description of the marked role of recent film in Brazil against the brutalisation of the lives of the impoverished urban class (pp. 143-63), related to the initiatives of the Non-Governmental Organisations (pp. 145- 48).

concern for their own lives, they embrace a life of crime. When a boy takes hold of a gun, he immediately has the attention and respect he craves. He 'exists' – even if just for a short while. Brazilian society and government have traditionally looked to repression, exclusion and removal to solve the problem. However these tactics have only aggravated the situation. The answer is clear: we must look to new solutions based on recognition and inclusion.

Film-maker Katia Lund's research on the universe of crime in Brazil, over the last six years, has led to the discovery that the lack of 'identity', recognition, and participation in society are the strongest causes leading young people to a life in crime.

Today, audio-visual language is the primary tool for identity-creation and definition. Unfortunately, it is also employed to exploit identity through consumerism, creating a desire to own 'status' clothing and costly brand-name products. As 'Nós students' become fluent in the audio-visual language, learning to 'read' and 'write' these images, they also learn the ways in which they are manipulated by advertising – which is a significant source of anxiety that compels them to consume products beyond their means.

Why Cinema?

Film-making is a joint effort that integrates many areas (general engineering, sound engineering, lighting, electronics, carpentry, transport, catering, accounting and budgeting, and administration) and the more specific ones of screenwriting, acting, casting, production, photography, law, costume design, makeup, painting, editing, and directing. Audio-visual productions can thus reach hundreds, thousands or millions of people, making these young men and women highly effective in creating a sense of identity.

Policies and Activities

Nós do Cinema has prepared approximately 200 students so far. It seeks to educate young people, produce original concepts and promote dialogue across socio-economic classes through work and cooperation. Participants are trained in workshops by professionals in the fields of media and communications. Experienced members complete the cycle by returning and teaching workshops for newcomers.
Nós do Cinema offers the following:
- Coursework in film-making and acting, which aims to use film and video as learning tools and a means of appropriating one's own image;
- Basic communication skills training via writing, computers, etcetera;
- Specific training in directing, screenwriting, journalism, lighting, sound, photography, production, and digital editing;
- Production of a short film, in which members partake in all aspects of film production as the culmination of the training.

After successfully completing coursework, students apply their knowledge in internships at production companies and group film projects. Of the 70 original participants, 74 percent were successful on the course and gained entry to the job market.

136

Nós do Cinema Productions

The project has been involved, directly or indirectly, in about 50 productions, which, in turn, have involved actors, technicians, production teams, *etcetera*. The productions are the voice of the group. They include fictional short films and documentaries that are shown in local schools and cultural centres. In addition, crews of students are hired to produce music videos and promotional advertisements, which are a source of income that helps maintain the organisation.

Nós productions so far include:

- *Citizen Silva* – awarded Best Fiction Film at the São Carlos International Short Film Festival, São Carlos, São Paulo, 2002;
- *Conversa no Banheiro* [*The Blind Man, the Devil and the Good Pastor*] – original short film;
- *Armas e Paz* [*Weapons and Peace*] – music video;
- *Sapukay* – promotional video for *Star One*, shot in an Indian village in Angra dos Reis;
- *Sem Violência, 100% Paz* [*No Violence, 100% Peace*] - video of a theatre piece by renowned Brazilian actress Zezé Motta;
- *Brazilian Personalities* – an international documentary;
- *Nova Baia* [*New Bay*] – promotional video for *IBG – Instituto Baia de Guanabara*;
- *Living and Learning* – promotional video for the NGO *Guardiões do Mar*;
- *Mini-Series Networks of Our Land* – a *Nós do Cinema* production for *Star One,* shot in the Amazon rainforest;
- *Rainforest Peoples Network* – documentary shown on popular TV Globo programme *Fantástico* in September of 2003.

More recent productions or participation in major feature films:

- *Olga* (directed by Jayme Monjardim, 2004). Participation of the *Nós do Cinema* trainee Ruy Vitório.
- *Quase Dois Irmãos* [*Almost Two Brothers*] (directed by Lúcia Murat, 2004) *Nós do Cinema* actor Renato de Souza (Marreco [Goose] in *City of God*) had a leading role; among others Eduardo Dorneles was in the cast. *Nós* also helped in the preparation of actors for the film.
- *Diabo a Quatro* (directed by Alice de Andrade, 2004). Participation of *Nós do Cinema* actors Diego Batista, Michel Gomes and Renato de Souza (Marreco).
- *Cafundó* (directed by Paulo Betti and Clóvis Bueno, premièring 2005). Participation of *Nós do Cinema* vice-president and actor Leandro Firmino.
- Series *Cidade dos Homens* [*City of Men*] (TV Globo, 2002–2004). The participation of *Nós do Cinema* included actors BR (Eduardo Dorneles) and Renato de Souza, the story for one of the episodes and students' training on the technical aspects of the series production.

Outreach Projects

Since 2003, *Nós do Cinema* has been producing events in schools, universities, cultural centres and other organisations, which consist, initially, of screenings of the film *City of God*, the Brazilian TV miniseries *City of Men*, as well as its own original films. The screenings are followed by discussions with the *Nós do Cinema* cast and crew of these productions. These events bring people together from different races, religions, classes and geographical areas, facilitating groundbreaking dialogue between groups that rarely have a chance to meet and exchange ideas openly. The objective is to use film to cut across social barriers, sparking conversation on a wide range of social issues, and present a positive image of young people from the *favelas*.

Outreach Visits of the *Get Together* Project

Get Together has visited over 70 public and private schools, cultural centres and other associations, including:

In Brazil: the American School of Rio de Janeiro; Graded American School of São Paulo; British School, Rio de Janeiro; Maria Immaculada American School, São Paulo; Festival de Tiradentes, Brazil; Festival Internacional de São Paulo; Festival Rio BR; Mostra Geração Futura; SESC, among others.

Internationally: the Cannes Film Festival, France; Encuentro Latinoamericano de Cine, Peru; Brown University, USA.

Get People Together England[2]

The purpose of *Get People Together England* is to help individuals from Brazil and Britain learn more about significant aspects of culture beyond their shared interests in football. Project *Get People Together England* offers a unique opportunity for its members and British students to expand and share views on theatre, music, politics and film. Cultural exchanges among young people from different countries also enable them to compare ideas on social equality and citizenship through audio-visual tools that everyone can understand. The creation of a link between young people from distant countries is also intended to break down barriers between nations and social classes and to diminish prejudice against disadvantaged groups.

In terms of strategy, *Nós do Cinema* will send three *City of God* cast members and three technicians to Britain to initiate the exchange (February 2005). During the seven days in Britain, *City of God* and other films will be screened to stimulate the discussion of technical and theoretical issues of Brazilian and British cinema. In turn, the *Nós do Cinema* team in Brazil will treat their European hosts to new films and discussions.

Specific Objectives of *Get People Together England*

- To establish a connection between *Nós do Cinema* participants (youth from poor areas of Rio de Janeiro) and British youth who participate in community projects in their own country. Extending this project to countries neighbouring Britain as well (Spain, Portugal, France, *etcetera*) is also envisaged.
- To organise meetings between youth from poor areas of Rio de Janeiro and university students in Britain and neighbouring countries.

---

[2] Editor's note: *England* here reflects the Brazilian usage that refers to the whole of the UK.

- To exchange audio-visual productions with British youth.
- To document the exchange between these young people.
- To arrange visits to historic sites, museums, libraries and natural attractions in Rio de Janeiro and in Britain with local youth.
- To show the feature film *City of God* and *Nós do Cinema's* original films, as well as watch and discuss films produced by young people from the cities visited.

Partnerships

Nós do Cinema has succeeded over the past three years thanks also to many corporate and individual partners. Corporate sponsors include Lumière, Grupo Lund and O2 Filmes. Production companies such as VideoFilmes, O2 Filmes and TV Zero have lent and donated equipment to the project. Educational partners which, in turn, have offered additional courses include among others, the Catholic University of Rio de Janeiro (PUC), Notre Dame University, Harvard University and Queen Mary, University of London. Eminent film-makers and professionals, besides Fenando Meirelles, director of *City of God*, and co-director Katia Lund, have also contributed along with Walter Salles, Daniela Thomaz, Roberto Berliner, André Horta and Rodrigo Letier.

19. Books and Studies on the Work of F. Meirelles by Brazilians
Maria do Rosário Caetano

Masters Theses and Doctoral Dissertations

Rodrigo, Márcio. *O Bangue-Bangue Mulato*: *Cidade de Deus, dos Homens e de Todas as Linguagens* [The Mulatto Bang-Bang: City of God, of Men, and of All Languages]. São Paulo: UNESP, Campus São Paulo, 2004 (mimeographed).

This is the first academic analysis in Brazil on the film *Cidade de Deus*, by Fernando Meirelles. The researcher uses as a theoretical base the concepts of hybridisation of means, introduced by Marshall McLuhan in *Understanding Media*, and dialogism, developed by the Russian Mikhail Bakhtin throughout his intellectual life. The work is divided into three parts. In the first segment, the author traces the historical panorama of the production and the aesthetics of Brazilian cinema and television, from 1990 to the present. The second part is a detailed analysis of Meirelles's film that looks at the sound track, narrative structure, editing, timing, *etcetera*. Finally, the author makes a comparison between *Cidade de Deus* and the television serial *Cidade dos Homens*, identifying the historical roots of the social question in Brazilian art.

Gatti, André P. *Distribuição e exibição na indústria cinematográfica brasileira (1993-2003)* [Distribution and exhibition in the Brazilian film industry]. Campinas: Universidade de Campinas (UNICAMP), 2005 (mimeographed).

In his doctoral dissertation, André Gatti discusses the strategies for making and marketing various Brazilian films, including *City of God*, in the Brazilian commercial marketplace. He briefly analyses the trajectory of Fernando Meirelles as a film-maker and emphasises the 'financial engineering' of the film, or how Meirelles wove the web of resources that made *City of God* possible. Gatti also examines the technical achievements of the film for the heritage of Brazilian cinema, and the polemics the film created among film critics and in Brazilian society. In addition, Gatti analyses the distribution of *City of God* in the national and international markets up to the year 2003 (the film's Brazilian première was on August 31, 2002).

Monograph

Meloni, Vitor. *Meu Nome Agora é Zé Pequeno, p... – um olhar sobre o Cinema da Retomada* [My Name is Now Zé Pequeno, G... – A Look at the Cinema of the Recovery]. Araçatuba: Unitoledo, 2004, 89 pages (mimeographed).

This experimental monograph, presented as a bachelor's thesis for journalism at Toledo University, offers a panoramic view of the *Retomada* – that is, the Brazilian Cinema of the Recovery (from 1995). The fact that Brazilian cinema has become a pressing subject both inside and outside the country, as seen with *City of God* (nominated for four Oscars) justifies Meloni's research. The first chapter focuses on the major films produced from 1995-2002. He draws on film-makers' statements (both veterans and newcomers) about their difficulties to help explain the stagnation of Brazilian cinema. He discusses the beginning of the Recovery, investigating public opinion and analysing the vital contribution to cinema of audio-visual technology. In a chapter on all of Brazil's candidates for the Oscar, he gives special attention to *City of God*, citing the distributor Miramax's struggle for its nominations, and the Oscar nominees involved in its production (Fernando Meirelles, the screenwriter Bráulio Mantovani, cinematographer César Charlone and editor Daniel Rezende). The polemics over aesthetic issues is also discussed. The third part posits a break in paradigms in Brazilian cinema, mainly in relation to the film *City of God*. It also looks at possible new tendencies and political directions for film production.

Books

Saraiva, Leandro and Cannito, Newton. *Manual de Roteiro ou Manuel, o Primo Pobre dos Manuais de Cinema e TV* [Script Manual, or Manuel, the Poor Cousin of the Cinema and TV Manuals]. São Paulo: Conrad Editora, 2004 (236 pages).

The book analyses *City of God* and episodes from the TV series *City of Men*. The preface is by Fernando Meirelles, 'Manuel is going to Become Your Best Friend' and is worth quoting in its entirety: 'On the cover it is written that this book is a manual, but this must be a printer's error. This is "Manuel", the poor cousin of the manuals. Poor but much smarter, because this Manuel does not make lists of rules or offer a recipe for how to write a script. He is more intelligent than that. He has a chat with the screenwriter, helping him to understand his own story from several angles. The Manual was written for a screenwriting course, in which I am involved, in which the series *Cidade dos Homens*, for example, was used. My good luck. Reading this, I was able to understand my own work better. In the third season of the series, we invited the authors of the Manual to become a part of our team. It is interesting to read the Manual in one sitting, as proposed in the introduction, but it makes even more sense to read it during the creative process of some project. It is there that the questions raised take on relevance and the reading becomes really useful. To close: the Manual likes intelligent films, but films popular with the public as well. What makes this work different and interesting is the fact that it does not base itself on the model of the North American film industry, but also that it does not look upon it with prejudice. Dziga Vertov, Truffaut, Antonioni, David Mamet, Sidney Lumet, Mike Leigh, Guel Arraes, Jorge Furtado, Godard, Billy Wilder. The best is here as reference material. This companion can become your best friend. "Manuel'" (see below for a special report on the launch of the book for *O Estado*).

Essays and Book Chapters

Nagib, Lúcia. 'A Língua da Bala' [Talking Bullets: The Language of Violence in *City of God*], 14 page essay by the professor of UNICAMP at the time and author of the book *O Cinema da Retomada* [The Cinema of the Recovery] (Editora 34, 2002).

Starting from a play on words ('The word balks, the bullet talks') by Paulo

Lins, who wrote the book, *City of God*, that inspired the film, Nagib analyses the rich stylistics of the novel and claims that 'the film-maker succeeded in creating an equivalent of the source work, giving criticism the difficult task of finding in the intersemiotic translation the corresponding techniques that are equally successful in both works'.

Oricchio, Luiz Zanin. *Cinema de Novo*: *Um Balanço Crítico da Retomada* [Cinema Anew: a Critical Assessment of the Recovery]. São Paulo: Editora Estação Liberdade, 2003, 256 pages.
In the last chapter of his book, Zanin analyses *City of God* and the schism that the film caused in Brazilian film criticism. 'His way of portraying the daily life of a *favela* in Rio was considered conservative by some critics and daring by others.' Zanin regards the film as 'an exemplary moment at the end of the process of Recovery of Brazilian Cinema and also as a point of encounter of the crisis of contemporary film languages'. Using, with little fuss, advertising and video clip techniques, he says, *City of God* is a point of no return in the style of representing Brazilian problems. This kind of film serves as a more contemporary strategy of audio-visual language to portray social conflicts and, with this procedure, is able to communicate with the public, especially the youngest section of it. This choice, however, is not ideologically neutral. It selects a slice of reality that does not aid the political understanding of the phenomenon portrayed. But beyond ideological discussions, the film uses a hybridisation of languages that, mixing television, cinema, advertising, and audio-visual, seems to have come to stay.

Xavier, Ismail, 'Angels with Dirty Faces', in *Sight & Sound*, January, 2003, London, pages 28-30.
This is a critique of the film *City of God* that offers information for the British public on the condition of Brazilian film as a 'social phenomenon'. Xavier argues for a sociological interpretation of the film based upon the strength of its theme and the effectiveness with which it develops the boys' drama within the classical structure of an action film, with an emphasis on intensity and speed. The article supplies data on the production and public reception, and features the work with the young people of the theatre group *Nós do Morro* [*Us from the Hills*], the main triumph of Meirelles as the creation of his 'effect of the real'. Also included is the commentary on the relationship of Paulo Lins, the author of the book on which the film is based, with film in general – his consultation work for João Moreira Salles and Katia Lund in the documentary *Notícia de uma Guerra Particular* [*News from a Personal War*] and in the case of Carlos Diegues's *Orfeu* [*Orpheus*]. The critique analyses the film's characters and their representation of poverty and crime, from the disparate fates of those who were present at the modernisation of crime to the arrival of drugs and access to greater sums of money and also greater operations of war – operations that the protagonist Buscapé [Rocket] escapes, as his fate is redirected by his encounter with photography. This is one more example of a Brazilian film that exemplifies the formula of the NGOs: art against barbarism.

Papers Presented at Annual Meetings of the SOCINE - *Sociedade Brasileira de Estudos de Cinema*

VIII Annual Meeting of SOCINE, 2004

Butcher, Pedro. '*Cidade de Deus, Cidade dos Homens* e a Nova Relação entre Cinema e TV no Brasil' [*Cidade de Deus, Cidade dos Homens* and the New Relationship between Cinema and TV in Brazil].

Mousinho, Luiz Antônio. 'Adaptação: Uólace e João Victor' [Adaptation: Uólace and João Vitor].
The paper examines the adaptation by Fernando Meirelles and Regina Casé (with the collaboration of the film-maker and screenwriter Jorge Furtado) of Rosa Amanda Strauss's children's book for one of the episodes in the first season of the Globo TV network series *Cidade dos Homens*.

VII Annual Meeting of SOCINE, 2003

Baptista, Mauro. '*Cidade de Deus* e a Matriz Clássica: Estilo e Gênero' [*Cidade de Deus* and the Classical Model: Style and Genre].
The paper discusses the dialogue Meirelles's film has with the classic tradition of the cinema.
Mascarello, Fernando. '*Cidade de Deus*: Crítica e Público' [*City of God*: Critics and the Public].
The critic from the periodical *Teorema*, published in Rio Grande do Sul, evaluates the critical and public reaction to Meirelles's film, placing it in a more comprehensive theme: representations of the *favela* in Brazilian cinema.

Others
City of God is the topic of a study of Ivana Bentes, professor of UFRJ, Federal University of Rio de Janeiro, who is preparing a book on the theme *Sertão e Favela*: *Da Estética à Cosmética da Fome* [Backlands and *Favela*: from the Aesthetics to the Cosmetics of Hunger].

It is also the theme of Esther Hamburger (Professor of USP, University of São Paulo): *Inclusão e Exclusão*: *a Política das Representações na Mídia em uma Favela Paulistana* [Inclusion and Exclusion: the Politics of Representation in the Media in a São Paulo *Favela*].

Lisandra Maioli produced a masters thesis *lato sensu, Comportamento da Crítica Jornalística Nacional em Época do Oscar*: *As Críticas ao Filme Cidade de Deus nos sites Estadao.com.br e na Folha Online* [Behaviour of National Journalistic Criticism at the time of the Academy Awards: the Criticism of the Film *Cidade de Deus* in the sites Estadao.com.br and Folha Online], for the course on Journalistic Communication at the Catholic University of São Paulo (2004).

At the SOCINE Meeting, other scholars spoke in their papers on *City of God*, including Fernando Vugman, of the Unisul, Santa Catarina.

Special Report for *O Estado*: The Young Authors of *Cidade dos Homens* Publish a Book with Script Notations for Cinema and TV
Maria do Rosário Caetano

Leandro Saraiva and Newton Cannito, who worked with Fernando Meirelles on the series *Cidade dos Homens*, will be signing their book on Tuesday, the 30th, at the Casa do Saber: *Manual de Roteiro, ou Manuel, o Primo Pobre dos Manuais do Cinema e TV*. The authors, who are a part of the FICs (Factory of Ideas for Cinema) pay homage to the innovative FEX (Factory of Eccentric Actors), which shook up Soviet Revolutionary Cinema. They wish to engage in dialogue with future screenwriters, 'people with open minds interested in renewing Brazilian audio-visual'. Those who prefer rigid norms and procedures like those found in the famous book by the American screenwriter Syd Field, the Screenwriters' Manual, should stay away from 'Manuel', its confessed poor cousin. 'We do not furnish cake recipes, nor are we a self-help book,' write the authors. 'What interests us is to engage in a dialogue with young screenwriters, without imposing any rules', for 'we believe that the writing of a script depends basically on individual processes, which cannot be reduced to absolute rules'. The book has a preface by Fernando Meirelles and the authors do not conceal their admiration for *City of God*. In the chapter where they analyse Bráulio Mantovani's screenplay, Saraiva and Cannito write: 'the synthesis of time and information (of the film) is enormous. In addition to the predominance of summaries, there are fragments of scenes within each one of them (like the killing of the dealer Aristóteles, carried out by his friend Sando Cenoura), there are accelerations of speed (in the narrative), there is a scene cut and taken up again three times. A real turn-around of dramatic classicism, very far from the small clips of passing time in more banal films'. So as not to leave any doubt as to what Meirelles's film has that is innovative and modern, the authors provoke the radical critics of *City of God*; everything in the film would be merely 'cosmetic', to use the current term, and not aesthetic, if the whole achievement did not work, precisely to brand on the consciousness of the audience, with the energy worthy of the protagonist, the polished phrase: 'Dadinho, my ass. My name is now Zé Pequeno, goddamn it'. The 'Manuel' of Saraiva and Cannito, in fact, came from the supplementary material from the workshop given by the authors, at the invitation of 02, of the producers Meirelles, Morelli & Olival, for 400 young screenwriters from all over the country. For four months, they did productive exercises in screenwriting, which formed the basis of the third season of *Cidade dos Homens*. The authors of the Manual ended up becoming a part of the team of writers. One of the episodes written by them was 'Hip Sampa Hop', which brought Acerola and Laranjinha (Douglas Silva and Darlam Cunha), now adolescents with fervid hormones, from the *favela* in Rio to take part in a lively adventure in the periphery of São Paulo. In the book, the two authors analyse sequences from films by Murnau (*Sunrise*), Ford (*The Man Who Shot Liberty Valance*), Godard (*Pierrot le Fou*), Sidney Lumet (*Dog Day Afternoon*) and give analyses of feature-length Brazilian films and TV programmes (especially those by Jorge Furtado and Guel Arraes). Besides detailed analyses of certain sequences from *City of God*, the book concentrates on the analysis of episodes from the first series of *Cidade dos Homens*, 'The Emperor's Crown' and 'Uólace and João Vitor'. And it closes most of its chapters with proposals for screenwriting exercises, of the type 'define the basic dramatic situation of your story in 10 lines', 'sketch out two versions for a scene in your script, one dramatic and one lyrical', 'write a wider argument of your story'. The authors show in the 10 chapters of their book the same good humour as their godfather, and preface-writer, Fernando Meirelles (who prefers the Manuel who carries on a dialogue with young screenwriters to the *Manual* that dictates rules. The text is easy-reading, even when the authors, backed by a good bibliography, discuss film genres, narrative focus, variations in time (flashbacks, summaries, and displacements), and give technical tips for making the director's version (with the technical and minutely detailed development of the script).

Translation by Thomas Laborie Burns

PART III
CONTEXT

20. The *Favelas* of Rio de Janeiro in Brazilian Cinema (1950 to 2000)[1]

Márcia Pereira Leite

Since the mid 1950s, with Nelson Pereira dos Santos's *Rio 40 Graus* [*Rio 40 Degrees*], the *favelas* have been present in modern Brazilian cinema. Sometimes they are broached as setting, at other times as theme. However, during the 1960s, especially with *Cinema Novo* – the movement that renewed Brazilian film production by dealing with national themes from a critical perspective and experimenting with unique forms and aesthetics – *favelas* were treated as one of the more perverse images of Brazilian urbanisation.

Cinema Novo: Misery, Violence and Nation

From the *Cinema Novo* film-makers' perspective, the *favelas* and the *sertão* (the hinterland in the Northeast), presented as dry and riddled with the *cangaço*[2], were the areas in which 'the problems were most radically concentrated' (Dahl, 1965: 246). However, if their focus was on the country's problems, at the time recognised as underdevelopment and misery, they were also gestating the solutions. If *Vidas Secas* [*Barren Lives*] (Nelson Pereira dos Santos, 1963) portrays suffering and resignation, *Os Fuzis* [*The Guns*] (Ruy Guerra, 1963) and *Deus e o Diabo na Terra do Sol* [*Black God White Devil*] (Glauber Rocha, 1964) both explode with revolt and violence. Ismail Xavier, commenting on this film, emphasises that in it Glauber discusses 'the relationship between hunger, religion and violence [...] to legitimise the response of the oppressed, lending evidence to the presence in Brazil of a tradition of rebellion which contradicts the official version, that of the pacific nature of the people' (1997: 46).

The aesthetics of violence, advocated by the film-maker Glauber Rocha (1965) and present in several of the *Cinema Novo* films, indeed confronted the myth of the intrinsic cordiality of Brazilians and Brazilian society. The films of the *cangaço* cycle recovered and fired the public imagination of the time with other forms of resistance, which, in a rural world dominated by the *latifundium*[3] system of large landed estates, amounted to social struggle, developed and organised by the Peasant Leagues.[4] Meanwhile, the films that depict the *favelas* would treat them

[1] Modified version of an article published in *Antropologia e Imagem,* vol. 11, n.2, Rio de Janeiro, 2000.

[2] Editor's note: Relating to *cangaceiros,* 'honourable' armed bandits who roamed the Northeastern region of the country from 1870-1940, taking over landed-estates and exercising justice.

[3] Editor's note: *Latifundium,* plural *latifundia*: 'Landed estate, or large rural property, which can be defined by size (an area greater than 600 times the average size of a family property) or by use (a rural estate with an area less than 600 times the average size of a family property whose lands are uncultivated' (Fernandes, Bernardo M. in Vieira 2003, landless-voices.org).

[4] Editor's note: A movement that began in mid-1954 in Pernambuco, Brazil. Among its founders was João Pedro Teixeira. Threatened with eviction, the peasants

as the background to a poverty uncontaminated by the values of capitalism, repositories of authentic popular culture and areas sensitive to class solidarity. The dimension of violence alluded to ties in with a political transformation of History. In the two areas an idealised perception of the Brazilian people is perfected in the vision of the intellectual who, like a demiurge, as Autran emphasises (1999), should reveal the people to itself, therefore awakening their conscience and stimulating action.

However, in the 1960s it was the rural world that was the central focus of Brazilian cinema, being thematised through a dialogue with literature; in particular via the works of writers who portrayed this rural reality – from Graciliano Ramos to José Lins do Rêgo. The perception of a great number of that generation's film-makers was strongly influenced by the theories of the Brazilian Communist Party, which regarded the alliance between the *latifundium* system of large landed estates and imperialism as the principal obstacle to the basic reforms championed by the *Projeto Nacional-Popular* [*National Popular Project*]. To their thinking, the agrarian question and the national question were articulated and would find their definitive solution in the social revolution.

Discussing the dialogue between modern Brazilian cinema and the national question, Ismail Xavier draws attention to, on the one hand, the connections between *Cinema Novo* and the National Popular Project, which, at the beginning of the 1960s animated the left in Brazil and reserved a place of distinction for the production of a critical culture against alienation. On the other hand, an international conjuncture of national liberation (in Africa and Asia, and in particular the Algerian and Cuban revolutions), provided a more incisive affirmation of the concept of nation (1997: 48-49). Moving the theme from backwardness to underdevelopment, from neo-colonialism to revolution, Brazilian cinema of the time demonstrated what Xavier calls a 'sociological profile of concerns' (1997: 61). It drew up an inventory of social questions, discussed collective solutions and thematised national identity and conscience.

This perspective found its translation in the *Esthetics of Hunger*, which Glauber Rocha, in defining the problem of hunger in Latin America as the 'nerve of society', defended as specific to *Cinema Novo*:

> From *Aruanda* (Linduarte Noronha, 1960) to *Vidas Secas* [*Barren Lives*], *Cinema Novo* narrated, described, poetised, discussed, analysed and raised the themes of hunger: characters eating earth, characters eating roots, characters stealing to eat, characters killing to eat, characters fleeing hunger; dirty, ugly, scrawny characters in their dirty, ugly, dark houses (1965: 167).

---

organised in 1955 a mutual aid association whose objectives were: to found an elementary school; to organise a funeral fund for the burial of children; to obtain aid to acquire agricultural supplies (seeds, *etcetera*.). In 1964 they were made illegal (From Vieira 2003, landless-voices.org).

It was an aesthetics that transformed the precariousness of technical and financial resources into language, namely, in Glauber's definition, into those 'ugly and sad films, clamorous and desperate films', which exposed the 'nerve of society' (1965: 168).

However, with the 1964 military coup, which defeated the National Popular Project and installed a dictatorial regime, urban themes were increasingly courted by Brazilian cinema. Again it is Xavier in his excellent article who points out the specificity of this urban cinema in relation to the period, in its persistence on the great national questions, while in Europe they debated 'subjectivity in the industrial environment in other terms' (1997: 52). The great question of *Terra em Transe* [*Land in Anguish*] (Glauber Rocha, 1967) related to the reasons for the Left's defeat in Brazil. Other films regarded as the most representative of the period, such as *São Paulo S/A* (Luis Sérgio Person, 1965) and *A Grande Cidade* [*The Big City*] (Carlos Diegues, 1966) were, in that period, valued above all for this thematisation. Gustavo Dahl, for example, considered Person's film to be seminal, 'an urban film *à la Cinema Novo*, utterly Brazilian' which undertook 'a denunciation of the middle classes' (Dahl et al. 1965: 245-246). Also, for Otávio Ianni, one of the greater virtues of *A Grande Cidade* was to show the futile rebellion of those who opted for individual solutions to collective problems: 'on leaving the *sertão*, they would transform their lives into an object of solitary flight' (1967: 201).

In recent years, in a certain sense, Brazilian cinema seems to have gone back down those avenues, discussing the nation and its dilemmas. Film and documentary makers are finding themselves leaning increasingly towards the *favelas,* as they once did towards the northeastern *sertão*, in the eagerness and in the hope of rediscovering Brazil. The *favelas* and their inhabitants are revisited in documentaries of varying formats, from *Santa Marta, Duas Semanas no Morro* [*Santa Marta, Two Weeks in the Favela*] (Eduardo Coutinho, 1997) to *Notícias de uma Guerra Particular* [*News from a Personal War*] (João Moreira Salles and Katia Lund, 1998), *Chapéu Mangueira e Babilônia* [*Mangueira Hat and Babylon*] (Consuelo Lins, 1999), *Santo Forte* [*Mighty Spirit*] (Eduardo Coutinho, 1999), *Somos Todos Filhos da Terra – Adão* [*We Are All Sons of the Earth – Adam*] (Walter Salles and Daniela Thomas, 1999), *Babilônia 2000* [*Babylon 2000*] (Eduardo Coutinho, 2000), and *O Rap do Pequeno Príncipe Contra as Almas Sebosas* [*The Rap of the Little Prince Versus the Greasy Souls*] (Marcelo Luna and Paulo Caldas, 2000), among others.

In fiction, too, it is the *favelas* of Rio de Janeiro which emerge either as theme or setting in such vigorous films as *Como Nascem os Anjos* [*How the Angels Are Born*] (Murillo Salles, 1996), *Orfeu* [*Orpheus*] (Carlos Diegues, 1999) and *O Primeiro Dia* [*Midnight*] (Walter Salles and Daniela Thomas, 1999).

In Rio de Janeiro in particular, the *favelas* invade the field of vision more and more, on the city's hillsides, in the media and in the cinema. In news articles in the papers and on television they are seen *en masse*, homogenised, almost always perceived as zones in a war which threatens the rest of the city (Leite, 2000). On the cinema screens they are beginning to be seen as heterogeneous realities, internally multifaceted, polysemous and polyphonous.

151

This article is interested in those films that thematise the *favela* and its relationship with the social imaginary with respect to themselves. It discusses some of Brazilian cinema's many perspectives towards the *favelas*, using as a point of reference, three periods in time: the 1950s via the films of Nelson Pereira dos Santos; the 1960s by means of *Cinco Vezes Favela* and, especially, the second half of the 1990s, through two films from Rio de Janeiro cinema: *Como Nascem os Anjos* [*How Angels are Born*] and *Orfeu* [*Orpheus*].

The Images of the *Favelas* in Brazilian Cinema in the 1950s and 1960s

Rio 40 Graus

This film [*Rio 40 Degrees*], directed by Nelson Pereira dos Santos (1955, 93 minutes, black and white), is usually referred to as the film which, under the strong influence of Italian Neo-Realism, inaugurated Brazilian modern cinema, representing, as it were, a precursor of *Cinema Novo* (Pereira, 1999: 36). For Hugo Sukman (1999), utilising naturalistic settings and dialogue and seeking to portray society through the humanity of its characters, as Rossellini did in *Roma città aperta* [*Rome Open City*], Nelson Pereira dos Santos bequeathed 'to Brazilian cinema the desire to open up the country on the screen. This engendered *Cinema Novo*. And all that came after.' For Xavier, Pereira dos Santos's cinema would have been, in its time, a 'proto-*Cinema Novo*', engaging in dialogue above all with Neo-Realism and popular Brazilian comedy (1997: 44).

The film features, to the accompaniment of the song *A voz do morro* [*The Voice of the Favela*][5], the city of Rio de Janeiro as its main character. The story unfolds in its streets, traversed one summer Sunday by five young boys, peanut sellers, and inhabitants of the Morro do Cabaçu, a *favela* in the suburbs of the city. As a counterpoint to the *favela* and the suburbs, the city emerges through the principal tourist attractions of the time. The Copacabana beach, the Sugar Loaf, the Corcovado with the Christ statue, and the Maracanã stadium successively appear as the boys' workplaces and leisure zones for the *Cariocas* (native inhabitants of Rio de Janeiro city) and tourists. This primary opposition between work and leisure is crucial to its narrative structure as it allows commercial, spatial and social relationships to operate in a Rio de Janeiro markedly divided between the poor and the rich, between the *favela* and the rest of the city. In accord with these relationships, the camera almost casually captures characters and dramas that intertwine on the streets. Contact on the physical plane emphasises the social frontiers, and above all perhaps, the diversity of values, behaviours and relationships in the different physical and social territories of the city. This constitutes the

---

[5] The *favelas* emerged in the late nineteenth century, when an urban reform destroyed popular housing in upcoming areas in the city; no effort was made to build or finance new houses. This way, the population began to occupy, usually with the tolerance of the government, the hills close to the neighbourhoods where jobs were available in factories, business or homes. The term *morro* [hill] has been interchangeably used ever since, even though later the *favelas* also developed in flat areas in the city suburbs.

second and definitive opposition, which informs the narrative.

Tributary to the representation of the 'national' and the 'popular' in the political imaginary of the era, the film idealises the *favelas* and territorialises poverty and popular culture. The *favela* in *Rio 40 Graus* is the hill partially taken up by the houses of the poor, representing the physical and cultural space in which develops a sociability which implies work, leisure and solidarity. The first point of view alludes to the low population density of the *favelas* of the time, the occupants of which nonchalantly occupy the football field, the *terreiro de samba* (*samba* ground); physical and cultural meeting points. The second presents the *favela* as a reservoir of the most authentic and elevated values of the Brazilian people. It is not by chance that the 'voice of the *favela*' is the *samba*. In contrast, the wealthier classes are shown to be futile, of dubious morality and given to foreign expressions, a recourse which reiterates the opposition between suburb and southern zone (the more affluent coastal area) present in the representations of the *cariocas* with respect to their city.

The *favela* is also a homogenous space, characterised by rudimentary social relationships, face-to-face contact and community existence, in which the neighbour substitutes for the family and poverty is shared with affection. Representations portray some of the traits of the *favela* archetype, formulated at the beginning of the twentieth century by journalists and state officials and which united the social imaginary in respect of these communities, being reproduced, as they were, in a major part of the sociological output of the subsequent period (Valladares, 2000). Also, in Brazilian popular music, the *favelas* are repeatedly represented as a resource of this homogeneity: a 'social space ... which is moved by the same emotions, *o morro sorri* [the *favela* smiles], *nós vivemos alegres a cantar* [we live happy to sing], *o morro está triste* [the *favela* is sad], *o morro está de luto* [the *favela* is in mourning] (Souto de Oliveira e Marcier, 1996: 80).

From another angle, the *favela* is the place of residence of the poor, presented as workers and 'decent people'. It is also the place of the *malandro*[6] of *samba* and *cachaça* (Brazilian cane spirit), of the martial dance *capoeira* and football, of card games and cockfights. However, we are not strictly dealing with two mutually exclusive logics; the ethics of *malandragem* (acts of the *malandro*), which is mythified and celebrated in popular song (Souto de Oliveira e Marcier, 1996: 94ff), and the ethics of work based on puritan values and the pursuit of productivity. Rather, in the particular construction of the film resides the alternative ethic that distances the *favela* as much from the bourgeois world as from urban marginalisation. Nelson Pereira dos Santos removes the stigma that surrounds the *favela* by means of the affirmation of another work ethic, which embraces class conscience and dignity. This perspective is commendably expressed in the drama which runs through the film, lending it tension: the lovers quarrel between the *malandro* [trickster] who is ignored, the mulatta and her boyfriend – this external to the

---

[6] Editor's note: see Roberto Schwarz's and Juliet Line's contributions for accounts of this Brazilian social actor.

favela. The quarrel is resolved in an anti-climax, at the moment in which the rivals find themselves united as textile workers and strikers. The same point of view is reiterated in the conversation between the mulatta and her boyfriend when he warns her that the dream of improving their lives is mere illusion if it is not a collective improvement.

In *Rio 40 Graus* there is no reference implicating the *favela* with the world of crime. While he criticises the bourgeois work ethic, Nelson Pereira dos Santos withdraws the figure of the *malandro* from the field of marginality and criminality, bestowing upon him the virtue of worker by the identification with a conscious working class, in this way undoing those symbolic connections which had been constructed and territorialised in the *favelas* of Rio de Janeiro (Valladares, 1991). The same occurs with the infant and adolescent *favela* dwellers: there is no association of these with violence, crime or delinquency. What dominates their lives is child labour, which appears natural in the face of the miserable conditions of their families and the absolute absence of the state. The focus of the film, therefore, is on the revelation of another type of marginality. By means of the poverty of the *favela*, the precarious nature of the homes, the absence of public services, there emerges a *favela* on the margins of society, i.e., with regards to its rights and public politics.

The one great omission in this portrait of the daily life of the inhabitants of the Rio de Janeiro *favela* is religion, as Jean-Claude Bernadet points out: 'It is surprising that in this film which seeks to be realistic, there is no religious element, in spite of the fact that there are situations favourable to it, such as the preparations for a wedding, a woman's illness and the death of a young boy' (1996: 188). And it is Bernadet who indicates to us the reasons for the elimination of religious traces: the left considers religion to be the alienating 'opium of the people'; it seems to be incompatible with the construction of a positive image of the people, repressed in solidarity and conscience.

Rio Zona Norte

In this film [*Rio Northern Zone*], directed by Nelson Pereira dos Santos (1957, 87 minutes, black and white), the *favela* appears mainly as a background to the life of a composer from a *samba* school, a suburban resident. Projected through this character, the image of the *carioca favela* is that of an almost rural ambience (few houses very spaced out, a fair amount of vegetation), conspicuous by its location and by the access to it by train. Beyond this, it is just extremely poor. Focusing on the poverty and on the lack of alternatives this offers, the film brings *favela*, hillside and suburb together, allowing the elements of social and economic identity to prevail over the geographic and spatial differences between the three terms.

On the other hand, contrary to *Rio 40 Graus*, the film does not tackle the relationship between the *favela* and the rest of the city, which appears strongly demarcated as a hostile and external world. It does not even offer any collective solution for the lives of its inhabitants. From the opening sequence, which shows the composer in agony after falling from a train, there follows a sequence of episodes without solution, which represent the key memories of his life. The beauty of his *samba* comes up against the problem of lack of access to radio and singers. The necessity to earn a living brings him to trust his songs to a crafty character who appropriates them. The search for a new love vanishes in the face of his miserable situation. Finally, his son, who has been lost to the world of crime, is found assassinated.

A comparison between the two films reveals that in *Rio Zona Norte* the vision of the *favela* is more lyrical, although in certain aspects less idealised, than the previous film. Nelson Pereira dos Santos continues to operate with several of the previously analysed elements, in particular offering a Manichean representation of the physical, social and moral territories of the city. He presents the *favela* as a space of poverty and of authentic popular culture, translated into *samba*, making the terms almost synonymous. What is added to the previously mentioned approach is the dynamic between *favela* and suburb inhabitants who are homogenised under the category of 'the poor'. The poor are simultaneously portrayed as guardians of Brazilian culture and bearers of the most elevated values and pure sentiments. The figure of the *samba* musician is emblematic in this sense, uniting creativity, ingenuity, good character and kindness to his fellow man. Contrarily, evil comes from outside the *favela*, represented by the false friend from the city who steals the rights to his *sambas*, suggested in the new wife who allows herself to be seduced for material goods and in the criminals who lead his son into crime and to his death. Expressions of evil, crime and violence are external to the *favela* but may contaminate it.

However, while *Rio 40 Graus* is a film which values the collectives of *favela* inhabitants and workers, and finishes on a note of hope indicating the possibility of a reversal of reality by the militant unions and/or politics, *Rio Zona Norte* is characterised by the observation of the precarious living conditions which undermine the expectations of the inhabitants of *favela*s and the suburbs, and which condemns them to a sad destiny. In this film the desire to compose a realistic portrait of the inhabitants of Rio de Janeiro's *favelas* and suburbs does not give in to the temptation to offer them collective solutions not inscribed in the immediacy of their lives. For this very reason, from the opening images, its central character appears to us to be inexorably defeated by poverty.

Cinco Vezes Favela

This film [*Five Times Favela*] (1962, 92 minutes, black and white) is composed of five episodes, five short films dealing with the difficulties and misfortunes of the inhabitants of Rio de Janeiro *favelas*: *Um Favelado* [*A Favela Dweller*] by Marcos Faria; *Zé da Cachorra* [*Zé of the Bitch*] by Miguel Borges; *Escola de Samba, Alegria de Viver* [*Samba School, Joy of Living*] by Carlos Diegues; *Couro de Gato* [*Cat Hide*] by Joaquim Pedro de Andrade, and *Pedreira de São Diogo* [*São Diogo Quarry*] by Leon Hirschman. The film was produced with the ambition of 'promoting the politicisation and the awareness of the popular masses' (Martins, 1999). This didactic dimension, characteristic of the political pedagogy of the time, seems to be mainly responsible for the linearity of the situations presented. Concerning theme, Bernadet, making special reference to the dramatic structure of the first three shorts, observes: 'each director begins his film with a given vision of society already schematised in terms of problems which derive more from the reading of sociology books than from a direct contact with the reality they would film: the *favela*' (1978: 30). Thus, none 'left to reality the least possibility of being richer, more complex than the problem the director wished to expose' (1965: 221). In this sense, we could say that rather than filming the *favelas* themselves they filmed their ideas in the *favelas*.

In fact, four of the shorts in *Cinco Vezes Favela* have fairly schematised characters and an idealised representation of the *favelas*, which are repeatedly shown to be communities opposing society. The tension between the two is expressed via the opposition of the values that permeate both, and in the permanent threat of material and symbolic destitution which society presents to the former. The only chance to stand up against this hostile world would be the affirmation of the *favelados* (the inhabitants of the *favela*) in collective action as one sees in the debate in each episode.

Um Favelado gives an account of the drama of an unemployed inhabitant who decides to steal. It shows the *favela* to be a miserable environment, punctuated by hunger, via the children who collect litter, by means of the women who wash clothes in the river and carry tins of water on their heads. The protagonist, on the verge of desperation and starving, threatened with the loss of his shack and without any prospects for the future, decides to accept the proposals of a delinquent who does not live in the *favela*. The transgression is therefore read on the key of social matters. However, the inability of the *favela* inhabitant to carry out the crime (he ends up being lynched and imprisoned) reveals that this is not the way out for workers.

The opposition between the solidarity of the *favela* and the corruption and greed of the world external to it is treated once again in *Zé da Cachorra*. The *favela* is portrayed as a community that tries to block the expulsion of a family by a person, who, with the support of a politician, falsely claims to be the landowner, charging rents and generally taking advantage of their misery.

The theme of collective action is re-explored in *Escola de Samba*, *Alegria de Viver* and *Pedreira de São Diogo*. The first proffers the different paths taken by a *samba* musician fighting against the lack of resources for his *samba* school to parade in the Carnival, and by his union activist wife. Accompanying both, the film portrays, via the futility of the *samba* musicians' efforts, *samba* and Carnival as a form of alienation of the popular classes. In *Pedreira de São Diogo*, the quarry workers ally themselves with the inhabitants of a *favela* to put a stop to the explosions that threaten them. The film celebrates, in Eisensteinian terms, the force of the people, demonstrating the solidarity between the poor and the exploited. There is no hesitation between one or the other. The answer lies in organisation. It just lacks a spark to start it.

Already *Couro de Gato*, produced two years previously, renounces the idealisation of the *favelas* and their inhabitants, adding complexity to the situation and the characters it presents. It accompanies a group of boys, who, close to Carnival, hunt cats in the city to sell them for the

156

manufacture of tambourines. The survival strategy of the boys prevails over affection, even if it does not exclude it. The friendship between one of the children and the cat does not stop him selling it, even though he is sad. And if the *favela* leads to child labour (the boys are shoe shiners, peanut or newspaper vendors), the themes of fear and order are also present. The inhabitants of the city are now not necessarily so hostile, since they treat a boy from the *favela* with sympathy and generosity. On the other hand the *favela* appears as a territory delimited by the absence of the state and its order, as much in the actions of the boy who steals a cat and shelters there, fleeing the police, as in the characters that pursue him and who remain powerless and fearful on the ascent to the *favela*. There too a *favelado* is arrested, attracted by the great commotion. The frontier between city and *favela* punctuates the deadlock in which everyone is placed.

Of the five shorts, *Couro de Gato* is the one which stands out, as much in terms of cinematographic language, particularly in the agile and creative editing, as in the breaking with the idealisation of the inhabitants of *favelas* and the Manicheism in the thought on their relationship with the rest of the city, therefore introducing a more nuanced vision of the Rio de Janeiro *favelas* into Brazilian cinema.

Representations of the *Favelas* of Rio de Janeiro in two Contemporary Brazilian Films

> I did not want to make a film about violence; I wanted to make a film about misery. About the relationship between misery and the wealth of Rio de Janeiro. I believe that this situation is what is violent.[7]
>
> The *favela* functions as social synthesis, it is a trailer of the plural Brazil that the country can still be. If we do not film this we have no role whatsoever in cinema.[8]

Como Nascem os Anjos

This film [*How Angels Are Born*] (1996, 96 minutes, colour, directed by Murillo Salles) introduced a new perspective over Rio's *favelas*. A long way from the lyricism and empathy with which the previously examined films approach the theme, Murillo Salas's film is denuded of any compassion for, or complicity with, the inhabitants of *favelas*. It portrays their lives as a brutal reality, accentuated by crude and unglamorous photography. The absurd derives from trivial situations, all of which are permeated by a violence without sense or solution.

The opening sequences announce how the film will be. In the first, Branquinha, an almost adolescent young female inhabitant of the Santa Marta *favela*, negotiates a fee with German television reporters, to record an interview. Cut to the drug-trafficking 'fortress' where, amid weapons, marijuana and cocaine, Maguila, a half-witted adult, later referred to as 'Branquinha's man', without meaning to, challenges the

---

[7] Murilo Salles, 1996: 26.
[8] Carlos Diegues, 1999.

authority of the local chief drug trafficker. Placed in the situation of kill or be killed, Maguila shoots him and flees the *favela*. Here the film really starts. There is another sequence in the *favela*, the interview with Branquinha. Asked what she hopes for her future, the young girl replies 'the coolest, streetwise girl of the *favela* of Santa Marta, respected by the in-crowd'. As to employment, she does not even think about it: 'What for? To work on the tills in the supermarket? As a domestic cleaner?' When the reporters inquire into how she supports herself, she says she has a husband. When they want to know if she has dreams, she refers to *jogo do bicho* (an illegal betting game involving animals or numbers)[9] which is very popular in Brazil: 'It is difficult to dream. Only sometimes about an elephant'. Thus, the absence of alternatives in her and others' young lives in the *favela* is demonstrated.

Here resides the radical freshness of Murillo Salles's film. Even if it is not strictly speaking a film about the *favela*, it appears as the background to a reality wrung dry by violence, by the despotism of drug-trafficking, by the lack of alternatives for its inhabitants, particularly the youngsters, and, finally, by their rejection of the world of labour (which offers them little or nothing), and by the seduction of the power and money provided by the trafficking of drugs. It is also a densely populated area, with precarious urbanisation, where every moment is marked by the absence of the state and its policies. The protagonists, Branquinha and her friend Japa, are neither good nor bad, simply without alternatives. The contrast the film establishes between the two protagonists is not sufficient to provide them with different destinies (Branquinha apparently does not study, instead she takes care of the house and of her two younger brothers. Japa's mother looks after him and his two brothers, he studies in a state school and does not want to get involved with the local gangs). The lack of alternatives derives from the *favela* itself. The violence to which they are submitted also turns them into characters who go through many mismatches and conflicts between the *favela* and the 'asphalt', already announced in the amazement of the German crew at the girl's answers.[10]

Murillo Salles stated in an interview (1996) that the original script was very extensive, that in fact it contained two films: the *favela* film and the house film, and that he opted to make the house film. In fact, from these sequences onwards, all of the action takes place in the more affluent areas of the city. Maguila and Branquinha leave the *favela*, fleeing the gang of traffickers and steal a car along with its occupants. In the confusion they take Japa, who had been trying to dissuade Branquinha from fleeing. At a certain moment, Maguila asks to be allowed to enter a house to urinate, refusing to do it in the street because he believes that doing so would take away his dignity, likening him to an animal. The subtlety of the distinction serves no purpose in a code that already regards the inhabitants of *favelas* as 'animalised' in their living

---

[9] Editor's note: See Rodríguez in this volume on betting games in Brazil.

[10] Editor's note: 'Men from the asphalt' relates to those who live in the urbanised areas and benefit from access to all services, in contrast to those who live in the unpaved *favelas* uphill.

hand-in-hand with misery, marginality and crime. Perceived as nonsense, the request seems to imply the intention of assault. Maguila takes a bullet from the house owners' security guard, and, out of revenge, kills him. From this moment onwards, with every move they make, they become more and more entangled in a web which wraps them in incomprehension and crime, forcing them to keep on going in the same direction. Thus, it reinforces the initial idea that the only destiny possible to the *favelados* (inhabitants of the *favela*) is misfortune. Entering the house to treat Maguila, Branquinha and Japa end up taking the house's inhabitants as hostages, creating a situation which is interpreted by the family, and later by the media and the police, as assault and kidnap.

The 'house film' concerns the difficult intimacy between the inhabitants of Rio de Janeiro's *favelas* and the citizens of the rest of the city, which is heightened by the fact that the latter are represented by a North American family (father and daughter). However, if the conflict and the misunderstanding derive in part from their incapacity to understand the language and the codes operating in Brazil, the greater estrangement between the Americans and Brazilians concerns this way of being a child in Brazil. Avoiding the theme of the street children, the film presents diverse aspects of the daily life of the children and adolescents in the Rio de Janeiro *favelas*: the attempt to distinguish themselves from the field of criminality in Japa's insistence in affirming that he is not a criminal; the children's fascination with the lifestyle and consumption of the Americans; the naturalisation of the violence of the drug traffickers; the recourse to the media and the human rights organisations to protect their rights and their lives from police violence; the manipulation of verbal and visual codes in their favour; the fascination with fame and the media which makes Japa breakdance in front of the police and the television cameras.

This mosaic resulted from the research preceding the film, an important tendency of Brazilian cinema in recent years as part of the numerous links which are being set up between documentary and fiction, as well as those between cinema and anthropology (Monte-Mór, 1998). More than 300 hours of statements were recorded from young boys and girls, inhabitants of *favelas*, for the construction of the characters. More than just for picking up vocabulary, producing dialogues and creating credible situations, this research allowed the director to reveal, with sensitivity, a multifaceted reality. It comes close to that fine tradition of the social sciences, to learn about the 'other' in all his/her complexity and difference.

It was this perspective which situated the making of the film. *Como Nascem os Anjos* does not propose to offer the viewer elements to classify its protagonists, to absolve or condemn them. They are neither completely innocent nor criminals. The film demonstrates how they move between the two universes with relative self-confidence and that it is not within their power to choose their destinies. As Ivana Bentes emphasises, they are victims of a violence that they trigger and yet do not control. A violence which, unlike what was happening in *Cinema Novo*, is deprived of any ethical finality: 'a violence without *telos* which will not lead to the Revolution, but...to diffuse and anarchic death (...) The sense of the violence, the anger of the victims of injustice is now juxtaposed with the random image of the violence' (1999: 93).

Orfeu

From the start, *Orfeu* [*Orpheus*] (1999, 111 minutes, colour, directed by Carlos Diegues) is a film about the *favela*. In transposing the Greek legend[11] to the Rio de Janeiro *favelas*, Carlos Diegues values the love between Orpheus and Eurydice as much as the conflict between civilisation and barbarism of which Orfeu and Lucinho (the chief local drug trafficker) are protagonists.

In the original 1956 theatre production *Orfeu da Conceição* [*Orpheus of the Conception*] by Vinícius de Moraes, with music by Tom Jobim, the transfer the classic myth to the hills of Rio de Janeiro did not have as its objective a discussion about the *favela*, but simply to use it as the setting for a love tragedy during Carnival. The first film version, *Orfeu Negro* [*Black Orpheus*] was made by Marcel Camus in 1959, winning the Palmes D'or at the Cannes Festival as well as the Oscar for best foreign film in the same year. It offers an almost folkloric, idealised vision of the hills and *favelas* of Rio de Janeiro. Its characters live and skip in idyllic harmony in a type of original paradise, characterised by the *samba*, by love and happiness. The conflicts of love are the only ones that disturb the lives of the characters. Nothing worries them except death. Here the *favela* is just scenery.

In Carlos Diegues's film, the love drama presents nothing new. In full Carnival-mode, Orfeu, a successful musician, director of the *samba* school *Unidos da Carioca* and composer of its *samba*, falls in love with Eurídice. The love ends in tragedy when she is accidentally killed by the drug traffickers of the *favela* where they live. In his pain and delirium, Orfeu goes to look for the body and ends up dying too. The great impact of the film comes from attempting to see the *favela* from the point of view of its inhabitants, instead of favouring the dominant point of view of the city which homogenises the *favelas*, treating them as territories of poverty, of marginality and of crime, and at the same time stigmatising the inhabitants as real or virtual members of the so called 'dangerous classes'. This perspective sees an opposition, if not a war, between the *favelas* and the rest of the city, and perceives the former by means of the conflicts, contradictions and dangers which they may represent for the latter.

In *Orfeu*, on the contrary, we come across a heterogeneous, urbanised, densely populated *favela*, which is just as much home to the miserable and the poor as the rest of the city is to comfortably-off families, who do not allow themselves to be defined by a linear and univocal reading. The image of the *favela* set-design, named and

---

[11] Orpheus, the son of the king of Traco, was a musician; his tunes were so melodious that they would charm even creatures devoid of sensibility. He used music to calm down the ferocious customs of the Tracos and make them shift from a barbaric life to a civilised one. He fell in love with Eurydices, who died on her wedding day; he went down to the underworld to fetch her but he died too as he ignored the prohibition of not looking at her before leaving the place (Commelin, 1997: 284-285).

160

especially constructed for the film, distances itself from the representations of the *favelas* in the cinema of the 1950s and 1960s which were little more than a few wooden shacks with corrugated iron roofs, beaten earth floors and a lot of black ditches. Carlos Diegues and his set designer climbed various hilltops to research today's *favelas* (Sukman, 1998). The result is a synthesis of the setting of contemporary Rio de Janeiro *favelas* that is complemented by location work in diverse areas around the city.

Carlos Diegues recently said that the best compliment the film received was from Nelson Pereira dos Santos who, in an interview stated: 'if *Rio 40 Graus* were made today, it would very much resemble *Orfeu*' (Almeida 2000). I believe that both refer to two connected facts: the *favelas* have changed and the perspectives (of film-makers, researchers, of the people) have changed too, with regards to the *favelas* of Rio de Janeiro.

The Rio *favela* is, above all else, a conflictive and tense space that breaks with the idyllic image of community. The conflicts which are presented are no longer reduced to the city versus *favela* type. As a matter of fact, the city hardly makes an appearance in the film. It is only a postcard scene which Diegues attempts to enhance by means of beautiful photography, or it is presented as the police, 'the only thing from the government which goes up to the *favela*', as one character states. Some of *Orfeu's* high points are the images of the police in the *favela* (which reveal police violence, disrespect for citizenship and human rights, and appeals to the media to denounce violence against the inhabitants) and the prejudice against the *favelados* (who are considered to be always ready to join the trafficking and crime) and, above all the promiscuity of the police with the traffickers, here linked to comradeship, but which the citizens of Rio de Janeiro usually only hear of via the media as being linked to corruption.

If the conflict between the police and the gang of drug traffickers and that between the police and the *favelados* runs through the film (and the *favela*), other conflicts between the *favelados* themselves now emerge. Especially the religious conflicts between the evangelists and the followers of the possession cults, represented in the relationship between Orfeu's parents. With regards to this aspect, there are two key scenes. Seu Inácio states, 'the word of Jesus expelled the Devil from my heart', referring to the bohemian lifestyle, to *samba* and alcohol. Dona Conceição turns to the *Orixás*, Afro-Brazilian religious entities, when in affliction. It is via the new and expressive presence of the evangelical religions, the circumscribed practitioners of the Afro-Brazilian religions, and the absence of the Catholic religion in the *favela* that the film, with sensitivity, brings religion to the surface, showing its capacity to redefine relationships and identities (Birman and Leite, 2000).

While the religious conflicts are organised into a confrontation between good and evil, another conflict punctuates the film, resisting a Manichean reading. It deals with the conflict that develops between the drug traffickers and the civilian population of the *favela*, here represented in the multiple possibilities of approximation and distancing between the two segments as a counterpoint to the relationship between the favour mechanisms that the former establish in Rio *favelas*. Its central axis is without doubt the relationship between Orfeu and Lucinho. On this basis the conflict assumes a double edge. On the one hand, the basic disagreement in relation to Lucinho's opting to traffic drugs – on the other, the absence of a rupture. Orfeu and Lucinho, raised together, can no longer be friends, yet neither can they turn against each other as enemies. Relationships are not suppressed with the conflict because both the physical and social spaces of the *favela* and the control of the drug traffickers demand and establish mediations and conviviality. It is this that Eurídice does not understand, coming as she does from outside the *favela,* and, as a city dweller, considers connivance.

The confrontation between Orfeu and Lucinho does not bring about a rupture (except in the final scenes via Eurídice's demands). But through the project to supplant barbarism with culture, the former, a modern *Orfeu*, aims to seduce the new barbarians, the traffickers, who boast that 'although living a little, this little I live well', and the youngsters who would follow them. Orfeu's ambition is to civilise them with his example of a *favelado* made good through music, as the film suggests happens to Maicon, an adolescent who seemed to be flirting with the fringes of the trafficking only to glimpse in painting another option.

Diegues was extremely happy to portray the vitality of the cultural life of the *Carioca favelas*, in which the *samba* no longer claims exclusivity, embracing *pagode*, funk (Brazilian popular musical styles) and hip-hop too. The new voices of the *favela* are present in *Orfeu*. On one hand, the drug trafficking and the evangelical churches, and on the other, *samba*, funk, and hip-hop with its cutting raps, which affirm the rights of the *favelados* and denounce police abuse and the community radio, which, in the first part of the film, represents a type of Greek chorus. Absent voices in *Orfeu* are the Catholic Church (as mentioned), the residents' associations, and the labour market. Of the first two, not a sign. Regarding work, it appears as part of the lives of *favelados*, who are referred to as dressmaker, cabinet maker, manicurist, taxi driver, domestic cleaner, musician, *etcetera*. However, neither work nor consumption are incorporated in the *favela's* day-to-day activities, neither does work constitute a significant dimension in the lives of the community. The world of work appears in *Orfeu* as doubly negative. In the same way as *Como Nascem os Anjos*, the film emphasises, on the one hand the difficulties of the labour market for the poor, young *favelados*, and on the other, an increasingly frequent denial of poorly paid or menial work. Lucinhos' statements ('Do what? Be a dustman or cleaner?') equate to those of Branquinha, the character in Murilo Salles's film in her choice of trafficking as an alternative life.

Right away *Orfeu* represents another of the new voices of the *favela*. Perhaps what receive more support from the rest of the city are specifically its non-governmental organisations. It is a voice that also represents the 'good things the *favela* has too' and thus achieves a mediation between the *favela* and the rest of the city, by means of art and culture, beyond *samba*. In Rio de Janeiro we are not lacking in these voices: Afro-Reggae, from Vigário Geral; *Companhia Étnica de Teatro e*

Dança do Andaraí [*The Andaraí Ethnic Company of Theatre and Dance*], *Corpo de Dança da Maré* [*The Maré Dance Corporation*], *Nós do Cinema* [*We in Cinema*], the theatre group *Nós da Favela* [*Us from the Hill*] and so many others groups, which aim to distance themselves from marginality and fuel the recognition and self-esteem of the *favela* populations by placing value on their cultural manifestations.

This is the image of the *favela* that Carlos Diegues wanted to illustrate in his film. In an interview at the time of shooting, he argued that the *favelas* found themselves in their third generation, and that Brazilian cinema was accompanying their development. For the film-maker, the 1950s *favela* with scant housing and an almost rural lifestyle was represented in a lyrical manner, as in *Rio 40 Graus* and *Orfeu da Conceição*. In the 1960s, with the migration to, and swelling of the cities, the *favelas* became an 'overpopulated place, marked by misery'. The 'era of the lament' had begun in which 'the *favela* was the ideal theme for film-makers who were looking for, at the same time, signs of injustice and identity', as in *Cinco Vezes Favela*. Today the *favela* 'fights for affirmation, for the pride to be a *favelado*, even living side-by-side with all of its problems, such as violence'. It is this *favela* which *Orfeu* wishes, perhaps for the first time, to depict on the screen' (Sukman, 1998). It was possibly this perspective that influenced Diegues to bring about the return of film to the *favelas*, shown with reasonable success in diverse towns and cities.

Thinking about the elements that these films bring to the *Carioca* political imaginary, especially in terms of the theme of violence in the city, it is worth emphasising the field of alternatives in operation. If Murilo Salles's film glimpses and proposes nothing, Carlos Diegues's work considers the exit from this universe by means of art and culture. However, neither sees any possibility of changing the situation by means of an affirmation of citizenship via the social movements or politics.

From another angle, I would like still to emphasise that while Orfeu looks to portray the pride in being a *favelado*, by means of a construction of an alternative which avoids drug trafficking as much as the *samba*, the previously analysed films of the 1950s and 1960s sought, above all, to stimulate the pride and the conscience of being a worker. In two recent interviews, Diegues explains how he sees that difference, which I believe can be applied also to Murilo Salles's film: 'It is that here we are not trying to tell the people what they should do, we do not have that pretension anymore. *Orfeu* is not *Cinema Novo*, it is contemporary cinema' (Graça, 2000). Also: 'the agenda of the *Cinema Novo* generation was [...] to change cinema, Brazil and the world. Today I know that a film does not change the world, but it can change the way of seeing it' (Diegues, 1999).

In a certain sense, however, *Como Nascem os Anjos* and *Orfeu* approach the *Cinema Novo* tradition. Both move from the theme of poverty to the theme of violence, and deal with violence and drug trafficking, the conflicts between the inhabitants of the *favelas* and the rest of the city, drug traffickers and police, the poor and the rich as if they touched the 'nerve of society' bringing it to the surface of the skin. They expose elements in the daily lives of the inhabitants of the *favelas* of Rio on the screen, which the greater part of the citizens of the wealthier areas of the city only know through the police news in the papers and on television and via the stories their domestic workers tell. In this movement, the characters who inhabit those stories are brought into focus (mainly the trafficker, the policeman, the adolescent without work options who is seduced by crime, also the rapper, the funk fan, the followers of the evangelical and Afro-Brazilian religions) as well as the themes of fear and crime, of the violence and the drug trafficking which have been taking place since the mid 1980s, the representations of the *favelas* and their occupants in the *Carioca* imaginary. In doing so, they point to new formats for the country's social questions, show new limits for a solution, present the new voices and images of the *favela*, as well as, in the case of *Orfeu*, the alternatives which are gestating. From this perspective, they advocate a meeting between the *favela* and the rest of the city which is frequently represented as 'divided'.

References

Almeida, Carlos Helí. 'Deus e Cacá são brasileiros'. In *Jornal do Brasil*, 30 April 2000.

Autran, Arthur. 'O nacional e o popular em *Eles Não Usam Black-Tie*'. In *Cinemais – Revista de Cinema e outras questões visuais*, n. 15, pp. 157-169, 1999.

Bentes, Ivana. 'Sertões e subúrbios no cinema brasileiro'. In *Cinemais – Revista de Cinema e outras questões visuais*, n. 15, pp. 85-96, 1999.

Bernadet, Jean-Claude. 'Para um cinema dinâmico'. In *Revista Civilização Brasileira*, n. 2, pp. 219-226, 1965.

Bernadet, Jean-Claude. *Brasil em tempo de cinema*: ensaios sobre o cinema brasileiro. 3rd Edition, Rio de Janeiro: Paz e Terra, 1978.

Bernadet, Jean-Claude. 'Cinema e religião'. In Xavier, Ismail (ed.). *O cinema no século.* Rio de Janeiro: Imago Editora, pp. 187-194, 1996.

Birman, Patrícia and Leite, Márcia P. 'Whatever happened to what used to be the largest Catholic country in the world?' In *Daedalus. Journal of the American Academy of Arts and Sciences*, vol. 129, n. 2, spring, pp. 271-290, 2000.

Commelin, P. *Mitologia grega e romana.* São Paulo, Martins Fontes, 1997.

Dahl, Gustavo et al. 'Vitória do Cinema Novo: Gênova, 1965 (debate with Gustavo Dahl, Carlos Diegues, David Neves, Paulo César Sarraceni and Alex Viany)'. *Revista Civilização Brasileira*, n. 2, pp. 227-248, 1965.

Diegues, Carlos. 'Cacá Diegues' (interview). *Jornal do Brasil*, 28 November 1999.

Graça, Eduardo. '*Orfeu* invade a terra de ninguém' (interview with Carlos Diegues). *Jornal do Brasil*, 11 May 2000.

Ianni, Otávio. 'A Grande Cidade'. *Revista Civilização Brasileira*, n. 13, pp. 199-202, 1967.

Leite, Márcia Pereira. 'Entre o individualismo e a solidariedade: dilemas da política e da cidadania no Rio de Janeiro'. *Revista Brasileira de Ciências Sociais*, vol. 15, n. 44, October 2000, pp. 73-90.

Martins, Carlos Estevam. 'Origem do CPC é Arena' (interview). *Jornal do Brasil*, 2 February 1999.

Monte-mór, Patrícia. 'Percorrendo o mundo: cinema etnográfico na tela'.

Catálogo da 5ª. Mostra Internacional do Filme Etnográfico. Rio de Janeiro: Museu do Folclore Edison Carneiro/Interior Produções, pp. 10-15.

Pécaud, Daniel. *Os intelectuais e a política no Brasil: entre o povo e a nação*. São Paulo: Editora Ática, 1990.

Rocha, Glauber. 'Uma estética da fome' (version cited in a paper presented at Resenha do Cinema Latino-Americano, in Geneva, January 1965). *Revista Civilização Brasileira*, n. 3, pp. 165-170, 1965.

Salles, Murilo. 'O chute na câmera na hora do pênalti' (interview). *Cinemais - Revista de Cinema e outras questões visuais*, n. 2, pp. 7-44, 1996.

Souto de Oliveira, Jane e Marcier, Maria Hortense. 'A palavra é: favela'. In Zaluar, Alba and Alvito, Marcos. (eds.) *Um século de favela*. Rio de Janeiro: Editora Fundação Getúlio Vargas, 1998, pp. 101-14.

Sukman, Hugo. 'É tudo cenário'. *O Globo*, 26 July 1998.

Sukman, Hugo. 'O nosso "Roma, cidade aberta"'. *O Globo*, 25 April 1999.

Valladares, Lícia. 'Cem anos pensando a pobreza (urbana) no Brasil'. In Boschi, Renato (ed.), *Corporativismo e desigualdade: a construção do espaço público no Brasil*. Rio de Janeiro: Rio Fundo/IUPERJ, 1991.

Valladares, Lícia. 'A gênese da favela carioca. A produção anterior às ciências sociais'. *Revista Brasileira de Ciências Sociais*, vol. 15, n. 44, October 2000, pp. 5-34.

Xavier, Ismail. 'O cinema moderno brasileiro'. *Cinemais - Revista de Cinema e Outras Questões Visuais*, n. 4, pp. 39-64, 1997.

Zaluar, Alba. 'As imagens da e na cidade: a superação da obscuridade'. *Cadernos de Antropologia e Imagem*, n. 4, pp. 107/119, 1997.

21. The Sociological Dimension of the Drug Traffic in the *Favelas* of Rio de Janeiro

Ricardo Vélez-Rodríguez

After the transfer of the federal capital to Brasília at the beginning of the 1960s, the city of Rio de Janeiro suffered its first socio-economic setback. Lacking the generous federal funds that made it a centre of services and intense political and cultural life, the former capital began to wane. A new blow came with the extinction of the State of Guanabara and its transformation into the State of Rio de Janeiro in the middle of the 1970s. Without any increase in its budget, the beautiful city had to share scant resources with the impoverished State of Rio. In the 1980s and 1990s, Rio de Janeiro succumbed to organised crime in the shape of drug trafficking, was exploited by delirious populism, and endured the general crisis of the stagnated Brazilian economy. Simultaneously, expressways cut through the city's suburbs permitting access to the rest of Brazil and the world – recalling the 'open veins of Latin America'[1] where the blood of citizens, mercilessly killed in bus and car accidents, flows.

Periods in the Evolution of the Drug Traffic

In the evolution of the Rio drug traffic, we may distinguish four historical periods:

First Period: From 1950 to 1980 we find, in the annals of crime, a predominance of the *jogo de bicho* [numbers game]. The city was full of *bicheiros*, or numbers bankers, but these people were somewhat folkloric figures, who in no way matched the dimensions of the violence unleashed nowadays in the hills and on the streets by the present-day drug dealers. Today, we would even feel naively nostalgic for rogues like Mineirinho (in the 1950s) and Tião Medonho (in the 1960s). The gangsters of subsequent years became much more violent, protected by the impunity enjoyed by the *bicheiros*. Gangsters like Lúcio Flávio (in the 1970s) or Escadinha (in the 1980s) became more sophisticated and more threatening.

Second Period: From 1980 to 1990, the fire-power of the numbers racketeers increased in the hillside slums, owing to the acquisition, by a part of this group, of long-range arms. The police no longer went up into the hills by the time of Brizola's first government (from 1983). On the other hand, the illegal drug market was consolidated, to the extent that the Colombian cartels began to be systematically combated by Brizola's government and the American Drug Enforcement Agency.

Third Period: Between 1990 and 2000, dealers consolidated the power of the numbers racketeers and began to systematically intimidate the population and build a businesslike organisation for their illicit trade. A comprehensive plan was designed that included broadening traditional betting places into rationally managed drug-dealing posts, diversifying

---

[1] Editor's note: A metaphor used by the Uruguayan thinker Eduardo Galeano to express the ruthless exploitation of human and natural resources by foreign powers in Latin America, in turn making it ever more vulnerable.

investments with front companies, laying down the foundations for exporting drugs, expanding the criminal drug business to other states in Brazil, and organising armies of death that enlisted police forces to ensure training and the acquisition of weapons and ammunition. The city was parcelled out among the *bicheiros* and criminal power in Rio de Janeiro gave way to a new generation of gangsters, the drug dealer-businessmen, one of whose most important representatives was Ernaldo Pinto Medeiros, nicknamed 'Uê'. Even in the maximum security prison of Bangu-I, Uê commanded the drug-selling posts in the hills.

Fourth period: From 2000 to 2003, Fernandinho Beira-Mar and Leonardo Dias Mendonça, the two most important Brazilian bosses, organised the *Suricartel*, a multinational company of crime and drug-trafficking whose headquarters was in Surinam under the protection of the ex-dictator Bouterse, which guaranteed arms to FARC, the Revolutionary Armed Forces of Colombia, and cocaine to the *favelas* of Rio, allowing Fernandinho Beira-Mar to dominate the other major drug dealers. Around this particular criminal the command of the drug traffic in Rio-São Paulo was unified and war against the establishment in Rio de Janeiro was declared.

Background: The Patrimonial State

The reality of the Rio drug traffic must be put into the context of the 'patrimonial' state, which was the mode of political organisation that prevailed in Brazil. Let us recall the fundamental characteristic of this socio-political formation. The State, in the context of Patrimonialism, according to Weber (1944; IV, 54-178), emerged as an excessive growth of an original patriarchal power, which enlarged its domestic domination over territories and people, and administered unowned as family (patrimonial) property. This strong tradition, on which the modernising forces that mark Brazilian history weigh, has not yet been surpassed. The state, as Faoro said (1958), 'has owners'. Republican history, in Brazil and the other countries of Latin America, is rich in examples of attempts by groups and political assemblies to privatise power. The 'politics of the governors' obeyed, in the context of the Brazilian Old Republic (1889-1930), an attempt by the regional elites to take hold of the state bureaucratic machinery as a means of enrichment. The long period of the rule of Getúlio Vargas (1943-1954), from 1930 to 1945, and, later, from 1951 to 1954, offered the opportunity to try to discipline traditional Patrimonialism, resulting in the emergence of a modernising project in tune with the overblown central executive power, which began to co-opt the regional patrimonial proprietors, the traditional oligarchies, to support a proposal that would establish the foundations for industrialisation. But this authoritarian, modernising effort, put into practice by the Second 'Castilhista' Generation[2], composed of the younger generation under Vargas's leadership that followed the teachings of Júlio de Castilhos (1860-1903), encountered strong opposition in the traditional oligarchical sectors, as well as in the context of their minute, servile bureaucracy, and in some intellectual and in certain political segments (a minority, to be

---

[2] See Vélez, 2000.

sure) of liberal inspiration.

The second half of the last century saw the emergence of two tributary modernising periods of the Vargas model: the goals of Juscelino Kubitschek (who governed from 1956 to 1961) and the military regime from 1964 to 1984.[3] The return to democratic life did not necessarily guarantee the preservation of the modernising elements, which survived alongside the traditional co-optive liturgy of the oligarchies, around the various republics in which Brazilian political experience of recent decades can be disseminated. One may speak, in succession, of the 'Republic of Maranhão' (presided over from 1985 to 1990 by José Sarney), of the 'Republic of Alagoas' (commanded by Fernando Collor de Mello from 1990 to 1992), of the 'Republic of Juiz de Fora' (organised around the government of Itamar Franco, from 1992 to 1994), and of the 'Republic of the Party of Brazilian Social Democracy' (presided over by Fernando Henrique Cardoso during two presidential administrations, which include the period from 1995 to 2003). In the present time of the national consolidation of the Labour Party leadership, with sensitive areas like health being parcelled out among the political clients of the party militants, we can speak of the 'Republic of the Steelworkers'. The bureaucratic machine is carefully filled at its federal and state levels with those who best represent the interests of the 'Republic of those on duty'. Is this a total absence of public spirit? It would be unjust to say such a thing, but it would also be utopian to think that we are in a strict republican regime, in which the *res publica* is not confused with the *cosa nostra* (our thing), with the private and clan interests of those who exercise power – a thing, let us say, which is still owed to Brazilian reality.

The Folkloric Numbers Racketeers

Marginality has been accommodated, in Brazil, to the essence of the patrimonial state. The traditional outlaw, the folkloric numbers banker, or *bicheiro*, has always lived well with the patrimonial structure of the region. An example of this model of accommodation was, in the old State of Guanabara, the administration of the governor Chagas Freitas (1970-1974), in which such men found their place in the sun without crossing the line of what was tolerated. The diligent bet-takers operated in places previously agreed on with the police, who religiously collected their small bribes, and things were kept peaceful in the local way. This type of law-breaker prevailed in the life of Rio until the 1980s. Was this an exclusively Brazilian reality in the Latin American context? Certainly not. A rather close parallel might be established between the *bicheiro* of Rio and the *chancero* of Medellín, both agents of an informal economy, in an activity much appreciated in contexts in which the 'shortcut ethic' replaces the 'work ethic': one attains wealth by the heroic path of war against the infidel, or through games of chance, which guarantee the desire for easy money at the drop of a hat and without the uncomfortable obligation to work. The social structure built around the traditional *bicheiro* had much in common with the practices of the Sicilian mafia:

---

[3] See Paim, 1994.

fidelity to agreements, a sense of family and honour, solidarity with the members of the clan, collaboration with other *bicheiros* in a kind of 'horizontal clientism', cruelty to deserters or to those who violate the rules of the game.

A New Outlaw: The Drug Dealer

With Brizola's first administration at the beginning of the 1980s, the *favelas* were converted into fortresses of criminality and there began to arise a new type of outlaw much more aggressive than the traditional *bicheiro*: the *traficante*, or drug dealer. This type does not arrive overnight, but appears first as an employee of the *bicheiro*, as that bold new salesman that assumes command of the new market in the city – drugs, marijuana initially. With the arrival of cocaine on the Rio scene during the1980s, and with the extraordinary profits made in this new business, some *bicheiros* abandoned the 'soft criminal' profile and turned themselves into common drug dealers. This is the case, for example, of Aniz Abraham David, who appears in the annals of the Rio numbers game as the one who broke the parental ties. What counts is immediate enrichment, or the maintenance, at any cost, of primacy obtained through terror. The testimony of Aniz's ex-wife is typical of this new kind of criminal, the *bicheiro* who became a *traficante*. Some of these men rise meteorically from the hosts who perform services for the old *bicheiros* and begin to increasingly gain control, based exclusively on intimidation and indiscriminate violence.

Men like Elias 'Maluco' [Crazy] illustrate this new type of character in the social panorama of Rio. In the areas where the drug traffic becomes strong, a new hierarchy of power arises. At the top is the *chefão* or Boss, the man who buys the cocaine to be distributed and who supplies the weapons; he is the *capo di tutti capi* in the *favela*. Then comes the *gerente*, the manager. Around these leaders, in a type of primitive *gard de corp*, are those in charge of the points where the drugs are sold, who are responsible for retail sales and managing profits, as well as the 'soldiers', many of whom are minors trained and armed by the Boss. On the lower end of the hierarchy are found the 'lookouts' (who by means of kites or fireworks warn of the arrival of strangers or the presence of the police) and the Boss's 'office boy' (who distributes the merchandise on the street). The authority exercised by the Boss, the manager, and the bosses of the sales-points is vertical and indisputable. The Boss in his fortress is a kind of satrap, with the power of life and death over the people who are hostages to his domination. He holds summary tribunals against his enemies, as in the case of Tim Lopes. Whoever is not directly connected with the business of drugs must allow himself to be co-opted by it: the law of silence is the first step to ensure the anonymity of the power structure in the face of the police.

Contrary to what happened in Medellín, in the golden age of the cartel of 'Don Pablo' (which forbade under pain of death the consumption of cocaine by its assistants so as not to interfere with business), in the Rio *favelas* the fuel for this frenzied traffic is usually the drug itself. An example of this can be seen in the account by the journalist Caco Barcellos of the activities of 'Cabeludo' [Hairy], one of the bosses of the *favela* Dona Marta. He writes:

> Cabeludo's extravagance derives from the consumption of cocaine. Away from drugs, in the restricted world of crime, he was a generous, thoughtful man. Before he became a boss, he transferred part of the money taken in the great robbery of the Mint to the relatives of the men killed in the operation. He always kept his promise to send money and drugs to those in prison. When he was not snorting coke, he liked to walk around the *favela* with children and tell curious stories of robberies to the retired, who sat on the doorsteps listening for hours. A thick white line on his badly trimmed moustache showed when Cabeludo was under the influence of cocaine. On such days, he became another man. People closest to him knew this and many of them avoided him to protect themselves from his unpredictable behaviour. Cabeludo often stayed awake for three days in a row, a period during which he had hallucinations and crises of suspicion (Barcellos, 2003: 92-93).

One can imagine the incredible potential for violence that the consumption of drugs has produced in the Rio drug traffic. Proof of this can be found in the repeated massacres, such as those that also happen every day in São Paulo, Belo Horizonte, Porto Alegre, and other Brazilian cities.

As a result of the daily contact with the criminal infrastructure and owing to a lack of professional training, some sectors of the police are corrupted. They no longer expect from the drug dealers the peaceful payment of small bribes, as was the custom with the *bicheiros*. They simply practice extortion on the bosses and their assistants. Violence in this context increases in an uncontrolled way. The settling of accounts between bosses and assistants, or between the assistants and consumers or the police takes place through the simple physical elimination of all those involved and their families. This explains the terrible growth of massacres in the large cities of Brazil since the end of the 1980s. The bosses ensure their domination over their assistants and in the communities that are hostage to their autocracy, through the mechanism that the Colombian sociologists called armed 'clientism', a subservience to the drug bosses based exclusively on fear. The corrupt police, for their part, organise themselves in extermination groups who systematically engage in massacres, such as that of Vigário Geral, which occurred in Rio de Janeiro in 1993.

The Narco-Guerrillas

The third figure characteristic of the Rio scene these days is the *chefe de cartel*, or Cartel Boss. He is differentiated from the *traficante* by belonging to a wider universe. The Cartel Boss is an international drug executive, one who buys cocaine directly from the foreign cartels and who negotiates sophisticated weapons with the arms-dealers, as was the case of Fernandinho Beira-Mar, when he belonged to the organisation Suricartel, which sold arms to FARC and cocaine to the Rio *favelas*. This type of boss appeared during the 1990s and is a hero to the youths who live under his domination. He has the women he desires, inspires the rap music of the funk dances, orders beneficial works in the *favelas* and poor neighbourhoods, becomes a television actor in a series produced by foreign networks, and a star in domestic films financed by politically correct bankers and businessmen, and is on the cover of a magazine or the subject of a best-seller, like the late Pablo Escobar or Marcinho VP.[4] He has the characteristics of a strategist and a businessman. He begins to co-opt mere bosses, charging them a suzerainty tax. He has inherited the will to fight from the ancient warriors, but unlike them he is an opportunist: on the one hand, he aims at profit and thus takes on the characteristics of a pragmatic negotiator, while on the other, he has a notable ability to plan war strategy and to occupy political space in society. The Latin-American guerrillas, orphans of the Soviet allowance after the fall of the Berlin Wall in 1989, began to approach the traditional cocaine cartels in Colombia, an opportunity for this new character, the Cartel Boss, a paradoxical mixture of Sancho Panzism and Quixotism.

The Cartel Boss is a kind of *condottiere*, like those who proliferated in Italian society in the Renaissance and planted unrest and violence in the land of Machiavelli. The best expressions of this type of character are found in Colombia, in the figure of Pablo Escobar, the first Cartel Boss of the Americas, or in the current figure of Mono Jojoy, the strategist of FARC, the armed organisation that during the last decade achieved a symbiosis with elements of the old Cali Cartel.[5] As is the case of the Colombian guerrillas, especially FARC and the Army of National Liberation (which have now joined forces against the Colombian Plan of President Uribe), the most important effect of the Cartel Boss's presence is the organisation of an army of drug-traffic soldiers, called 'narco-guerrillas', who are under a single command and rigorous military discipline, and the establishment of a sophisticated business structure with executives who speak several languages and wear fashionable clothes. These executives are engineers, lawyers, and public relations men. The purpose is not the direct takeover of power, but the strengthening of power by terror so that the drug traffic can work 'in peace'. In this attempt at the organisation of a regular force, the enlisting of former armed forces officers and soldiers is an important factor, which has taken place in Colombia and is now taking place in Brazil.

The journalist Percival de Souza properly defined the climate created by narco-guerrillas in the Rio *favelas* as a 'narco-dictatorship'. Souza complains that society (read the middle and upper classes) treats with excessive benevolence the murderers who guarantee their drug-propelled dreams. In this respect, he asks: 'Why are these dictatorships treated differently? What is it about drugs that inspires charm and glamour, and why do consumers respect and admire the bosses to the extent of defending them when the subject comes up? The recipe for being implacable with the seller of dreams in the form of substances is unknown. The idea that the user cannot live without the dealer is quite

---

[4] See Barcellos, 2003; Salazar, 2001.
[5] See Villamarín, 1996:11-12.

troublesome. They confuse philanthropy with misanthropy. The narco-dictatorship orders undesirables, those who do not pay the bill when it is due, to be killed. Not paying one's bills is unknown to the vocabulary of the narco-dictator. The same thing goes for bankruptcy, forced agreements, or closures, all unheard of. Civil suits are very helpful in understanding the economy of the country. In the narco-dictatorship, the market is regulated by gunshots, stabbings, torture, and cremations. The narco-dictatorship succeeds in implanting an education ignored by the majority of those who talk about drugs' (Souza, 2002: 251).

The narco-guerrillas began to co-opt elements of civil society, notably candidates to national or regional legislatures, as well as judges, police chiefs, and (as was pointed out) officers of the armed forces. If it is necessary, as happens in Colombia, it will engage in an outright military confrontation with government agents, but the ideal is to maintain a low intensity conflict to ensure profits, without having to spend a lot of resources on a regular armed struggle. Here, the principle of 'variable administrative rentability' may be applied, as formulated by Paul Milukov for societies governed by patrimonial states.[6]

In the context of this flexible and pragmatic logic, the drug traffic accommodated itself in Latin America, and in Brazil in particular, to the wave of service-sharing and privatisation sweeping Latin American countries during the 1990s. The old Colombian cartels have been ground down into hundreds of small cartels that carry on business as strongly as ever. On this phenomenon, Argemiro Procópio has written: 'The drug traffic in Latin America dances according to the music that corrupts the three powers. It may seem bold to say so, but the deregimentation has included both the selling and the production of drugs. In the 1970s, only two Colombian cartels were really in action. At the end of the 1990s, the drug traffic had broken down into mafias, gangs, bands, and cartels of different geographical origins. This deregimentation has become flexible and out of the reach of the traditional strategies of repression' (Procópio, 1999: 242-243).

The effort to establish administrative rationality takes place as long as the lords of power need to maintain unquestionable supremacy. The tactics of the urban and rural guerrilla were incorporated by the narco-guerrillas, with all the resulting institutional breakdown, continued violence, high crime rates, growing insecurity for citizens, lack of stimulus for foreign investment, breakdown of tourism, and incentive to profitable kinds of crime, like the systematic kidnapping of businessmen, industrialists, politicians, and professionals. In the world of global terror, the Cartel Boss and the narco-guerrilla are an open door to professional terrorists, who find in them effective collaborators. Pablo Escobar's joint actions with the Basque terrorists of ETA are known (for example, a Boeing from the Colombian company Avianca was brought down in Bogota in the mid-1980s). Recently, we may recall the attacks perpetrated by the FARC in Columbia alongside IRA activists. What is happening in Colombia is beginning to also become established in Brazilian society, a tragic fate, all a consequence of the consolidation of

---

[6] See Wittfogel, 1977:69-70.

this new power – that of the Cartel Bosses aided by the narco-guerrillas. Fernandinho Beira-Mar is, no doubt, the great Brazilian paradigm of this new type of criminality. Will the Brazilian Patrimonial State succeed in confronting this new wave of disintegration and backwardness?

Translation by Thomas Laborie Burns

References

Amorim, Carlos. *Comando Vermelho*: *a história secreta do crime organizado*.
3rd ed. Rio de Janeiro: Record, 1993.

Barcellos, Caco. *Abusado*: *o dono do morro Dona Marta.* Rio de Janeiro: São Paulo: Editora Record, 2003.

Cavalcanti, Sandra. *A escalada da insegurança.* Rio de Janeiro: Expressão e Cultura, 2002.

Faoro, Raimundo. *Os donos do poder*: *formação do patronato político brasileiro*. 1st ed. Porto Alegre: Globo, 1958. 2 v.

Paim, Antônio. *A querela do estatismo*: *a natureza dos sistemas econômicos*: *o caso brasileiro*. 2nd edition, expanded and revised. Rio de Janeiro: Tempo Brasileiro, 1994.

Procópio, Argemiro. *O Brasil no mundo das drogas*. 2nd ed. Petrópolis: Vozes, 1999.

Salazar, Alonso. *La parábola de Pablo*: *auge y caída de un gran capo del narcotráfico*. Bogotá: Planeta, 2001.

Souza, Percival de. *Narcoditadura*: *caso Tim Lopes, crime organizado e jornalismo investigativo no Brasil*. São Paulo: Labortexto Editorial, 2002.

Vélez-Rodríguez, Ricardo. *Castilhismo*: *Uma filosofia da República*. 2nd edition, revised and expanded. Brasília: Senado Federal, 2000. Coleção Brasil Quinhentos Anos.

Vianna, Francisco José de Oliveira. *Populações meridionais do Brasil*: *Instituições políticas brasileiras*. First edition in one volume. Compiled by Antônio Paim. Brasília: Câmara dos Deputados, 1982. Coleção Pensamento Político Republicano.

Villamarín Pulido, Luis Alberto. *El cartel de las FARC*: *la más completa documentación escrita y testimonial sobre el que ahora es el cartel más grande y peligroso de Colombia*. Bogotá: Ediciones El Faraón, 1996.

Weber, Max. *Economía y Sociedad.* Trad. José Medina Echavarría *et alii*. 1 México: Fondo de Cultura Económica, 1944, 4 vol.

Wittfogel. *Le despotisme oriental*: *étude comparative du pouvoir total*. Trad. Micheline Pouteau. Paris: Minuit, 1977.

Notes on the Contributors

Arnaldo Jabor is a journalist and film-maker. His most renowned films are *All Nudity Shall Be Punished* (Silver Berlin Bear 1974), *I Love You* (official representative to Cannes 1981), *Love Me Forever or Never* (Golden Palm, Cannes 1986). As a journalist, he is known for his polemical articles in the dailies *O Estado de São Paulo*, *O Globo* (in Rio de Janeiro) and *Correio Popular* (Campinas), among others. He is also a political commentator for the TV news programmes 'Jornal Nacional', 'Jornal da Globo' and 'Bom Dia Brasil', for Globo TV, CBN Radio and Globo FM.

Walter Salles is a renowned Brazilian film-maker whose directing credits include *The Motorcycle Diaries*, *Central Station*, *Behind the Sun* and *Foreign Land*. Salles has also produced or co-produced the films of such up-and-coming Brazilian directors as Fernando Mereilles (*City of God*), Katia Lund (*News From a Personal War*), Karim Aïnouz (*Madame Satã*) and Sérgio Machado (*At the Edge of the Earth*). He began his film career making documentaries.

Roberto Schwarz is an eminent Latin American intellectual and Professor of Literary Theory at the University of Campinas. His materialist interpretation of cultural history has produced many works of critical theory over a span 25 years, including the books *A sereia e o desconfiado*, *Ao vencedor as batatas*: *forma literária e proceso social nos inícios do romance* (1977), *O pai de família* (1978), *Que horas são?* (1987), *Um mestre na periferia do capitalismo*: *Machado de Assis* (1990) and *Misplaced Ideas*: *Essays on Brazilian Culture* (1992).

Fernando Meirelles is the Brazilian director of the international box-office hit, *City of God* (2002), awarded the Best Foreign Film prize at the British Independent Film Awards, and the first Latin American film to have been nominated for four Academy Awards (best director, best cinematography, best film editing and best adapted screenplay). Alongside his prolific work for TV and his advertising company O2, Meirelles has co-directed *The Nutty Boy 2* and *Maids.* He is currently working on the post-production of a British film that he has directed, *The Constant Gardener,* starring Ralph Fiennes.

Jean Oppenheimer is a contributing writer at *American Cinematographer* magazine and a freelancer for *The New York Times* syndicate. Additionally, she reviews films on National Public Radio, as well as in print for *Screen International* and the *New Times* organisation, and is the former president of the Los Angeles Film Critics Association. She studied international relations at Cambridge University and The London School of Economics.

Lúcia Nagib holds the Centenary Chair of World Cinema at the University of Leeds, UK. She is the author of several books, including *Werner*

Herzog: *Film as Reality, Born of the Ashes*: *the Auteur and the Individual in Oshima's Films, The Japanese Nouvelle Vague, The Recovery of Brazilian Cinema*: *Interviews with 90 Film-Makers of the 1990s,* and she has edited, among others, *The New Brazilian Cinema* (2003).

André Gatti conducts research on cinematography for the Cultural Centre of São Paulo and teaches Cinema History at the Fundação Armando Álvares Penteado. He has an MA in Cinema (School of Communication and Art of the University of São Paulo), a PhD in Cinema (Institute of Arts of the University of Campinas). He contributes to many journals, including *D'Art, Marketing Cultural*, and *Sinopse*.

Leandro Saraiva is one of the editors of the periodical *Revista Sinopse*, is a film critic (*Revista Reportagem*), a researcher for documentaries (*Peões*, by Eduardo Coutinho, 2004 and *Em Trânsito*, by Henri Gervaiseau, to be released), and a telescreen writer (*Cidade dos Homens* series, Globo/O2 Filmes). He is the author, with Newton Cannito, of the recent *Manual de roteiro ou Manuel, o primo pobre dos manuais* (2004). He has a doctorate in cinema from the University of São Paulo.

Miranda Shaw's previous research projects concentrated mainly on Brazil and film, particularly on *Cinema Novo* and *City of God*; her comparative studies have considered Brazilian and Spanish Cinema. Her MA dissertation (Queen Mary, University of London) focuses on the gender-class intersection in *Cinema Novo*. Her forthcoming PhD thesis will be on *Novo Cinema Novo.*

Juliet Line holds an MA by research in Brazilian Cultural Studies at the University of Nottingham, with a dissertation on the film *City of God*. Other areas of her research have been the Tropicalia Movement, 1930s *sambas* and the films of Ruy Guerra. Her forthcoming PhD will look at cultural exchanges between Brazil and Mozambique.

Ivana Bentes teaches and researches on cinema and communication at the School of Communication of the Federal University of Rio de Janeiro. She is the author of *Joaquim Pedro de Andrade*: *a revolução intimista* (1996) and editor of *Cartas ao mundo*: *Glauber Rocha* (1997). Her current research is on images of the backlands and of the *favela* in contemporary Brazilian Film.

Ismail Xavier. Professor at the University of São Paulo, Department of Cinema, Radio and Television. Visiting Professor: New York University (1995), University of Iowa (1998), Université Paris III-Sorbonne Nouvelle (1999). His major books include: *Allegories of Underdevelopment*: *Aesthetics and Politics in Modern Brazilian Cinema* (Minneapolis-London,1997), *O olhar e a cena*: *melodrama, Hollywood, Cinema Novo, Nelson Rodrigues* (São Paulo, 2004) and *Cinema brasileiro moderno* (São Paulo, 2002). He has a PhD in Cinema Studies from New York University.

Luiz Inácio Lula da Silva is the President of Brazil. He started working at the age of 12 as a shoeshine boy, and two years later in industry, as a metal worker; he became the president of the Metalworkers' Labour Union. In 1980, while president of the Workers' Party, he was arrested for 30 days, on a charge of leading a strike of 200, 000 workers for 41 days. In 1983, he led the campaign 'Diretas Já', to demand free direct elections for President. He also helped the Workers' Party found the Central Única dos Trabalhadores [Workers' Central Union]. He took office in January, 2003 as the first President from the Workers' Party in Brazil's history.

Luiz Eduardo Soares is an Anthropologist and Political Scientist, former National Secretary of Public Security, Coordinator of Security, Justice, and Citizenship of the State of Rio de Janeiro. He formulated the Police Reform Policies of President Lula's government. Among his many books, *Meu casaco de general*: *500 dias no front da segurança pública do Rio de Janeiro* [*My General's Coat*: *500 days on the Front of Public Security in Rio de Janeiro*] (2000). Professor at the State University of Rio de Janeiro; visiting scholar at Columbia, among others; researcher at the Vera Institute of Justice in New York.

Ely Azeredo has been a cinema critic for over 50 years. Also a journalist and cinema professor, he has contributed to about 20 publications, among them, the magazines *O Cruzeiro* and *Senhor*. He wrote for the newspaper *Jornal do Brasil* from 1965 to 1982. He coined the term *Cinema Novo*, and authored the books *Infinito cinema* and *Roteiro*: *escrita do olhar*. His article about *City of God* marks his new start in writing for *Jornal do Brasil*.

M V Bill (Mensageiro da Verdade Bill, or Alex Pereira Barbosa) [M V stands for Messenger of Truth], 30, the well-known rapper, was born and still lives at Cidade de Deus whose reality he dreams of changing. He became acquainted with hip-hop in 1980 and helped to create CUFA, *Central Única das Favelas* [The Favelas' Central Union], the largest Brazilian organisation of hip-hop. As an activist he has been awarded several titles for social and political works. A prominent black leader and creator and president of PPPomar [Popular Party Power for the Majority], whose membership comprises solely blacks.

Paulo Lins, a native of Cidade de Deus, is a professor at the Universidade Federal do Rio de Janeiro. He published his novel *City of God* in 1997 (adapted for the screen in 2002). A bestseller in Brazil, it is considered one of the greatest works in Brazilian contemporary literature and has been translated into 12 major languages.

Maria do Rosário Caetano is a journalist and researcher. She wrote *Cinema latino-americano*: *entrevistas e filmes* (1997), *João Batista de Andrade*: *alguma solidão e muitas histórias* (2003) and *Fernando Meirelles*: *biografia precoce* (forthcoming). She has contributed to *Enciclopédia do cinema brasileiro* (1997), *Trinta anos de Gramado* (2002), *Guia do cinema brasileiro* (2003) and *Alle Radici del Cinema Brasiliano* (Pagani-Salerno, 2003) and *Jorge Amado e o cinema* (in the press). She writes regularly for the magazine *Revista de Cinema* and the supplement *Caderno 2*, of the newspaper *O Estado de São Paulo*.

Márcia Pereira Leite has a PhD in Sociology and is Professor of Social Sciences at the State University of Rio de Janeiro. She has various articles and book chapters published on images and citizenship, violence and human rights, social movements, religion and politics. Co-editor of *A trama dos espaços na Grande Tijuca* (Rio de Janeiro, Ibase, 2003) and *Um mural para a dor: movimentos cívicos religiosos sobre justiça e paz* (Porto Alegre, 2004, forthcoming).

Ricardo Vélez-Rodríguez. Born in Bogotá. BA (University Javeriana, Colombia), MA (Catholic University of Rio de Janeiro) and PhD (Gama Filho University in Rio) in Philosophy. Research at the Centre for Political Research Raymond Aron, Paris. Postgraduate Studies Director, University of Medellín; Professor at Gama Filho University; Visiting Professor at the Catholic University of Lisbon. Author of *Liberalismo e conservadorismo na América Latina* (1978); *A ditadura positivista no Brasil* (1982); *A democracia liberal segundo Tocqueville* (1998); *Keynes, Teoria e Crítica* (1999); *Estado, cultura e sociedade na América Latina* (2000).

Else R P Vieira is a Reader in Brazilian and Comparative Latin American Studies, at Queen Mary, University of London; former Visiting Professor at the Centre for Brazilian Studies, University of Oxford (1999) and a Senior Research Fellow at the University of Nottingham (2001-02); previous career in Comparative Literature at the Federal University of Minas Gerais, Brazil. Among her major projects, she is the Director of Research and Editor of the website *The Sights and Images of Dispossession: The Fight for the Land and the Emerging Culture of the MST* (landless-voices.org). Her present AHRB-funded project involves a comparative study of documentaries in Brazil and Argentina.

Index

ALSO AVAILABLE

Our publications are sent POST FREE anywhere in the world if ordered from our website, **www.cccpress.co.uk**. The same website additionally offers our titles in e-book format at a considerably cheaper price. Our publications can also be purchased from **Amazon.co.uk** or ordered through any good bookseller.

Silviano Santiago in Conversation ed. Macdonald Daly and Else Vieira

This book is the first to introduce Silviano Santiago, the renowned Brazilian novelist, theorist and critic, to an English-speaking audience. It surveys Santiago's theorisations of Brazilian modernism (including his key concepts of 'inbetweenness' and 'hybridity'); examines his literary critical and fictional relations to postmodernism; and presents Santiago's voice in a unique five-way dialogue with some of his most celebrated readers.

Haroldo de Campos in Conversation ed. Else Vieira and Bernard McGuirk

This book provides an indispensable introduction to the critical theoretical stance, the literary criticism, the translation theory, the poetics, and the poetry of de Campos. A highly accessible reference guide, it juxtaposes his seminal texts with original essays on his work by eminent critics. Here the reader will find, for example, the 1958 "Pilot Plan for Concrete Poetry", several of his theoretical reflections on translation as transcreation, as well as illuminating texts by Severo Sarduy, Ángel Rama, Octavio Paz, Jacques Derrida, and Umberto Eco, among other distinguished intellectuals. A restless innovator who played from the earliest with a legacy of Mallarmé, Pound, the Brazilian modernists, João Cabral de Melo Neto and, especially, the concept of the materiality of words, de Campos later abandoned concretism in its strict sense of a visual poetry and recognized the end of both utopia and the avant-gardes, broaching a post-utopian poetry. As the contributors to this memorial collection definitively show, he will be acknowledged not only as an inspired poet and as a daring critic but also as a *sans pareil* translator himself who, as the formulator of a new translation theory, has left many extraordinary "transcreations". It is Umberto Eco who best captures the stature of Haroldo de Campos when he describes him as "a fine connoisseur of many literatures" and "one of the great poets of our time".

Brazilian Feminisms
ed. Judith Still and Solange Ribeiro de Oliveira

This collection of specially commissioned essays includes contributions from Brazil and North America as well as scholars working in the UK. Still provides an Introduction to Brazilian feminism, entitled "Identity and Difference". The essays cover the period from the sixteenth century to the present day, but focus on the twentieth century, and, in particular, literary criticism and the analysis of Brazilian writing.

NB – not available as an e-book.

Post-conflict Cultures: Rituals of Representation
ed. Cristina Demaria and Colin Wright

Bringing together international scholars from fields as diverse as semiotics, media studies, critical theory, visual culture, history, political science, literary theory and international law, *Post-conflict Cultures: Rituals of Representation* adopts a calculatedly interdisciplinary approach to address the omission of the cultural dimension from most examinations of post-conflict. Each contribution focuses on texts and practices and thus on representations; but on representations as events, agency, as spaces in which strategic thinking is inscribed and produced, and meaning is communicated and negotiated.

This revised edition of this classic work is the first to appear for thirty years. It retains the original extensive editorial material with supplementary annotation and a new Preface which reflects the changes in the field over the past three decades.

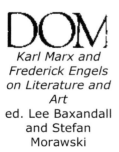

Karl Marx and Frederick Engels on Literature and Art
ed. Lee Baxandall and Stefan Morawski

Macdonald Daly

a
primer
in
marxist
aesthetics

A Primer in Marxist Aesthetics is aimed at readers with little or no knowledge of the field or its vocabulary. In an attempt to build an understanding of the subject in a step by step manner, each chapter contains exercises and questions which prompt reflection on and enquiry into the material. As a result, Marxist aesthetics is seen as an area of contention rather than a settled body of knowledge. The book will be useful to students, whether working alone or as part of a formal course of study.

Susan Wilson

a
primer
in
feminist
criticism
and
theory

A Primer in Feminist Criticism and Theory focuses upon those aspects of feminism which form a distinct critical approach to literature. No foundational statement of the tenets of feminist criticism is provided. Instead, readers are encouraged to engage with and critically assess the work of the key feminist writers and theorists presented here. This book will be useful to students, whether working alone or as part of a formal course of study.

Felicia Chan

a
primer
in
film
narratives
and
cultures

A Primer in Film Narratives and Cultures introduces readers to the notion of film cultures expressed and experienced through popular film. It aims not to approach film from a prescribed theoretical perspective but rather to explore the different processes involved in reading film through culture and culture through film. Through the analyses of a range of film texts, readers are encouraged to explore modes of reading and understanding film narratives.

Constance Goh

a
primer
in
deconstruction

A Primer in Deconstruction is designed to introduce deconstruction to readers new to this critical approach. It aims to clarify the more challenging aspects of deconstruction and explain how it aids textual analysis. As deconstruction is fundamentally interrogative, the book demonstrates the ways in which writing can be dismantled, exposing the underlying assumptions that influence reception.